CUBICLE TALES

WALTER H SOLOMON

ISBN-13: 9781494403126
ISBN-10: 1494403129
Library of Congress Control Number: 2013922766
CreateSpace Independent Publishing Platform
North Charleston, South Carolina

DEDICATION

I'd like to dedicate this book to my grand daddy, Morris Ness, who was an extraordinarily gentle, humble and gracious man. He taught me to love books, as he read them well beyond the point where age had taken his sight but not his vision. He also taught me to appreciate the telling (and the teller) of good stories, many of which he shared during my childhood late into the night when he stayed in my bedroom on his visits.

TABLE OF CONTENS

FORWARD

WHEN MY MIDDLE son was six years old, he was asked by some unsuspecting adult "what does your dad do for a living?" He responded like any six year old would, based on the world as he sees it.

"My dad sits in a cubicle and types," he replied before running off to do something more interesting that speaking with an adult, which is probably just about *anything else* to a six year old.

I suspect his observation of my vocation wasn't too far from the truth. I have spent a good portion of my career in a proverbial cubicle and have a lot of stories to tell as a result. This book is a collection of my tales of work - of my *life in the cubicle*. Consequently, this book is largely autobiographical and therefore mostly true. Accent on *mostly*.

My primary purpose in writing this book is to capture and to retell many of the unusual stories I have experienced in my relatively unusual career — before I get too old and forget them. While the stories have always been entertaining to me, I've always wondered if others might also find them to be entertaining.

I'll let you be the judge of that.

PROLOGUE

BRISTOL

"THEY'RE READY FOR you now," she said as she tapped him gently on the left shoulder.

Michael Elliot sat in front of the broad windows of the Turn Four Luxury Suite, surveying the expansive view of Bristol Motor Speedway and the Blue Ridge mountains beyond. It was late August and he watched the sun recede, illuminating the balmy haze that lay like a sheer veil settled gently over the mountains on the border of Northeast Tennessee and Southwest Virginia. This tranquil view was in stark contrast to the "beatin' and bangin'" that was about to transpire in the auto race below it.

It was the Bristol Night Race, one of the premier races on the NASCAR Sprint Cup Circuit, rivaled perhaps only by the Daytona 500. The "Night Race" as it was known, was sold out, and had done so for each of the previous ten years. The track's owners had expanded the seating to accommodate 165,000 fans, appearing from a distance like a high rise version of the famed Rose Bowl – only this was Tennessee, not Pasadena. The half mile concrete track, banked at an advertised and quite steep 36 degrees, stood in the center of the bowl – the stage for the bullfight that would ensue that evening. Or at least that's what fans called this auto race – a bullfight. Men in machines competing in tight confines, often fighting to the death – of the machines, that is. As much as fans love watching racing at Bristol, NASCAR drivers experience a mix of challenge and dread, having described racing at Bristol to be like flying fighter jets in a gymnasium.

Fans were filling the stadium, anxiously awaiting driver introductions, the patriotic rendition of the National Anthem, and the most famous words in motorsports, "Racers, start your engines".

Michael loved it all -- the sounds, the smells, the vibrations — the visceral sensations created when those 43 engines all cranked at once, and each of those 850 horsepower, hand-assembled beauties roared to life. He reveled in the notion that each engine was built for this specific race, would diligently serve its master for more than 500 laps, and then be torn down, cleaned up and rebuilt again at the behest of master engine builders. He loved that what he did for a living served as the engine's lifeblood.

Michael Elliot was Senior Vice President & General Manager of The Valvoline Company, America's oldest manufacturer of engine oils, and a brand synonymous with racing. Valvoline motor oil was in the engine of the car that won the first recorded race, at the birth of motorsports -- over 100 years before — and many great races since including the Indianapois 500 and the Daytona 500.

"They'll be doing driver introductions in about 15 minutes, so they asked that we come down to the track now," whispered Sherry Gaze, Valvoline's Director of Corporate Communications, gently interrupting his conversation. "I'm ready to escort you down if you're ready to go."

Michael excused himself graciously from the collection of 50 or so customers that Valvoline was hosting for the race. He made no indication where he was going, though many suspected it was for some notable reason. Valvoline had just announced earlier in the week that it had become the exclusive motor oil sponsor to Bristol Motor Speedway, and many of the guests had seen the famous Valvoline "V" logo adorning many parts of the track and every 55-gallon trashcan in the surrounding parking lots. Nothing was subtle in NASCAR, especially when it came to sponsorship.

Michael and Sherry strolled down the hallway to the elevator to take the five floor ride down to the tunnel that ran underneath the track and led to the pits and the stage where driver introductions would take place.

In the elevator, Michael looked at Sherry. "So the Track officials were not offended at my insistence *not* to address the crowd prior to driver introductions?"

"No, they understood why you didn't feel any need to address the crowd. So they'll introduce you, and you can step back on the stage and just shake hands with the drivers as they are introduced."

"Perfect. I think I can handle the handshaking challenge," he said with a sarcastic smile. "Thanks for taking care of that for me."

THE ELEVATOR DOORS opened and they passed through the security gauntlet guarding the gate into the tunnel under the track. Michael chuckled to himself as he walked through the gate, remembering what happened the previous year at the Night Race when he was walking the opposite way – coming out of the tunnel toward the gate.

Michael had just finished a discussion with Ray Evernham at the red #9 Dodge hauler in the track's infield. The hauler was the customized 18 wheel truck that carried the race cars and equipment to and from the tracks. A hauler typically had a small office behind the cab, where Michael and Ray hashed a few more details of their secret new racing partnership. Michael always found the term "hauler" amusing, as it said so much about the familiar and friendly nature of NASCAR drivers, owners, crews and families. The same vehicle in Indy Car and Formula One racing was called a "transporter". In NASCAR, it was just a "hauler".

The previous year, Valvoline became a co-owner of a NASCAR Sprint Cup Team with Ray Evernham. Ray had a notable history as the three-time championship crew chief for Jeff Gordon and fabled car owner Rick Hendrick. Valvoline had been among the first to sponsor Ray when he became an owner of two new NASCAR Cup teams. And now Ray was looking to expand his successful endeavor. Valvoline brought sponsorship dollars and a history of racing commitment to the partnership. Ray brought technical capability, experience and most importantly, an understanding of what it takes to be a champion in this tough sport. It was a marriage made in heaven, one built on mutual respect, trust, a history of success and a genuine love of the sport.

As Ray and Michael were walking through the tunnel toward the security gate, fans immediately recognized Ray and began reaching across the fence, asking for his autograph. "Let me greet a few fans here if you don't mind, Mike," Ray said. Not many people called him "Mike"; but if that's what Ray wanted, it was just fine with Michael.

"I'm sure they'll appreciate that, Ray. I'll see you back in the suite later," Michael smiled. NASCAR was well known for demanding fan indulgence from its racers, and that extended to crew chiefs, car owners and everyone else who made a living from the sport. The quickest way to exact the wrath of NASCAR management was to do anything perceived as dissing a fan. And rightly so.

As Michael approached the security gate, a young woman reached over the fence, pushed a program and a sharpie pen into his face, and asked "how about an autograph?"

Surprised, Michael asked "You want *my* autograph?" He was genuinely astounded. "Honestly, ma'am, I'm nobody you'd want an autograph from."

"Sure I would. You're with Valvoline," she replied as she nodded at the iconic "V" embroidered over his heart on his oxford cotton, buttoned down shirt.

Michael thought about how embarrassed she might feel once she realized that she got an autograph from a nobody such as himself. But then he considered how aloof and fan-unfriendly he might appear if he refused an autograph – and, more importantly, how poorly it would reflect on the Valvoline brand and possibly NASCAR. He'd have harsh words for a Valvoline driver who refused a fan request for an autograph. Why shouldn't that apply to any other Valvoline employee, including himself?

"Well OK then," he smiled and took the sharpie and the program and signed his name – the lesser evil of the two choices. "Here you go, and thanks for your loyalty to Valvoline. It means a lot to us."

As he started to walk off, she said, "How about a picture?" Sure, why not. She was already going to be embarrassed when her friends asked whose autograph she had. At least with a picture of Michael she would have an answer: "the poser in this picture."

So she leaned over the fence, and put her arm around Michael's shoulder while her husband took a picture of their ginning faces.

It was the camera flash that drew the mob. Before Michael knew what was happening, people were leaning over the fence with requests for autographs on caps, mugs, programs, t-shirts – and yes, even particular body parts. You gotta love NASCAR fans. Michael was ferociously signing autographs, scratching his name illegibly so they wouldn't be disappointed when they realized they had no idea who he was.

He could hear people in the crowd murmuring "Who is that?"

"I'm not sure exactly. He looks like one of the up and coming Valvoline drivers."

"Probably so, he's about the size of a driver." Drivers are notoriously small - generally between five and six feet tall – to fit in those tight cockpits.

"Well, get his autograph now while we can. Maybe we can sell it for something on eBay."

So Michael stood there for 10 minutes diligently signing autographs and thanking the crowd for being loyal to Valvoline, feeling quite sheepish and trying to find a way to gracefully extract himself from this awkward situation. Then he heard a muffled voice behind him.

"Do any of these people know who you really are?" It was Lorne Joseph, Valvoline's Vice President of Sales, with a sarcastic chuckle.

"Apparently not, or they wouldn't be asking for my autograph," Michael murmured out of the corner of his mouth, out of earshot of the autograph seekers.

"Do you want out?" Lorne asked quietly.

"Please. Before I completely embarrass myself."

So Lorne stepped between Michael and the crowd and announced in an official tone, "I'm sorry Ladies and Gentlemen, but he's running late and we have to get him to his next fan appearance. Thank you and please root for all the Valvoline drivers in tonight's race!"

And with that, Lorne and Michael scurried through the security gate and into the elevator amid flashbulbs and cheers for a successful race.

So much for those famous 15 minutes of fame.....

—∞∞—

MICHAEL AND SHERRY came through the tunnel under the track and walked through the pits toward the main stage. Michael nodded gracious greetings to the faces in the pits he had known over the years, the NASCAR family that got together every week, 38 times a year, for many years, to put on what NASCAR demanded -- *a good show for the fans*. As he reached the stage, he was greeted by Jeff Byrd, the track's president, and joined the others hovering around Jeff. They included two other gentlemen – the president of Sharpie Pens (that night's race sponsor), and the Governor of Virginia. The city of Bristol's main street straddled the boundary line between the states of Tennessee and Virginia. Of course, the track was on the southern side of that boundary in Tennessee. Nonetheless, there was only one venue in the area that attracted 165,000 possible voters – it was late August and November elections were just around the corner. The Governor of Virginia couldn't resist. It must not have been an election year in Tennessee.

"OK, here's the plan," Jeff said. "Michael, I'm going to introduce you first as the track's newest general sponsor, and then you'll come on stage and address the crowd. Then, John, I'm going to introduce you as the sponsor of tonight's race and you'll address the crowd. Then, Governor, I'll introduce you last and I'm sure you'll take it just fine from there!" Jeff winked the Governor a knowing smile.

Michael was a bit shocked, but hid it well. "That's a fine plan, Jeff, but please permit me to offer one modification," Michael asked awkwardly. "When you introduce me, I'll just come up, wave to the crowd, step back and then let these fine gentlemen offer their remarks. There's nothing Valvoline needs to say tonight. We're just proud to have the opportunity to be part of this great track and tonight's race. These gentlemen have earned the right to speak. I'll just smile and shake hands with drivers as they're introduced."

That was, hopefully, a gracious way to redirect the situation more to his liking.

"Oh, no!" responded Jeff immediately, much to Michael's surprise. "You represent Valvoline. Valvoline is *legendary* in this sport. The fans *want* to hear from you. The fans *need* to hear from you!" And with that, Jeff walked up on the stage and began addressing the crowd.

Michael looked at Sherry and her mouth was agape, even more surprised than he was. Michael asked, "Well it looks like I'm going to have to address the crowd. Any suggestions on what I should say?"

Sherry's mouth was still agape. No ideas emerged. In fact, no words escaped her lips. The only voice Michael heard was Jeff Byrd's echoing through the stadium, "...and I'm proud to introduce the Senior Vice President of Bristol Motor Speedway's newest sponsor, Michael Elliot of The Legendary... Valvoline... Company!"

Michael had no choice but to walk calmly up the stairs to the stage, doing all he could to collect himself, noticing his face projected on the four-sided Sony JumboTron towering above him, to the polite applause of the crowd and the smiling face and outstretched handshake of Jeff Byrd.

Michael prayed he didn't soil himself as 165,000 sets of eyes stared upon him, waiting for him to say something...anything.

1

The Plan

I, Michael Elliot, grew up in Charleston, South Carolina in the 1960's and 1970's. Charleston is a magical city, tracing its colonial history back to the 1600's, beautiful in its preserved streetscapes and architecture, and rich in culture and tradition. Charleston is referred to in travel periodicals as the "Holy City", ostensibly due to the number of centuries-old churches and synagogues that adorn its downtown streets and low slung skyline – a building in Charleston cannot be taller than its tallest church steeple. Religion aside, however, the Charleston native fervently believes that the "Holy City" moniker was actually chosen to reflect Charleston's rightful role as the center of the universe. When true Charlestonians -- the ones with brackish water coursing through their veins and ancestry gripping the holy terra firma south of Broad Street -- refer to the two rivers that flank the city's peninsula, they firmly assert that "the Ashley and Cooper Rivers come together in Charleston Harbor to *form* the Atlantic Ocean."

As you may readily surmise, there are no self-esteem issues in Charleston.

I was fortunate enough to have various after-school jobs during my formative years in Charleston, usually just enough work to provide a bit of pocket money, but not enough to get in the way of the school, sports, and religious activities that my fervently Jewish parents established as priorities. My first job was mowing lawns in our neighborhood at the age of ten. I would ride my bicycle up to the gas station in the nearby South Windermere Shopping Center, fill a two-gallon gas can using just pocket change, and mow an entire lawn for the enormous sum of $5.00.

One of my favorite customers was Ms. Hardcastle, the retired school teacher on our street who had three notable qualities: 1) foremost, she was very kind, in that wonderful schoolmarm-ish way; 2) for a reason I neither knew nor cared, she had an 8 foot, full-color drawing of Woody Woodpecker on the back wall of her garage, of which my friends and I always tried to catch a glimpse when her garage door was open; and 3) she couldn't hear worth a lick. She always called me Carmichael, which I thought was odd, but I didn't mind. I just didn't think it was my place to correct a teacher.

A job I had later in high school was inherited from one of my brother's friends when he went off to college. It was the ultimate flex-time job. I worked for a company in that far-off and mystical place called New York City (typical Charleston attitude toward New York: why would anyone want to be there when you can be here in Charleston?). My job was to take inventory of the hats they sold at a local department store.

It was not a very demanding job. I drove to the two store locations in Charleston once a month, and counted hats — both on display and in storage - reporting them by style and color on the printed form that I received in the mail. I then mailed the form to New York to a strange zip code that didn't start with a 2 like all other zip codes in South Carolina. I was not familiar with those. I didn't realize they existed.

This job took me about two hours each month to cover both stores, and I got paid $30 for each visit. That was the equivalent of mowing six lawns — and I was working in air conditioning instead of Charleston's sweltering humidity. A definite step up the evolutionary ladder of employment.

The teen job that truly shaped my career interests was working at Charleston Abstract Company. My mother managed Charleston Abstract, as she called it, a business that provided title insurance for real estate transactions. I had no idea what title insurance was — and didn't really understand its purpose (which was why I thought the business was aptly named Charleston *Abstract* Company). Now, later in life, as I've purchased title insurance with real estate, I'm still pretty baffled as to its real value. It's still pretty abstract to me. Nonetheless, it paid me a few dollars an hour and provided more frequent and abundant income than the hat job. Just to stretch myself, I kept the demanding hat job, too. You see, that way, I could prove my manliness by holding down two jobs at once.

My job at Charleston Abstract was gopher, as in "go fer this" and "go fer that". I was the errand boy, delivering documents to lawyers' offices, getting food, buying stamps, watering plants, filing, etc. Whatever was needed. If it was low skilled labor, I did it. While the work itself was not very exciting, the environs were pretty amazing. The law district of downtown Charleston was about a four block segment of Broad Street between King and East Bay Streets. It included such notable historical locations such as where the Ordinance of Secession was signed in 1860, the official document that initiated what became the Confederacy. Had President Lincoln not been success-ful in holding the Union together that document might have had the same historical significance as the Declaration of Independence. Fortunately, it didn't.

Broad Street was, and still is, a fabulous street. It hadn't changed that much in 300 years, why would one expect it to change much in the last 35? Broad Street is simply one historic building after another, and in 1977, it housed banks, law firms, real estate brokerages, small restaurants, upscale clothing stores (the famed *Berlin's*, no less), an apothecary (it was not to be called a mere drug store in downtown Charleston, mind you), and even a grocery store (yes, the southern icon Piggly Wiggly). The sidewalks were made of flagstone -- not to be quaint or fashionable; that was just the material that was readily available in the 1700's. Charleston takes the ordinary, and embellishes it with stories to suggest it has some grander design. I'm OK with that. It adds color to life. Some people even call it *marketing* and people pay a price premium for excel-lent versions of it. Go figure.

There was also Washington Square, with its gated entrances on both Broad and Meeting Streets, and the pastel colors of its vibrant azaleas ablaze in March. Washington Square's focal point was a miniature version of the Washington Monument. After all, why bother to travel all the way to Washington, when you can stay in Charleston AND have a delightful little Washington Monument? Flanking Broad Street were cobble-stone streets that dated back to the 1700's, paved out of the stones that served as ballast from ships sailing empty to the new world to bring the colonies' bounty back to England. Today, these streets are tough on the ankles and automobile suspension; however, when you're a teenager, you could hop from stone to stone and it was strangely fun. Twisted ankles be damned.

Now, let me tell you, the people-watching on Broad Street was something else. You had bankers in their pin-striped suits; ladies dressed elegantly in their pumps, stockings and white gloves; lawyers in their blue blazers, khaki pants, buttoned-down oxford cloth shirts, guards ties and penny loafers; and women from the sea islands who had come to town to sell their sweetgrass baskets -- known more commonly as *reeds*, drawn straight from the salt marshes. *Sweetgrass* sounds more expensive. Yes, more ordinary stuff embellished. Charleston at its finest.

Something about this four-block microcosm excited me, and I visualized myself in the future as one of those attorneys in the blue blazers, speaking with clients, rushing to the courthouse, grabbing a sandwich at lunch, and solving the Lowcountry's problems — one lazy Charleston day at a time. Even to this day, I still feel quite at home in a blue blazer, an Oxford cotton shirt, and khakis. Although the comfort of Cole Haan's with rubber soles (from *Bob Ellis Shoes* on King Street in Charleston, no less) has trumped the penny loafers.

And as you might believe it would be, being a Broad Street lawyer is the visualization that drove me all through college. My plan was to study what interested me in undergraduate school, do well enough to get into law school at the University of South Carolina, and get a job as an attorney on Broad Street. That was honey on cornbread to me. All I needed.

Or so I thought…

———

I HAD THE Plan. A well-developed plan, if I must say so myself. And I followed The Plan. After graduating from high school, I enrolled at the University of Virginia and traded the historic structures, the colonial tradition, and the blue blazers and khaki pants of Charleston for the historic structures, the colonial tradition, and the blue blazers and khaki pants of Charlottesville. I was nothing if not consistent.

I had The Plan. A well-developed plan. And I followed it. At UVA, I studied whatever interested me. After all, I was going to attend Law School and you could study just about anything in undergraduate school in preparation for graduate studies in law. I didn't really like sciences so I enrolled in more math-based studies. I enjoyed business courses so I transferred from the College of Arts & Sciences to the McIntire School of Commerce for my third and fourth years at UVA. I seemed to have a knack for psychology and arrogantly telling people what to do so I concentrated my business courses in management. I focused on courses taught by the professors that I thought were cool and the subjects that seemed to be worth the distraction from my primary objective in undergraduate school — social activities.

I had The Plan. A well-developed plan. And not only did I follow it, I even allowed it to evolve. Yessir. When the appropriate time came during the summer between my third and fourth years of college, I not only took the LSAT's in preparation for law school, but I went one step further. I also took the GMAT's, because I had this idea that I would get two graduate degrees concurrently – a law degree AND a Masters in Business Administration. That was what I thought was the huge *evolution* of The Plan. A new added plank to The Plan. A demonstration of my flexible and innovative thinking. Totally *out there*.

I had The Plan. A well-developed plan. And I followed it.

Until The Plan started to spring a few leaks.

The first leak in The Plan started showing up in the form of apathy in my fourth year of college. I was simply getting tired of this whole *education thing* – read a book, hear a lecture, take a test, write a paper, get a grade. It seemed so....academic (duh). I needed something more practical. I needed something I could do every day that was outside the staid, impractical confines of academia. I needed the real world. I needed a change.

But....I had The Plan. A well-developed plan. And what I was feeling did not conform to The Plan.

So I did what every Type A, list generating, left brain-driven, over-achiever does. I rationalized away my feelings.

One of my favorite films of all time is one from the 80's entitled *The Big Chill*. The character played by Jeff Goldblum had a great line I'll never forget: "I don't know anyone who can get through the day without two or three juicy rationalizations. They're more important than sex".

In my case, this would have been a *Venti* rationalization. I suppressed that urge to escape academia and focused on the things I needed to do to secure my well-planned future. I focused on completing applications to Law School with the MBA twist. And I successfully compartmentalized those feelings and drove them away. Problem solved.

The second leak in The Plan was a doozy. This leak was so seductive, so completely invisible to me, that it mesmerized me like a rattlesnake does to a gerbil. And it struck with such veracity that I never knew what hit me. Before I realized what was happening I was bound head first down the viper's gullet, en route to abandoning The Plan forever. The Plan was a goner and I was spiraling out of control, off the defined path, and therefore.....lost.

As PART OF my scholarship and loan program to attend the University of Virginia, I had to participate in a work-study program each year. Participation in work-study was not a problem for me. I only had to work about 10 hours each week and it paid $3.00 per hour. In 1978, with a housing and meal plan in place, $30 a week in pocket money bought a reasonable amount of socializing.

My original work-study job was working in the University's cafeteria, paying $2.00 per hour. I received a letter with my assignment to the cafeteria the first week of school. I did the math and realized I could make more money in less time typing papers for other students. At three minutes and 25 cents per page, I could generate $5 an hour – two and a half times the rate the cafeteria was paying. So I blew off the work-study job and instead put up signs around the dorm advertising my first entrepreneurial venture -- a typing service. Of note, back in the *old days*, the way one interfaced with computers was through punch cards not keyboards. So typing was a somewhat unique skill and in demand -- not remotely as common as it is today.

This venture worked out pretty well. I had more business than I could handle. Life was good and cash flow was exceptional. For about a month. Then my first venture came to an abrupt end. I received a letter asking me to report to Miller Hall, UVA's Office of Financial Aid. To my dismay, Miller Hall was not named for the beer. According to the letter, since I did not show up for my work-study job in the cafeteria, my "scholarship was now in jeopardy". I didn't need Alex Trebek to tell me this was a problem.

The university official in the Office of Financial Aid explained to me that work-study was not an option -- it was an *expectation* – an inseparable part of my financial aid package and I could not, in her words, "choose to opt out". Clearly, she expected me to reply "yes ma'am" and head off to the cafeteria. But "yes ma'am" would have implied that I engage in compliant behavior. And I was *anything* but compliant. So I explained to her what I was doing and why I thought it was a better idea than working in the cafeteria.

"Oh, so you can type?" the official's eyebrows arched.

"Yes, ma'am," replied the Mouse.

"Well, I can't let you out of work study in as a program, but I can assign you to a *different* work study job – one that requires typing skills. In fact, I believe I have one right here. Lesseee....yes, report to the Chemical Engineering Department. They have a need for a part-time secretary. And because you must have typing skills, it pays $3.00 per hour instead of $2.00."

So off I went. Yes, Mom, you were right. Taking the typing class you made me take in high school paid off in spades. I will never question your judgment again. I swear. No, *really*.

I showed up in the Chemical Engineering Department where I proceeded to spend the next two years. Ten hours per week at $3.00 an hour due to my advanced typing skills....doing absolutely nothing. I don't recall typing a single page while at work (except my school papers on their generally unused, super cool IBM Selectric Typewriter). Every now and then I'd make a copy of a thesis on the Xerox machine. I might have to go straighten up the lab. Once, I ran a package over to another department. But mostly, I tried to ignore the other two secretaries' discussions and did my homework. They had nothing for me to do and paid me the saintly sum of $3.00 per hour to do it. And most college students had to do their homework for FREE!!

At the end of the first year, when I was invited back to the same job for a second year (ostensibly due my stellar performance at doing my homework), I asked the Department secretary why they have my role and pay me to do nothing.

"If the Chairman doesn't spend the money in his budget, he'll get a lower budget next year." Ah, my first lesson in appropriate behavior in a bureaucracy. Our government at work. Spend the budget no matter what — even if it makes no sense. Now I know why four years of college costs more than the average home in America and why we have government deficits larger than most countries' GDP.

So that's what I did for my work study job for two years.

Until I took a required course in career planning the second semester of my second year in college. And I absolutely LOVED it. The principles of career planning were logical -- they made so much sense to me. Why wouldn't you pursue a job that reflects your values, skills and interests? Why shouldn't a resume be an advertisement for yourself rather than merely a listing of your job history? Why shouldn't you assess fit between yourself and a prospective job? It all seemed very logical and insightful to me. This career planning course took a lot of disparate, yet interdependent, ideas and wove them together into a practical approach to deciding what you wanted to do with your life.

And I really loved the professor, Tom Schertzer. What a terrific fellow. We got along very well. One day, in providing an example of *bad* career planning, I was sharing with him my frustration with my work study job. How I felt I was not only wasting my time, but I was wasting the University's dollars.

Wise Tom came up with a neat solution. He hired me to be the Office of Career Planning and Placement's work study student for my final two years of college. I became a teaching assistant for his Career Planning Courses and did a variety of odd projects for the Director of Career Planning and Placement, Len Singletary. As you may recall, I had become pretty adept at doing odd jobs in beautiful environs. I simply traded Broad Street in Charleston, South Carolina, for Mr. Jefferson's Academical Village in Charlottesville, Virginia. Who could ask for more? I turned mundane work into something I love. I was career planning in action! Yet little did I know how much *in action* I'd be....

———— ∞ ————

ONE DAY, DURING the fall of my fourth year of college, Len Singletary, the Director of Career Planning and Placement, called me into his office.

"I have a problem, and I need help solving it. Michael, I'll bet you can help me."

"I'll do whatever I can. But what could I possibly help *you* solve?" I idolized Len.

"In two weeks, Procter & Gamble is going to be conducting on-campus interviews here at UVA. They will only have 24 interview slots and I know we will have a lot more than 24 people trying to get a job with them. (Note: the unemployment rate in 1981 was just shy of gi-normous)

"Normally, I would treat it like we treat ACC Tournament Basketball tickets. Let those who want it badly enough line up, even the night before or the week before. But, as you know, there was a sexual assault late at night on the Grounds last week and I don't want people to be put in danger, lining up all night. Come up with a solution."

"Yes, sir," replied the Mouse. I had my marching orders. And off I went. Even did a fake salute.

I pondered the problem overnight and came back with a suggestion the next day. I sat before Len and began to unfold my brainchild.

"OK. So here's the crux of the challenge as I see it: how do we reward the people who will go the extra mile to get the interview, but have them prove it in a way that doesn't put them in any danger?"

"You've captured the essence of the problem," Len retorted sarcastically, yet unbeknownst to me at the time. Yes, I had attained a firm grasp of the obvious and was very proud of it.

"So here's what I suggest. Put an ad in the student newspaper, as we usually do, announcing sign-up's for interviews. Mention that P&G is one of the companies interviewing students Also mention that sign-up's begin at the usual time of 9:00AM. However, make a note in the announcement that no lines for sign-up's will be recognized until 5:00AM that morning, when we'll unlock the doors of the Office of Career Planning and Placement."

"I think that's a great suggestion. If a college student gets up at 5:00AM, it means they want something pretty bad. I think that'll work," Len replied. "Go write up the ad and place it now."

I beamed. Knocked that one out of the park. You could see me proverbially dropping the bat and going into my home run trot. Yup, another problem solved.

"Except," Len continued, "there's no one here to unlock the doors at 5:00AM." Drat, the devil is always in the details. "But no problem. *You* can be here to unlock the door. Remind me to give you the key the day before."

He could have asked me to pick up my jaw on the way out of his office.

THE ONLY PART of 4:30AM that most college students see is the part that is a continuation from the night before. And that tends to be, as Mick Jagger describes in the Rolling Stones' song *The Girl With Faraway Eyes*, a little *bleary*. This was not, however, the case for me on this day (but just *this* day). Even though the alarm clock sounds like the apocalypse at 4:30AM.

As I stumbled my way to the Office of Career Planning and Placement to unlock the door and to recognize the line for P&G interview sign-ups, I stumbled upon something of a revelation, an incredible idea! I was the teaching assistant in the OCCP's course on interviewing that semester. P&G had a reputation for being very tough interviewers. What if I were to use the P&G Interview as a case study for students in the class? I could show students via a real life example of how to prepare for the interview, do research on the company, practice mock interview questions and answers, frame the resume so it fits P&G's interests, develop thoughtful questions about the job and P&G, do a follow-up thank you note. The students and I could do this whole process *by the book* together and the students could get a taste of what it's really like to interview with a Fortune 50 company -- without any of the associated risk. Perfect! Damn, I'm brilliant! I added a bit of spring to my step, very proud of my new idea.

So I unlocked the door, went inside, waited until 9:00AM with the rest of the folks, and signed my name first on the list. As I scratched out my name, I felt a tinge of guilt knowing I was pirating a spot from some ambitious MBA candidate who had gone through two years of graduate school JUST to get a chance at a job at P&G. After all, I had The Plan and it called for me to attend law school. I wasn't legitimately seeking a job at P&G. But I rationalized away the guilt (thanks to Jeff Goldblum once again), as I was acting in the name of creative education. So many students would benefit from my new case study. It was well worth it.

And that is exactly what I did. I prepared for the interview with the class. By the book. Step by step. Modeling the exact way it is supposed to be done. I was as prepared as one could be for what would end up being an excellent interview.

Except for one thing.

—◦◦◦—

P&G CONDUCTS A tough interview. They train their people to ask penetrating questions, to "peel back the onion" as they say to get to the facts of the situation. If you're bluffing, they'll sniff it out fast. No softball questions with patsy answers, like "What's your greatest weakness?" What a goofy question. "Oh, I work myself too hard. Oh, I'll drive myself until I'm sick." People could easily turn the purported weakness into one of their strengths. When asked the question of one's greatest weakness, I advise people to answer "chocolate."

But I digress. Back to the tough P&G interview. I was calm, prepared, was pausing and giving thoughtful responses, and asking good questions about P&G. The P&G interviewer and I parted with a firm handshake and a smile. I was feeling good. I had the right finish to a great case study for my students. Again, the spring in that step; I was very pleased with myself.

I didn't count on the telephone call I got that evening from the P&G interviewer: "Would you be available to come back tomorrow to interview with the other P&G manager who's here with me? He's the Marketing Director of P&G's Paper Products Division."

"Sure," I replied, a little shaky. "Jjjjust tell me when and where."

I didn't see that one coming. I didn't anticipate the possible *consequence* of doing well in the interview. Or well enough that they'd want to speak with me again. I just thought I'd interview, they'd pick candidates from UVA's MBA Program rather than a lowly undergraduate like me, and that we'd both move on. After all, I'd heard that P&G only hires MBA's in their Brand Management program, don't they?

But flexibility is a hallmark. You have to adjust on the fly. I knew just what I'd do. I'd simply extend my case study, now to include the second interview. Yes, this topic would be entitled "how to be sure to cover the important things that got you to the second interview; how to add a new dimension to your capability set so they see even more of what you have to offer." Yes, as Jon Lovitz used to say on *Saturday Night Live*, "that's the ticket."

The next day's interview with the Marketing Director seemed to go well, too. The perfect extra chapter in the case study on the follow-up interview.

Except for one thing.

I didn't count on the letter I got the following week inviting me to come to Cincinnati, Ohio, for a full day of interviews with a variety of P&G managers at P&G's corporate headquarters. They were bringing two candidates from UVA to Cincinnati – one of the MBA candidates from the Darden School…and me.

Now I felt *really* guilty. And I was too deep into this to say "uh, just joking. I was just doing this for the benefit of the interviewing class. I'm not really serious about your company. After all, I'm going to law school. That's The Plan!"

Saying something like that would reflect poorly on UVA; it might even dissuade P&G from wanting to interview at UVA in the future. I couldn't bear to have been responsible for that, not with my *critical* role as a work study student at the Office of Career Planning and Placement!

I had no choice but to see this through. So I graciously called P&G and made plans to travel to their headquarters in Cincinnati. Okay, I kept telling myself to just think of this as another chapter in the ever enlarging case study. We'll call this chapter "The Home Office Interview". This case study was getting very long.

And I was starting to feel like maybe I was in a little too deep. Maybe this case study idea wasn't such a good one.

Yet, at the same time, I became aware of some different feelings I was experiencing. The second leak in The Plan was emerging. I really was getting tired of school. I really felt like an extended break from the classroom would be good. Do something *practical* for a few years.

Yes, I had to admit that I was finding the Brand Management job at P&G, well, *interesting*. While I was studying the role methodically, in an academically detached fashion for purposes of the case study of course, it sure seemed like a very good fit with my skills, interests and values inventories. I liked the strategic thinking challenges, the general management approach to business, the high level of responsibility. According to the precepts of career planning, of which I was a devotee, this job seemed like a good fit for me.

But it wasn't part of The Plan.

THE FIRST SIGN I saw when I got off the plane from Charlottesville to Cincinnati said "Welcome to Northern Kentucky". Panic! Did I get on the wrong plane? Did I really mess this up? Why on earth was I in Northern Kentucky?

It took me just until I got to Baggage Claim to realize that Cincinnati is tucked away in the Southwest corner of Ohio, just a few miles away from both Indiana and Kentucky. So the Greater Cincinnati airport was actually located in Northern Kentucky? OK. I guess geography was not a strength area for me. Especially Ohio geography. I had never been to Ohio, Kentucky *or* Indiana before. And Google Maps didn't exist back then.

That evening, I was taken to dinner by a friendly fellow, Tim Gorman, who was an Assistant Brand Manager on the Bounty Paper Towel Brand. Tim helped me to understand the benefits of Bounty being the "quicker picker upper" (Bounty's advertising tag line), and how much harder it was than it appeared to be both absorbent and strong! I actually found the discussion fascinating (as hard as that is to believe). At the same time, he put me at ease and helped me understand what to expect in my interviews the next day. It liked this Gorman guy.

When I arrived at P&G's offices the next day, I looked at a full schedule of what would be tough P&G interviews. The first three one-hour interviews were with two Brand Managers and a Marketing Director. All seasoned interviewers – they don't mess around at P&G. But I was well prepared – right by the book. The interviews were tough but I felt like I had managed through them reasonably well.

I was taken out to lunch by another Assistant Brand Manager, Barbara Crittenden, who was equally gracious and very impressive. She worked on the Charmin brand, and taught me more than I wanted to know about the two key market segments for bathroom tissue – folders and crumplers. Oooh, my first real live experience in market segmentation. This was cool. Barbara was loving P&G and assured me that I would, too. Guilt. Guilt. Guilt. Because only I knew I wasn't there to actually get a job. We returned to the office after lunch, and I was girding myself for the afternoon's grueling interviews.

Except for one thing.

When I got back in the office, I met with the Marketing Director who invited me into his office. He got right down to it.

"Michael, you've impressed a lot of people this morning. So we want to skip this afternoon's interviews and offer you a job right now as a Brand Assistant here in the Paper Products Division."

What? He was offering me a job with P&G right on the spot?

"Well, what about the afternoon's interviews?" I asked, quite taken back by the offer, reverting to the agenda for the day I was given. What else would a normal Type A person do?

"We don't believe we need them. We've seen all we need to know to offer you the job. In fact, all that's left is to find out when you want to start," he replied with great confidence.

It was at the point that I realized that I was not only in this really deep, I was in so far over my head that I was probably going to drown. My life was flashing before my eyes. A great light formed in the distance. A voice was beckoning me to "come to the light...."

The Marketing Director was not used to anyone saying anything other than "yes, I'll accept right now!" Especially if you weren't an MBA graduating from Harvard, Stanford, Wharton, University of Chicago, Northwestern, MIT, Columbia, and UVA (just to name a few). Which I wasn't. Not even close. If you were outside that elite circle and got a P&G offer, you should have been thankful not to have sacrificed your first born child for it. And I wasn't prepared to say yes to anything that wasn't part of The Plan!

So I said nothing; I had nothing to say. Certainly the truth wouldn't do in this circumstance.

"So when do you want to start, Michael?" The Marketing Director was cleverly using the *assumptive close* – not asking *if* I would accept the job, but *when* would I choose to start. And why wouldn't he?

I needed a diversionary tactic and I needed one fast. But I was fresh out of smoke bombs and no fire alarms to pull were in sight.

"Thank you very much for the offer. I'm quite flattered. When do you need to know my answer?" asked the Mouse. "It's just that I'm surprised to be receiving your offer today and am considering some options other than employment for next year. So I probably need to do a little more thinking on this."

There it was. I put it out there. It's not that I was going to take another job; rather, I was considering a *different life direction*. Yeah, that's it. We were going to see how this concept played in Peoria, or at least in Cincinnati, very quickly. The concept was either going to test well…or I was in *a heap of trouble*.

"Well, we'd want you to have all the time you think you reasonably need to consider our offer," the Marketing Director said with great political dexterity. Now I saw how he got to the job he had. "Perhaps a few weeks might be long enough?"

Good news: I wasn't in *a heap of trouble*.

"I'm sure a few weeks would be sufficient," I replied, wondering if I was going to need some of P&G's Charmin bath tissue -- or more likely, a very large Pampers diaper.

"Well, let me give you this official offer letter to take with you and this packet full of information on P&G Brands, our benefit programs, and what will undoubtedly be your bright future here. Also know that we'll be in touch. When we decide we really want someone to come join us, we will work hard to ensure you do. Is there anyone else you might like to speak with today that may help you with your decision before you leave?"

"Nnnnnot at the moment," I cowered, still pondering whether this situation was acceptable to use an emergency-only exit.

"Well then, you've got my number, so call me anytime." And with that, I was off to the airport with an unexpected offer in hand, ready to return to school.

What was I going to do now? I had really stepped in it…..

———

"BOURBON, PLEASE. ON the rocks."

"You look like you could use one," the perky flight attendant chirped as she searched the cart for a mini-bottle of Maker's Mark. I thought bourbon to be appropriate since we were somewhere over Kentucky en route to Virginia. She quickly poured the bourbon over ice and then looked sympathetically at me. "Are you OK?"

"I just got an unexpected job offer from Procter & Gamble," I replied shakily.

"And that's a bad thing?" she asked with more than a bit of sarcasm. A simple question, but as I paused to reflect on it, she had a good point.

"No, I guess not. Just an *unexpected* thing more than a *bad* thing, I guess. To tell you the truth, it just wasn't in my Plan," I said with perhaps a bit more consternation than intended.

"Then maybe you need a new plan," she laughed.

———

AT TIMES, ADVICE and opportunity share a commonality — they can come from where you'd least expect. That flight attendant's advice was perhaps the simplest and most profound piece of perspective I've ever received. And I certainly didn't expect the advice that would shape the balance of my career — and life -- to have come from an academic misadventure to develop a case study and a flight attendant who woke me up to what was likely an opportunity of a lifetime.

The Plan was officially dead.

2

MOVIN' ON UP...TO A DEE-LUXE APARTMENT IN THE SKY

AT ONE TIME, Procter & Gamble's Laundry Division — the collection of businesses that included brands like Tide, Cheer, Oxydol, Gain, Dawn, and Cascade — was affectionately referred to as 3M. Or at least its Brand Management department was.

Not 3M, as in the famous company Minnesota Mining and Manufacturing. Procter would never deign to voluntarily compare itself to another company. The US Marine Corps would not compare itself to anyone else. Heck, the Marines like to refer to the US Navy as its *taxi service*! P&G's Laundry Division was known as 3M because virtually everybody who worked there at the time fit into one of the three "M" classifications: 1) Military; 2) Male; or 3) Michigan. Generally, Laundry marketers were either ex-military, male or graduates of the University of Michigan. Sometimes, you had even multiple qualifications — like two-time P&G Chairman and CEO AG Lafley, who was both in the Military and a Male. Having two of three M's is what probably got him the top job at the world's largest consumer products company - twice. Just imagine how much further he might have gone in his career if he had all three M's!

The marketing staff of the Beauty Care Division at P&G — what Laundry Division snobs might call a collection of *lesser* P&G brands such as Head & Shoulders Shampoo, Prell Shampoo, and Lilt Homeperms — was not quite as homogeneous. Or pedigreed. We were more the mutts of the company and instead of having graduates of the University of Michigan, we actually had some from — brace yourself - Michigan

State. Clearly, we dared to differ – as long as you stayed within the state of Michigan. Clearly, P&G is comfortable with Midwestern accents and hard A's.

So P&G's Beauty Care Division leadership really stepped out of the proverbial box when they took in, dare I say it, an *undergraduate* from the University of Virginia. Mind you, they didn't actually *hire* me. It was more like they were *assigned* me. P&G's Paper Products Division did the actual hiring. As you may recall, I was studying the science of being a *quicker picker upper* and the nuanced differences between crumplers and folders during the interview stage of my early P&G experience.

When I got the phone call, I happened to be packing the U-Haul trailer for the move to Cincinnati in front of my parents' home in Charleston, SC. My mother yelled out of the back door, "Someone from P&G is on the phone for you. Better come quick." That didn't sound good.

"Hello," inquired the Mouse.

"Hi Michael, this is Cindy Mooreland from P&G's Human Resources department. I just called to let you know there's been a change of plans." I had met Cindy on my earlier visits to Cincinnati. A wonderful lady…delivering what appeared to be an ominous message.

"Change of Plans?" I inquired. Omigosh. I had an apartment rented in Cincinnati already. I had the U-Haul all loaded and was ready for what the cheerful U-Haul counter clerk promised to be an "Adventure in Moving". And I had abandoned The Plan! The Plan!! Would all of this elaborate diversion from The Plan be flushed at the last minute??? Would I be left at the altar??? P&G must have somehow discovered that I was a disingenuous interview….that I really wasn't serious when I interviewed for the job. How did they figure that out? Damn, they're even smarter than I thought they were. And I already thought they were pretty darn smart! Oh, this was devastating! What was I going to do?

"Yes, it turns out that our Beauty Care Division has an immediate need for a Brand Assistant on an important brand they're readying for test market. So we're going to move you from Paper to Beauty Care," Cindy informed me.

"So I still have a job?"

"Oh, goodness yes," Cindy reassured. Whew, OK. Level set. Breathe again. But don't sit down; your shorts may be soiled. Once again.

"Well that's good to hear. I was a little concerned there for a second."

"We just wanted to make sure you were OK with the transfer to Beauty Care."

Was I OK with it? I was OK with anything that had a paycheck attached to it at this point. I had abandoned The Plan for goodness sake!

"Sure, if that's where you need me that's where I'll be. By the way, is that still in Cincinnati? I'm getting ready to drive the moving truck up to Cincinnati now and if I have to drive somewhere else, just point it out and I'll get a new map." Ever the flexible one I was. Or so I liked to project.

"No. The only move you're making will be from the 4th floor to 6th floor in our headquarters," Cindy quipped. "Come see me at my office on your first day next week just as we planned and I'll take you to where you need to go."

And so it was. Just like that, I had moved from Diapers to Dandruff.

THE FIRST NIGHT in Cincinnati was a memorable one.

For almost everything at P&G there was a policy. And moving was no exception. The moving policy allowed for transporting the contents of your abode from one location to Cincinnati. And this was no *low rent* move, let me assure you. Professional packers, uniformed movers, furniture pads, boxes, the whole nine yards. P&G certainly provided more care in moving my things than they probably deserved. Like there was anything I owned a professional mover wouldn't look at and vomit, "you want me to touch that?"

My problem, relative to P&G's moving policy, was that the sum contents of my estate were located in two cities – Charlottesville, Virginia, where I had gone to school, and Charleston, South Carolina, where my dad had kindly offered to provide me with a few pieces of furniture from his store.

I had proposed to P&G what I thought was a win-win proposal to solve this problem. Instead of paying for professional movers, if I moved everything myself, would P&G pay for a U-Haul, a one way plane ticket for someone to help me move, and the associated food and gas costs? It didn't take P&G long to do the math on that proposal and realize they were getting a good deal.

So that's what we had – food, gas, a moving truck and sweat equity. One of my lifelong friends, Bernie Crane, agreed to help me move. Bernie and I went back a long way, all the way to the crib. I don't recall living life without Bernie. I think we may have been more like twins than Bernie was with his actual twin brother (they were fraternal, not identical). Bernie was a generally affable guy, if not a little wired. To say he didn't need to drink coffee was an understatement. Which is one of the many things I love about him. Always *on*. And a lot of fun. So he was totally up for the trip when I asked if he might help me move to Cincinnati.

We loaded up the truck in Charleston at my dad's furniture store and embarked upon the first leg of the road trip to Charlottesville. There, we packed all my possessions from college, completed the load and headed for Cincinnati. I drove the truck and Bernie followed in my car.

We arrived at my new apartment in Cincinnati about 2pm on a Saturday afternoon in June. The apartment was a one bedroom unit in a transitional area called Mt. Adams. It was what I could afford: $300 a month, heat included, off-street parking. Couldn't beat it. In 2013, condo's in the same neighborhood with the same view would set you back about $1 million. A far cry from $300 a month. Go figure.

The apartment overlooked the city and you could see Riverfront Stadium, the home of the Cincinnati Reds. As we passed Riverfront Stadium driving into Cincinnati, we noticed that the Los Angeles Dodgers were in town and the Saturday afternoon game was just underway. This was a major league city and we were *major league* excited.

It took us about three hours to unload the truck, set up the apartment and return the truck. At the U-Haul rental location, the attendant took us through the check-out process, accepted that despite our appearances we had not done unlawful damage to the truck and refunded our deposit.

At that moment Bernie had a great idea.

"Where can you get the best steak in Cincinnati?" Bernie asked the attendant.

"I've never been there myself, but I hear the best steak is at a restaurant not far from here called The Precinct. All the Reds and Bengals players hang out there. Gonna cost you a bundle though," the attendant told us.

Bernie and I locked eyes and our minds met like they had since we were in kindergarten: "Not if P&G's paying."

The U-Haul attendant did not steer us wrong. After a pair of much needed showers, Bernie and I took the short drive along Columbia Parkway, weaving along the Ohio River from Mt. Adams to The Precinct. We were not disappointed. This was a high end steak house in a remodeled police station, replete with a small jail, ostensibly for unruly guests. I was hopeful that we would not qualify that night; but given the way we were feeling, there were no guarantees on that matter!

After a few drinks in the bar, we were informed by the vivacious blonde hostess that we were ready to be seated. We had different ideas of what that could mean, but were also painfully aware that we were not in her league! So instead, we focused on the food. Bernie had the Steak Collinsworth and I had the Steak Anderson, named for former Cincinnati Bengals receiver Cris Collinsworth and quarterback Kenny Anderson. For two boys who had never even seen a live NFL football game – or eaten steaks of this caliber -- we were wide-eyed and in high cotton. The food was awesome. The environs were well above our pay grades. Especially since neither of us even *had* pay grades.

In a well-veiled effort to seat other guests for dinner, the management offered us a complimentary dessert upstairs in the disco (yes, disco, it was the early 80's). Sounded good to us. They seated us at a prime corner booth and we enjoyed the complimentary champagne and dessert. Three girls sauntered up to our table – why not? We were living large! They suggested we all head to the dance floor and that's exactly what the five of us did. This evening was just getting better and better. Was every night in Cincinnati like this? If so, I had made a very good call deviating from The Plan.

As the song on the dance floor transitioned, the DJ announced that he wanted to dedicate the next song, Frank Sinatra's legendary *New York, New York*, to Tommy Lasorda, manager of the Los Angeles Dodgers. We got the LA vs. New York joke; we even thought it was funny! Then we noticed an older couple dancing on the floor and as we looked closer, we realized that the gentleman was, in fact, Tommy Lasorda!

Perhaps it was the excitement of it being our first evening in Cincinnati. Perhaps it was the number of drinks we had that night (but I *seriously* doubt that could have been it). Perhaps it was simply fate. No matter which, we decided at the same moment that it was a good idea to *greet* Mr. Lasorda personally.

Perhaps our choice of greetings would not have been approved by the Greater Cincinnati Welcome Wagon.

"Hey Tommy, I hope Fernando Valenzuela is pitching tomorrow so the Reds can rough him up!" yelled Bernie, impressed with himself, and leaning over to high five me.

Where did that come from? What in the world made one of us say that? We'd been in town for a few hours and all of a sudden, we were die hard Reds fans ready to see *our* team beat up on the newest major league phenom pitcher?!

Clearly though, Tommy was not a novice at such welcomes. He knew how to handle this. He gently spoke to the woman he was dancing with, "Excuse me a moment, dear" and escorted her to the side of the dance floor. Then he walked back toward us, without menace, and said quite simply, "Hey boys?"

"Yeah, Tommy?" We eagerly awaited his response, smiles abounding.

"Hey boys, fuck off!" said Lasorda with an attitude a little more like New York than Los Angeles. We learned very quickly that Tommy Lasorda can be candid and direct. He then turned and walked back to dance with his partner, wearing a big smile.

We looked at Tommy, we looked at the girls, we looked at each other — and burst out laughing. High fives abounded! Was this the greatest night in the world or what? Great steaks, great times, beautiful women and Tommy Lasorda gave us his personalized *well wishes*.

It doesn't get much better than that for two 21 year old boys on their first night in the big city. An auspicious beginning to what would be an eventful next chapter of life.

3

CUBICLE LIFE

THE P&G DESK. Gunmetal gray. Army surplus. Laminate top surface. A multi-line telephone, replete with flashing lights. Flanking file drawers on the lower right and left. Small drawers above each of them; the left one for active papers, the right reserved for a special item. Locking middle drawer with enough room for four #2 pencils, two pens, a stapler and staple remover, and about 30 square paper clips.

Yes, you heard me. SQUARE paper clips.

I once attended a P&G training program conducted by an outside consultant. One of the topics was corporate culture and dealing with the softer aspects of succeeding at work. The consultant asked the group "Can anyone give me an example of the power of corporate culture?"

Silence. The typical P&G manager was trained to deal in the currency of data, cold hard facts. Nothing soft and mamby-pamby like *culture*. That was for psychologists, HR specialists, democrats, and those less fit for the marketplace combat of P&G Brand Management – such as people who worked at Unilever or Clorox or, dare I utter it, Kimberly-Clark.

"OK, the culture of a company is often defined by the unspoken, yet broadly accepted, practices prevalent in an organization. Can you think of one here at P&G?"

Still silence.

"OK. I'm going to draw something on the board. See if you can tell me what this is." He proceeded to draw a picture of a square paper clip, similar to the ones that sat in each member of the audience's middle drawer.

"Can anyone tell me what this is?"

Someone finally raised a hand and waited patiently to be selected.

"It's OK, just blurt it out," implored the facilitator, pleased that someone was finally participating.

"Yes, uh, it's a paper clip."

"Excellent. What else is it?"

"What do you mean, 'what else is it'?"

"You might think it's just a paper clip, but it's more than that. It's a cultural artifact. And you know why I assert that? Because I've consulted at a lot of companies, and there's only one other company than P&G where I've seen square paper clips – and that's Lenscrafters. What do 'eyeglasses in about an hour' have to do with square paper clips... or P&G? Nothing, but Lenscrafters was founded by ex-P&G people. And the culture of P&G is so powerful that they felt they had to have square paper clips instead of those dastardly round ones that virtually every other company in the world uses. I suspect it wasn't even a conscious choice; in fact, I'd be quite surprised if it were. Rather, when they ordered paper clips, they just assumed that square paper clips were the *right kind to have* – a reflexive choice. That's a cultural artifact, and what you get when you have a defined corporate culture. You're not even conscious of the choices you make."

The clarity of that observation has stuck with me for a lot of years. Culture is powerful.

P&G desks also came equipped with one other indispensable item -- the fact book. What in the world, you might ask, is a *fact book?* Well, let me assure you, there is no room in a fact book for, dare I say it.....*opinion*.

The fact book is a three ring binder with multiple tabs. In the fact book, one would place the most relevant business information to have at one's fingertips. Your assistant typed it on a piece of paper (hand-written data was considered *unprofessional*). You three-holed punched the typed sheet. You put it behind the appropriate tab in the fact book. That way, if you were in a meeting with Management (with a capital "M"), and were asked a specific question about your business, the appropriate fact would immediately available. As an entry level Brand Assistant, you brought your fact book with you to every meeting (along with a mechanical pencil and a calculator). I even saw a few carrying fact books into the bathroom! I imagine they were *folders* and not *crumplers*. Office paper doesn't crumple very well.

The fact book had a specific home in every P&G desk. It resided in that drawer of the gunmetal gray desk that I noted was for a *special item* -- the upper right hand drawer. The fact book was a very special item, and it lived in that drawer. *Locked* in that drawer, especially at night. You may have been forgetful enough to lose your house key; you may have on occasion misplaced your car key; but you NEVER dared to lose your desk key. And you had to keep the desk with the fact book locked, because you never knew when a Unilever or Kimberly-Clark employee dressed as a janitor would be lurking around the office at night.

Once a P&G Brand Manager left his fact book at the Cincinnati airport. An airport security guard found the binder and called P&G's headquarters to inform them the item was found. P&G's security team went out to the airport immediately to retrieve the fact book and assess how compromised P&G may have been. (You can almost see the black Chevrolet Suburbans screeching in front of the airport terminal!!) The Brand Manager to whom it belonged was never heard from again. There was a term for that – it was called *special assignment*. People *were sent on special assignment*....and never returned. It was like being drummed out of the corps of cadets at one of the Military Academies, only less ceremoniously. Since I first heard that term *special assignment*, I have always held the word *special* at a certain distance – the distance one would carry a soiled diaper or a spent uranium rod.

KEEPING THE FACT book updated was THE challenge. The end of every month brought new data, and thus, new reports. People would often just stuff new fact book materials in their desks, or in folders labeled *Fact Book Info to be Updated*. Clever folder title. A label like that would confuse even the CIA. And of course, people would inevitably get behind in filing. Because, after all, is there anyone in the world who likes filing? Anyone? Anyone? Bueller? Nonetheless, falling behind is what happened, which could prove to be perilous, or at least contribute to early aging and, if prolonged, special assignment.

I witnessed this problem with one of my mates in the Brand Bullpen, Marcia Natick. Marcia had a shock of strawberry blond hair, freckles, and drank, cussed and smoked like a sailor. Marcia will never get cancer from smoking. Cancer would be too intimidated to attack her. Cancer is too smart. It will target victims less likely to kick its butt. Like... General Patton.

Marcia was a blast to be around. Always something entertaining happening. And even if not, she found some way to ensure we ended up laughing – sometimes by design, sometimes by happenstance. Sometimes even with her signature snort after a belly laugh. She helped to train me from a Brand Pup and I learned a ton from her.

Marcia was one of the Assistant Brand Managers on the Ivory Shampoo and Conditioner Brand. Ivory was in its second test market, totally revamped after an initial test market failure. P&G tested products rigorously to ensure they got it right. Marcia had authored the written document, reverently called the *Reco* (short for *Recommendation*), describing the plan to expand Ivory nationally after the successful second test market. The Reco was making its way up P&G's management chain. Once forwarded to management, one never knew at any given time exactly which level of management a Reco resided. If there were questions, you got a call. If not, the Reco was passed up the food chain. So we often used the relationships that existed between administrative assistants to identify on whose desk the Reco sat. Reco Reconnaissance.

And let's be clear, NOTHING happened at P&G without a written, well-thought-through Reco. The famed P&G one-page memo was the transactional currency at P&G. It was *how business got done*. I wrote the reco to purchase the first personal computer in Beauty Care. I had to rewrite it a mere 18 times before it was acceptable.

But I digress.

Marcia's national expansion Reco was the *Granddaddy* of all P&G documents. Marcia's reco involved more than $150 million in marketing spending to support the business economics of the national introduction of a new brand. The Reco had probably been edited and revised more than 100 times before it was sent forward for approval. It was *that* important.

Suffice it to say, Marcia sat on pins and needles as the Reco moved its way through the system. The latest admin reconnaissance indicated Marcia's Reco had moved off the Executive Vice President's desk and was sitting on the desk of then P&G Chairman & CEO, John Smale. The final step before going to the Board of Directors.

John Smale was one of the most iconic of P&G's Chairmen. Brilliant, sharp, insightful. Committed to doing the right thing for the long term. A great Canadian. He served on numerous Boards of Directors, including serving as Chairman of GM's Board after his retirement. Having a major reco such as a national expansion of a new brand approved by Smale was a career-making move. And Smale knew career-making moves. I never read a single article in any publication about John Smale that didn't mention that he turned Crest into the #1 US toothpaste in the 1950's by securing the endorsement of the American Dental Association. Smale ran major multi-national corporations, but his claim to fame, the thing people remembered him for, was inevitably a toothpaste claim. It was even in his obituary when he passed away in 2011. Go figure.

So Marcia was awaiting her *Smale moment*.

About 11:30am one morning, Mr. Smale's administrative assistant called Marcia and asked if the Brand Group could be available to speak with him regarding the Reco. Like the answer would be "uh, no, we were planning to go to Shillito's during our lunch hour to shop. Would next Tuesday do?" A mad scramble ensued. We had thirty minutes before meeting with Smale. It took Marcia ten minutes to smoke a cigarette, hair spray the shock, dab on a little more make-up, and gather herself. At the T-minus twenty minute mark, she realized her fact book was not updated.

"Oh gawd," she exclaimed in her Michigan accent. Hard a's and expletives abounding.

"I'll help," I offered. "You hand me the sheet you want, I'll three hole punch it, and you can put it behind the right tab in the fact book. Go!" And that's what we did. Papers flying everywhere, white round paper punches all over. We finished at exactly two minutes to 12, with just enough time to take all the stray sheets of paper and hide them behind one of the desks. We had our coats on (you never met with *Management with a Capital M* without your suit coat on) and were ready as Mr. Smale turned the corner. Following briskly behind him were the Ivory Brand Manager, Associate Advertising Manager, Advertising Manager and Division Vice President, as word spread quickly Smale was on the floor. Like on a naval ship, "Officer On Board"!! And everyone was certainly standing at attention. I had never even seen Mr. Smale in the flesh before. He struck me as strangely human, for someone who was larger than life, the kingpin of Procter celebrity.

"Shall we meet in a conference room, Mr. Smale?" asked Marcia's boss, the Ivory Brand Manager, feeling the need to take charge of the situation. Marcia braced for what was sure to be the grilling of her life. It was a great moment of truth. This was the moment in which she was going to make her career, her *American Dental Association Moment*. And she was ready, fact book and all.

"No need," said Mr. Smale. "I'll just ask my question right here: where was the original Ivory Shampoo test market, the one that failed?"

"St. Louis," replied Marcia immediately and efficiently.

"Excellent," retorted Smale. "That's all I need to know at this point. I'll let you know when I'm ready to discuss the expansion Reco."

And Smale wheeled out of the bull pen.

We all stared at each other dumbfounded. That was it? A call a half hour ahead of time announcing a royal visit, a mad scramble to have the fact book as pristine as possible, cigarettes smoked, hair sprayed and freckles dabbed with make-up — just to answer that question???

"Well, at least I got my fact book updated," quipped Marcia, as we all chuckled. "Anyone got any business questions?"

BEFORE MODERN DAY office systems were created, P&G desks were arranged in pods by Brand group. All the Tide Brand Assistants and Assistant Brand Managers sat in a collective pod across the hall from the Tide Brand Manager, who had a real office with a real door, that was frequently closed. Probably taking calls from Executive Recruiters. The P&G Brand Manager was expert at self-advancement. Elevated it to an art form.

The pod which held all the people that reported to the Brand Manager -- the Brand Assistants and Assistant Brand Managers -- was affectionately known as the Bull Pen.

The bull pen — the 1980's version of the work cubicle — was where it happened. Imagine a U-shaped wall, with 3-6 desks flat against the walls. When chairs rolled back they bumped into each other. When telephones rang, when group conversations ensued, when someone smoked a cigarette, when someone spilled coffee (Folgers of course — 15 cents a cup), when someone murmured a quick "I love you" on the phone, when someone quietly tried to suppress a burp after lunch — everyone heard it!! Nothing went unnoticed. They were no secrets in the bull pen. It was all out there. As such, the members of the bull pen became your family. It was a tight-knit group, designed to build camaraderie fast and to foster a team environment. And it worked.

For 12-15 hours a day every weekday. Often one day a weekend, too. Sometimes two. And it was not only where the work was….it was also where the fun was. A lot of *bull* was slung in the bull pen.

SOME CALL IT *welcoming new employees*. Some call it *hazing*. I suspect what went on in the bull pen for newly hired Brand Assistants landed somewhere in between. All of it was good spirited and perhaps even a bit fun. Depending upon whether you are the giver or the receiver I guess.

The king of hazing on the 6th floor was a guy named Jim Bedrosian. Jim was an above-average sized guy. Six-four or so, probably 250 pounds. Had the largest head I've ever seen on a human being. And from this huge cranium emitted a huge, booming voice. You could hear him coming down the hall as his voice carried over the bull pen walls.

"Oh, oh. I hear Bedrosian coming," muttered Marcia. No one seemed to call him Jim. Only "Bedrosian". A single name. Like Madonna. Or Mussolini.

"Who's Bedrosian?" asked the Mouse.

"You'll find out," said Marcia, somewhat ominously.

"And who might we have here?" boomed Bedrosian, as he turned into the Ivory bull pen, boring down on me. "I heard we have a new baby brand assistant aboard."

"Shut up, Bedrosian," Marcia said protectively. "Michael, meet Bedrosian."

"Pleased to meet you," said the Mouse as I stood and extended a tiny paw. It was met by a meat cleaver of a hand, extended from somewhere behind the heifer of a head that had engulfed my field of vision.

"Nice to meet you too, Michael. Hey, by chance, do you play racquetball? We love to play after work, up on the 11th floor. We're always happy to have another."

"Don't do it, Michael," warned Marcia, as she blew out a puff of smoke from her cigarette. She didn't deign to even lift her head out of her work when in Bedrosian's presence. "It's a set up. Don't fall for it."

"Damn, Natick, you are no fun whatsoever," Bedrosian groused and turned to leave. "Does no one have fun around here anymore?" he called to no one in particular. "Are we all so serious that we can't have any fun at the expense of a baby brand assistant anymore?"

"Not when it's *my* baby brand assistant," scolded Natick, as she lifted one eyebrow and eyeballed him with a motherly scowl. I loved that Marcia protected me. "Now beat it, Bedrosian."

"What is this world coming to…" Bedrosian muttered as he beat a frustrated retreat, shaking his huge head. He knew better than to mess with Marcia.

"What was that all about?" the Mouse asked.

"It's a Procter time-honored pimp whose time has passed," Marcia responded in a protective tone.

"A pimp? He's a pimp AND an Assistant Brand Manager? How does the company feel about that?" I was clearly confused.

"No. *Pimp* is the term used around here for a practical joke. He doesn't manage prostitutes, although it might be a better fit for his skill set. He was about to make a fool out of you."

"How?" inquired the Mouse.

"It goes like this. They tell you there are racquetball courts on the 11th floor. They have you bring in your racquetball clothes the next day and change in the office bathroom after work. They tell you to meet them on the northeast part of the 11th floor at 5:00pm. So you change into your tennis shoes and whites, hop in the northeast elevators, and hit the button for the 11th floor. When the elevator door opens, you're peering right into eyes of John Smale's administrative assistant, who sits right in front of his office, which is directly in front of you.

"The 11th floor isn't a health club", Marcia continued. "It's the executive floor. Mahogany paneled walls, green crushed velvet carpeting, quiet as a library, smells like your grandma's closet. You just *know* you're not supposed to be there. And as the embarrassment you're experiencing sets in, you paste yourself against the interior wall of the elevator and hit the down button as fast as you can. The quiet of the 11th floor makes it easier to hear all the laughing that greets you when you come back to the 6th floor, completely and utterly humiliated. Isn't that a great joke?"

"Well, I have to admit. It's pretty clever and probably pretty funny."

"Not if it's *you* in the elevator. At least not at that particular moment. Maybe later, but not then." I got the visual of Marcia standing there in her white tennis dress, shock of strawberry blonde perfectly coifed, lip gloss perfect....totally blushed a shade of red that does not occur in nature, and drowning in a sea of embarrassment. I couldn't visualize myself in that position. Or didn't want to.

"Then thanks for saving me, Marcia. I really appreciate it."

"Yea, you owe me one. You'll owe me many. I'll collect someday."

———— ∞∞∞ ————

THE FIRST 45 minutes of Monday mornings were one of my favorite times in the bull pen.

It always started out slow. Everyone stumbled in between 7:45 and 8:00am, shaking out the cob webs of the weekend. Some sat at their desk staring at a document; not reading it, just staring at it with fixed eyes. Some glanced across the headlines of the *Wall Street Journal*. Others quietly made a list of what they needed to do that day, yet there was very little talking.

At least not until the bell rang. Not an alarm or a bell like you would hear in high school to signal the change in classes. Not even church bells. It was a little tinkle bell, like a self-important member of the elite would use to call for a servant to lift the silver cover off their breakfast in bed.

It was almost Pavlovian. When the ball rang, you could see people's eyes perk up. You watched them smack their lips, their mouths beginning to water.

Folgers. Yes, coffee. And it most certainly was called "Folgers", not *coffee*. This is the land where Brands are King. It would have been like calling "Kleenex" *tissues* at Kimberly-Clark. It just isn't done. At least not in polite company.

The tinkle was the coffee cart. P&G had a coffee cart on each floor that served Folgers and carried assorted danish and doughnuts. And Priscilla, the coffee cart *lady*, dressed in a freshly pressed uniform, would push the cart around our floor. She reminded me of Hazel, the maid of the eponymous 60's sitcom. Priscilla would tinkle the bell, and brand pups of all shapes, sizes and colors would pour out of the bull pens with their two dimes in hand. A 15 cent cup of Folgers and a 5 cent chocolate doughnut. Breakfast of Champions.

As the caffeine began to course through the bloodstream, the brand group would begin to come to life. The ritual was to begin the week by retelling stories of what transpired over the weekend.

THE OTHER ASSISTANT Brand Manager on Ivory Shampoo and Conditioner was Mark Shapiro. Mark had recently been promoted into this role, having just returned from a training assignment with the Sales organization in the field. Mark grew up in Chattanooga, Tennessee, and came to P&G by way of the Kellogg School of Business at Northwestern University. The Kellogg School was perhaps the best marketing MBA one could get, and P&G had begun recruiting furiously there (outside of the Laundry Division, of course – it wasn't Michigan). This would have been a good reason for Mark to be arrogant. But that wouldn't have been Mark. The man didn't have an arrogant bone in his body.

Mark was just plain ol' fun. And funny. And this humor actually belied the brilliant mind behind it. Mark and I hit it off right away. Perhaps it was that we had common backgrounds, both being Jewish boys from the South working for a WASPy company in a German Catholic city. That's OK, we were used to being in the minority. We kinda liked it that way. It strengthened our secret alliance. Jewish humor and Yiddish swear words were our secret code.

"So what were you guys up to this weekend?" asked Marcia, kicking off the Monday Update with a freshly lit cigarette to compliment her black Folgers. "I hope it was better than mine, because all I did was spend the whole weekend here. N-O-F-U-N!"

"Sharon and I went to Chattanooga to visit my parents," said Mark. Sharon was his blond haired, blue eyed girlfriend – the girl every Southern Jewish boy pursues as soon as he moves away from his parents' house and is therefore allowed to date someone other than one of the twelve Jewish girls with whom he grew up. Sharon was also an Assistant Brand Manager on the Sure Deodorant Brand and worked in a bull pen down the hall. So she had a lot more going for her than blue eyes and blond hair. No blond jokes here. Sharon was sharp!

"The issue of the weekend was my dad trying to deal with my grandfather. You will NOT believe this one!" Mark exclaimed. We had heard a few stories before on this topic, never to be disappointed.

"Do tell," said Marcia. "But wait until I get back. I gotta get another cup of Joe."

MARK'S GRANDFATHER HAD come to America from Poland in the early 1900's. Like many Jewish immigrants at the time, they came to the US through Ellis Island in New York, and with the few dollars they had, took a train to whatever town in which they had some family. For Mark's grandfather, it was Atlanta, Georgia.

And like many of his time, he worked for his cousin or uncle or friend as a peddler, using a horse-drawn cart to travel from town to town selling wares. It was not an easy life. But it was a helluva lot better than the pogroms of Russia and Eastern Europe, and eventually, the Third Reich.

Eager to build a new life in this land of religious freedom, Marks's grandfather, like so many like him, made friends easily and built up a nice business. You could tell where Mark got his amiability. Mark's grandfather met a woman in Atlanta and soon they were married. With the money he had saved, he opened a Dry Goods store in one of the small towns up in the North Georgia mountains in which he had peddled and had come to know the people of the town of Dalton. They were the only Jews in this small, mill town. But they lived piously and did their best not to stand out too much. While they stayed true to their Jewish values and traditions, it was a private observance. They raised their only son, Mark's father, with the same sense of values and humor, taking him on the weekends to nearby Chattanooga so he could also get a sense of Jewish community.

Over time, Mark's grandfather decided that he could live a more complete Jewish life in Chattanooga. But what would he do for a living? He understood the clothing business so he secured a Hanes underwear distributorship with rights for the southeast Tennessee and North Georgia region and, as they say, moved up the value chain. He closed the store in Dalton, rented it for income, and moved his family to Chattanooga. There, he bought a small warehouse, where he stored the Hanes products, while his wife and son lived on the second floor of the building. Mark's father studied hard in high school, and later graduated from the University of Tennessee-Chattanooga with a degree in Accounting. He joined his father in the business and helped to transform it into a thriving business. As the business grew, they moved the distribution center into a modern and much larger facility in Chattanooga. Yet Mark's grandparents refused to move from their apartment above the original warehouse. It was *home*.

Years later, they were offered a tidy sum for the Hanes distributorship and smartly sold. Being financially secure, but not likely to retire, Mark's father decided to open a restaurant on the ground floor of the original warehouse, which, due to his amiability and hard work, became an instant success. It was expanded a number of times to add dining rooms and quickly became the highest grossing restaurant in Chattanooga. However, despite the growth, Mark's grandfather never wanted to move again, especially after his wife passed away and left him alone. So they grew the restaurant *around* his grandfather's tiny, original apartment on the second floor and his grandfather continued to live there happily.

"You gotta hear the latest with my granddad," Mark quipped. He had this look in his eye like you knew there was a good story coming.

"He's now 86 and still drives. But in a single week, Pops had three accidents, nearly killing himself in the last one. He wasn't really hurt, but he put the car right near the edge of a lake. If it had rolled in, he would have drowned for sure. So my dad tells me that he just had to take Pops' keys. It broke his heart but he had no choice."

"So how did your Grandfather take it?" Marcia asked, blowing a puff of smoke in the air.

"About as well as you'd expect anyone who was losing his freedom. But thinking ahead, my father promised him that he would hire someone in the restaurant whose primary job would be to drive Pops wherever he wanted to go."

"A sort of 'Driving *Mr.* Daisy'?" I asked with a smile.

"Yeah, but I don't think Morgan Freeman would have taken this job," Mark replied.

"Dad told Pops that he was going to interview a fellow for the job and he wanted Pops to sit in on the interview. Pops was not happy. He didn't like the idea, didn't want any part of it. Dad made him come to the interview anyway and Pops sat in the back silently with his arms crossed and a scowl on his face. As my father interviewed the fellow, Pops said nothing."

"At the end of the interview, my father looked at Pops and asked, 'Well, Pops, do you have any questions you'd like to ask?'"

Pops sat there with the same sour look on his face and thought for a moment. Then he responded in the most even voice he could muster, staring at the young interviewee.

"Young man, you seem like a fine boy. Good character, upstanding, hard working, earnest. Congratulations. Your parents have done a fine job raising you."

"Thank you, sir."

"So, young man, I only have one question for you: do you own a gun?"

"No sir," replied *young man*.

"Do you know how to shoot a gun?"

"No sir. I've never shot a gun in my life," *young man* eagerly responded, proud even.

"I see," said Pops. And then he went quiet.

"So what does having never shot a gun have to do with this driving job?" mistakenly asked *young man*.

Pops looked him straight in the eye and dropped the kindly demeanor.

"Not having a gun, well…that's just unfortunate for you," Pops began, his voice even and icy. "Because, you see, I *do* have a gun. It's a .32 pistol in fact. I keep it in my pocket. All the time. And I *do* know how to shoot this gun. And I will tell you this as sure as I'm sitting here today. If you take this job, if you step into the front seat of my car and try to drive me around in my own car, here's what I'm going to do. I'm going to take out my gun someday, not the first day, nor the second. Likely when you least expect it. I'm going to quietly take out my gun and I'm going to shoot you with it…."

in the back of the head....from the back seat of the car ....as many times as it takes until you're stone dead! Now, with that in mind, do you think you still want to take this job?"

"Is he crazy?" *young man* looked at Mark's dad incredulously, wide eyed. "I mean, is he really crazy?"

"No," Mark's dad lamented, begrudging a smile, knowing he'd be beaten. "He's quite sane...and he knows exactly what he's doing."

And they both had a nice laugh as *young man* scampered out the door like he was running for his life. Experience will trump good intentions every time.

—⚬⚬⚬—

"I DON'T THINK I can top that one," I said. "In fact, I'm not sure I've heard a story in my life that tops that. But Toni and I surely had an unusual thing happen this weekend while we were in Charlottesville."

We had travelled back to Charlottesville to meet some college friends for Homecoming Weekend and a football game. Which was largely an excuse to get to Charlottesville, Virginia, to see the leaves change in the fall. If anyone ever doubts there is a God, then you should visit Charlottesville in the fall when the leaves are in full color. It is as if God painted the leaves himself, only for the sheer joy of watching them fall softly to His earth.

Of course, the hotels are always full during football weekends, so we opted for alternate accommodations. Once when I was in Charlottesville, I got a brochure for a network of private homes that offered bed & breakfast accommodations for overnight stays. There was one large home only two blocks from UVA's central grounds so we booked a room for the weekend.

We arrived Friday afternoon around 4:30pm after driving all day. Mrs. Wellington, the owner of the home, greeted us at the door, shooing back her rather large English Bulldog who was barking rather loudly. This did not start well.

"Quiet, Winston!" she scolded the dog. Fortunately, the dog heeled as commanded.

"Welcome to Wellington Place," she intoned, with a voice bearing the timbre and continental dialect of Julia Child. Mrs. Wellington was about 5' 2", a rather barrel chested woman, in her late 60's to my estimation. She explained that she and the late Professor Wellington had lived in Wellington Place for the last 40 years. After the good Professor had passed, she chose to rent a few rooms in the west wing of

Wellington Place to some law students. However, they were so distracted with studies, that she became bored with them and decided to rent a guest room for greater entertainment value.

"Oh, and here I am prattling on while I'm sure you'd like to get to your room and clean up. Come along, Winston, let's show our guests to their room." Winston, of course, was a bit distracted as all sixty pounds of him were dry humping my leg. Mrs. Wellington had not noticed and I was trying to be polite by tolerating it. Apparently, now, Winston liked me. A little too much, I believe.

"Winston, please. How dreadfully rude you are," she scolded the dog when she finally noticed his, er, affinity for my leg. Fortunately for me, Winston heeded her word. "Bulldogs can be so terribly affectionate, can't they?" she said pretty much to no one as she had already turned to escort us to our rooms. That was an understatement. I hoped he would be affectionate with someone else.

"After cleaning up, you absolutely must join me in the courtyard for cocktails," she announced. "It's nearly five o'clock and according to my watch, it's officially the cocktail hour!" I had gotten the impression that her notion of cocktail *hour* might not have necessarily been time-bound. But I was OK with that.

Wellington Hall had what you might call *outlier* architecture for the city of Charlottesville, which boasted more red brick two story colonials than you could shake a stick at. Settled in a 100+ year old neighborhood, Wellington Hall was hardly English. Rather it was a Mediterranean style villa, built of stone and wood, with a red-tiled roof and an elaborate stone courtyard. There were not many similar homes nearby – or in the state of Virginia.

After she poured us her cocktails of choice – Bourbon on the rocks – we got the grand tour, with Winston in tow. Fortunately, Winston was keeping his distance, but I could swear he was eying my leg with a look of lust that made me shudder.

As we ended the tour in the stone courtyard, I noticed there was a green patch of grass in the Southwest corner of the courtyard. As I wandered over to get a better look, I noticed that the green patch had three prominent headstones.

"Professor Wellington, I presume?" I asked, nodding toward the green patch.

"Oh, heavens no," she replied quite dramatically. "Professor Wellington is buried in the University's cemetery, adjacent to Echols Dorm up on Alderman Road. Just a few stones down from William Faulkner, whom I consider to be the *second* most famous English professor to have taught here at the University!" She was quite proud of her reference and chuckled lightly, no doubt reliving a fond remembrance of the dear old professor. Or perhaps it was of Faulkner. I couldn't quite tell. There was definitely something about this odd woman that I quite enjoyed.

"Then who is buried in your courtyard?" I inquired, wondering if I was going to regret having asked the question.

"Have a closer look then, dear," she chided. "You'll see that these are the hallowed grounds where we have laid to rest Winston's three predecessors. We love English Bulldogs so."

And there they were. The three headstones read "Winston", "Winston II" and "Winston III". She had buried her dogs in the courtyard. And purchased headstones for them, too! I was willing to bet that Winston IV pissed on each of them every day, just to show them who's still around!

"And I presume this would be Winston IV then", nodding to my overly amorous friend.

"Quite," she responded and then she lowered her voice, ostensibly so Winston IV wouldn't hear what she was about to say. "But, let me tell you, Winston III was actually my favorite. He was such a sweet creature. Have a look at the inscription on the headstone."

The headstone read in old English font, "Winston III: Born a Dog. Died a Gentleman."

We all laughed heartily.

To which Mark quipped, "Yeah, if Winston IV had been a gentleman, he would have at least taken you out to dinner before having sex with your leg!"

— ∞ —

ON OCCASION, WHEN a story was too funny to resist, one would hear chuckling coming over the wall of the Bull Pen, from one of the adjacent Bull Pens. This morning the chuckling came from John Edward Hasse.

The *Hasse-Man* as he was called, was the Brand Assistant on Head & Shoulders shampoo. Hasse-Man was an unusual hire, given the general P&G standards. He was not your typical "go for the throat, self-promoting, can't wait to become CEO tomorrow" type A personality that P&G loved to hire.

Hasse-Man was what you might call *educated*. John was about 10 years older than me, had a Bachelors degree, Masters degree, and PhD -- all in Music -- and was a highly accomplished pianist. Something had motivated him to go to the Wharton

School of Business at the University of Pennsylvania, and from there he came to P&G. Not one to give up his passion for music, on the weekends, Hasse-Man would do lectures at regional universities on the work of his PhD dissertation, Ragtime Music. Hasse-Man would flash up a few slides on the musicians of Ragtime such as Scott Joplin, and then play for you his own version of the *Maple Leaf Rag* that would have made you think you were back in time. What a talented guy.

Perhaps you've probably heard of the many P&G alumni who have gone on to become CEO's of famous global companies – perhaps Jeff Immelt (GE), Meg Whitman (e-Bay, Hewlett-Packard), Steve Case (AOL), Steve Ballmer (Microsoft), Paul Polman (Unilever), Scott Cook (Intuit), and the list goes on. But none of the P&G alumni did what the Hasse-Man did.

After two years of the grind at P&G, Hasse-Man decided that the rat race was not for him. So he went to Washington, DC, to become the Curator of American Music at the Smithsonian Institution, a role he held for at least the next three decades. And, let me tell you, you haven't heard the Ella Fitzgerald story until you've heard the Hasse-Man tell it!

Chuckling, Hasse-Man came around the corner into the Ivory Bull Pen. "I hope you don't mind me eavesdropping, but those were pretty funny stories. I don't have anything quite as colorful, but I thought you guys might like hearing about our meeting with Carmichael on Friday."

Carmichael was Bob Carmichael (not the little boy who mowed Mrs. Hardcastle's lawn), the much-loved and quite eclectic Vice President of P&G's Beauty Care business. Bob was the original tough guy with a soft heart. Despite having become a rather wealthy man as an officer at P&G, he never forgot that he grew up on a farm in Nebraska, rode a motorcycle because he couldn't afford a car, had lived in a trailer (and not even a double-wide) for a period of time, and had his nose broken in a few places in more than one drunken brawl. As Carmichael used to say, "I have a lot of class; but most of it's *third*."

We all loved Carmichael because he was *real* – no airs about him. What you saw was what you got and we respected that. He also genuinely cared about us as people – *his* people. He cared enough to complement us when we did well, usually through a quickly penned note. If you got one of those notes, you kept it in a secret file. It was a treasure. He also cared enough to point out when we screwed up and gave us an appropriately swift kick in the rear to let us know. When that happened we only wanted to work harder to please Bob. I had what I considered to be a true honor to work on Bob's team for eight years.

"So the purpose of the meeting Friday was to show Carmichael casting tapes for the latest Head & Shoulders commercial we're getting ready to shoot," continued Hasse-Man. "As we showed him the five finalists for the spot, he just kinda scrunched up his brow. You know how he does that?" Yes, we'd all seen that before. And it was not usually followed with a complement.

"You do realize that the target audience for a Head & Shoulders commercial is largely male?" Carmichael offered.

"Yes, we do," replied Hasse-Man, the appointed representative of the Head & Shoulders brand. It's amazing how quickly the responsibility for a project moves down the hierarchy as soon as Management expresses concern.

"Then why did you cast all these *girly-men?*" Carmichael did not find this comment the least bit offensive. He did not harbor a racist or elitist bone in his body. To him, his observation was just a *fact*.

"Uh, *girly men*, sir?" replied Hasse-Man.

"Yes, *girly men*! How much more plainly do I need to say it?" Clearly, Carmichael was not too worried about being politically correct or insensitive.

"Well, these are the types of male models we typically get from our usual talent scouts at the Advertising Agency," Hasse-Man explained, treading carefully.

"Then they're scouting the wrong talent to appeal to the Head and Shoulders consumer. And I can tell you how to fix that," replied Carmichael with quite a bit of confidence and a wry smile. "Tell the Agency that when they're screening male models, ask each model *just one* question; this question: 'if you're in the shower and you realize you have to pee, do you get out of the shower?' Eliminate anyone who answers *yes!*"

We all howled. The Gospel According to Carmichael. More life in the Cubicle.

4

THE GREATEST SALES REP IN THE CAROLINAS

At Procter & Gamble in 1983, the best job in the Company was NOT the job of Chief Executive Officer. Sure, the CEO got paid the most money in the Company; sure, the CEO had a car and driver waiting at his call; sure the CEO had a grand, mahogany-paneled office and a door electronically controlled by the button under his desk; sure, the CEO got on his gulfstream jet (which Bob Carmichael dubbed "The Wretched Excess") and flew off to wherever he needed to go. And it's possible that if anyone was afforded the privilege, it was the CEO who would get to drink his morning coffee from the original Folger's sterling silver coffee service....for 15 cents, of course.

But I'd still contend that was not the best job in the Company.

In my humble opinion, the best job at Procter & Gamble was a job that doesn't exist anymore. There's no need for it the way the world works today. But back then, people would kill for this job.

The District Sales Manager. The best job in the Company.

Yes, you heard me right. The District Sales Manager. "Why?" you might ask, for which I'd be eternally grateful, because it would allow me to proceed with an explanation....and a story or two.

You see, the DSM was the best job in the Company because he was akin to an Emperor (and they were nearly all "he's" back then). The DSM had a regional territory (there were about 25 in the US – per P&G Division) with a number of customers, primarily grocery stores. After all, P&G at the time was largely a soap and detergent company. In fact, P&G created the original soap opera concept as media content to carry their radio and later television advertising. Thus the moniker *soap operas*. How's that for a fun fact to know and tell? OK, you can get back in your chair and recover from your shock.

But I digress.

At the time, grocery stores were where soap and detergents were primarily purchased. The DSM's empire often included at least one major regional grocery store chain (such as Kroger in the midwest, Winn-Dixie in the southeast, Pathmark in the northeast, and Von's on the west coast) and a number of smaller ones also. His goal was to get P&G products distributed in any store that could pay on P&G's not so generous business terms. Woe to an account that was a day late on payments to P&G.

At the time, there were really no global, national or super-regional grocery retailers as there are today. Wal-Mart was a relatively small regional mass merchandiser (it didn't even sell groceries then). So the sales function of P&G was largely administered regionally. Or, more accurately, in little *empires*.

There were no scanners in the grocery stores like there are today, so the data revolution that was created by scanners was just a dream in some lab at IBM back then.

Today, data gathered in stores from scanners impact an incredible amount of the way retailers operate – how they order products, manage inventories, decide what goes on the shelf and on display, price products, and manage profit margins. Not to mention, how retailers watch and analyze what we as consumers buy. These abilities were only dreams back then.

As such, instead of those things being managed at centralized headquarters through data and cyber connections as they are today, they were influenced by *feet on the street* -- the *feet* of sales people and grocery store clerks, at the store level, armed with shelf tags for pricing, header cards to build displays, and sales presentations to store managers who made all those decisions, store by store. So the DSM and his team were P&G's ability to influence at the retail level, *in the field*, as it was called.

This was the power base of the DSM, his *Empire*. He commanded legions of sales rep's, had lieutenants called Unit Managers to manage the sales rep's day-to-day and call on the major accounts. What the DSM spent most of his time doing was presiding over the Empire and sandbagging head quarters on his monthly sales estimates. *Sandbagging* was the time honored practice of negotiating downward one's sales goals through expertly created and documented excuses, and then over-delivering goals. That meant better bonuses, and more importantly, the ability to brag as to how much better your empire was than someone else's. Most importantly though, if one sand-bagged well, presided well, and was savvy enough to get a warm weather empire, then one generally became an accomplished golfer too.

A good DSM was probably akin to a good military Captain – not a military General. They did not need to be a military strategist. They did not plan wars; they figured out how to *take hills*. They were good at taking orders from headquarters. And they were good at motivating and commanding troops to turn those orders into ground level actions. Actions that got results. Results that generated cases sold. Not profit, mind you; that was the role of the military strategists at headquarters. Volume. Their objective was simple: grow volume. And they used every tool at their disposal to do so.

The DSM who was expert at moving volume, at this single-minded goal, had the best job in the world. If he delivered his numbers, no one looked over his shoulder. If headquarters people had questions about a customer, they had to go through the DSM. He had *control* over his Empire. And in a very large Fortune 50 company, having control of *anything* usually translated to some measure of comfort, some measure of security. If you managed your Empire well, you didn't need to be promoted. You didn't *want* to be promoted. You simply raised your family, had a great job, and retired a millionaire on P&G stock. Not a bad plan.

That describes many happy DSM's. All P&G's CEO's retired as millionaires, too. But look what they had to go through – relatively speaking – to get there. CEO's lived to their 70's. DSM's lived to their 90's. That's why the DSM job was the best job in the company.

OK, I'll admit it. These guys had it figured out and I was envious. Wouldn't you be?

⸺⸙⸺

P&G FELT IT was essential for every Brand Manager, and ultimately every general manager, to have a keen understanding of consumers. CEO AG Lafley later coined the mantra "The Consumer is King" to ensure that was the focus of the company, which was a change from the past, where I believe P&G thought "The Brand is King." In addition to understanding consumers, P&G expected Brand Managers to have a good understanding of retailers, too; but for different reasons. Back then, P&G viewed the retailer as an *impediment* between the company and its ultimate customer -- the consumer. P&G viewed retailers as an unfortunate and unnec-essary link in the chain between product idea and consumer purchase, sapping dollars from P&G's preferred method of marketing – advertising – which simply translated to sapping profit from the P&G shareholder. If money wasn't spent on advertising, it was generally wasted according to the P&G mantra Brand Assistants were drilled on. And like any other evil in the world that you couldn't make go away, P&G had to find a way to work productively with it, much to P&G's chagrin. P&G, after all, was practical.

So every Brand Assistant had to spend some time in the field working with the Sales organization before they could become a Brand Manager at P&G. It was a pro-gram, creatively dubbed *Sales Training* (go figure!), in which a P&G manager would transfer for a 2-3 month period from Marketing into Sales, reporting to a DSM. Many DSM's didn't particularly like Sales Trainees from headquarters. They were nuisances, work-creators as opposed to work-providers, and quite possibly, spies. Yes, spies from headquarters who might report back on how things really happened in the Empire. A potential threat to the Emperor who had to be ever-vigilant, on guard for distur-bances in the Force.

Some less defensive DSM's chose to embrace the Sales Trainee. After all, Brand Managers controlled big budgets. And budgets were the equivalent of taxes to the Emperor. A well cultivated relationship with a number of Brand Managers could mean the Emperor might generate more taxes, taxes that could be spent to buy more volume. More volume equaled more independence. And more independence propa-gated the Emperor's way of life.

———

WHILE THERE WERE mixed views among the Emperors as to the value of Sales Trainees, there was no question as to the desirability of becoming a Sales Trainee to Brand Assistants. Of course, this had nothing to do with the desirability of the content of the work (as you'll see later). It had everything to do with advancement in P&G. It was the first promotion one would get in Brand Management. The entry level job at the time was entitled Brand Assistant, followed by Assistant Brand Manager and then Brand Manager. Only one-third of people hired into Brand Assistant jobs eventually made it to Brand Manager. The rest failed and were summarily dismissed from the company, deemed not good enough. *Went on special assignment*. It's a cold world.

Sales Training was desirable because getting sent on Sales Training meant you had accomplished all the requirements of being a Brand Assistant, and were therefore being released from Boot Camp. When you returned from Sales Training, you came back promoted into the Assistant Brand Manager role. So by definition, Sales Training was a good thing, no matter what perils or disappointments the job may have held.

And the disappointments were many.

As a Brand Assistant, one was given a tremendous amount of responsibility. Typically, you worked on one of the world's best known brands (even if it was only shampoo, Pantene was still *sexy*). And you managed budgets in the tens, sometimes hundreds, of millions of dollars, planned promotions that generated millions in profit, and developed packaging that could be seen in every grocery store you entered. It had caché.

And after doing all this wildy sexy marketing, you....experienced sales training. Which was like another form of boot camp. Sales people at P&G often felt the Brand Managers didn't respect the sales function like it should. Personally, I loved hanging with the Sales guys. They tended to be a lot less uptight than the Brand Managers and more likely to go drinking. So there. It worked for me.

But Sales Training had a purpose. Sales Training was there to teach you; not just skills, but *lessons*. Lessons on how hard it was to sell at the store level; how much grunt work was involved in pricing product at the shelf, building displays when it was 95 degrees outside, persuading store clerks to set shelves so they'd carry P&G's full lines of products. It took skill, guile, persuasiveness, a strong back and an eager and aggressive personality.

Brand Assistants got 8-12 weeks to experience it, to master it, and to learn to *respect* it. And DSM's ensured you respected it.

While on Sales Training, I was assigned to call on an independent grocery store that did so little volume, it hadn't been seen by a P&G rep in years, maybe even decades. When I arrived and introduced myself as the P&G Sales Representative, the store manager said "I've been waiting for someone from your company to show up. I've got some out-of-date product that you need to credit me for." He took me into the back of his store and showed me three cases of Head & Shoulders shampoo that was so old, it was in glass bottles (last sold about 15 years earlier). He made me dust his shelves, rotate stock, and put new price tags on the shelf. I spent three hours in the store, walked out with spider webs in my hair, and hadn't sold a thing. Two weeks prior, I was fashioning P&G's plans to introduce a new shampoo and conditioner product designed to generate a couple hundred million in sales in its first year; now I was dusting shelves. How did this happen? How did my life deteriorate so fast?

———

ONE DAY WHILE on Sales Training, I was summoned to the Emperor's office. As I entered the sanctum sanctorum, the DSM had his feet up on his desk and instructed me to sit down. He had his wingtips strategically placed at eye level on the desk between himself and me, blocking eye contact between us. Apparently, as a lowly Sales Trainee, I had not earned the right to gaze directly upon the Emperor. Over time, I would come to learn that when I had made a point worthy of acknowledgment, the DSM would spread the wing tips far enough apart to make eye contact and nod approvingly. Not smile, just nod. Those were special moments between us.

"I have an opportunity for you, a rare treat", the DSM said. This was a confusing statement to me. In P&G lingo, an *opportunity* usually meant it was something you were not going to like doing, but doing so would curry favor with the asking manager. As such, you were expected to do it, regardless. Translated into the language of the movie, *Caddyshack*: "You'll get nothing and like it, Spalding."

So I experienced what psychologists would refer to as cognitive dissonance over anything that would be considered both an *opportunity* and a *rare treat*. How could something at P&G be both? *Unicorn* would have been a more real term.

"You are going to get to spend the day selling with the *Greatest Sales Rep in the Carolinas*. This is a rare treat. You are going to learn how to sell at store level from the *Master*, from the guy who invented it, from the guy who knows no peer. You will get to watch a genius in action."

The DSM knew no bounds of oversell.

"What a rare opportunity indeed," I responded, having learned how to be appropriately deferent to the Emperor at this point in my Sales Training experience. I learned the definition of the word *obsequious*. It sounded classier than *ass kisser*.

"So what's the Plan?" It was all the restraint I could muster to not include *your highness* in there.

"You will drive from our offices here in Charlotte to Columbia, SC, on Tuesday evening. You will meet Bob Grace, the Greatest Sales Rep in the Carolinas, at 6:30am sharp on Wednesday morning, and you will be completely in awe for the rest of the day. He will show you the way it is done. You will return to Charlotte Wednesday night, enlightened." The Emperor's orders were issued. I was to follow them. The wingtips closed, signaling my dismissal. I wasn't sure if I should kiss the ring or not. So I beat a hasty retreat from the throne room.

———

I MET BOB Grace for breakfast at 6:30am sharp as prescribed. Truth be told, I was actually excited about it. P&G had legendary sales skills, and I was excited to actually learn from someone who was exceptional at it – regardless of the Emperor's oversell. It's always a treat to learn from someone who's genuinely good at what they do.

Bob was a burly fellow and congenial as all get-out (that's *Carolina-speak* – I readjusted quickly to being back in the Carolinas). Based on the build-up the Emperor gave Bob, I expected an intolerable level of arrogance; I was wrong. Bob had a self-deprecating, unassuming way about him. His way struck me as both appealing and familiar, having grown up in South Carolina. For some reason, though, I neglected to bring the commonality of our birth origins forward upon introduction. That oversight would turn out to be a problem later, or fortuitous, depending upon your point of view.

Bob informed me that we were going to tour the back roads of South Carolina that day, visiting grocery stores in a number of small towns. Our route would form a circle, starting out southernly, that would turn east and eventually have us heading back northwesternly to Columbia by dinner time. I made note of the directions, with regret that I had not packed a compass.

We stopped at more Piggly Wiggly's, Bi-Lo's, A&P's and IGA stores than you can imagine that day, each time following the same pattern, each move crafted from years of perfecting the art of selling to grocers. We'd park a distance away from the store's front door -- "the retailer doesn't want a salesman to take the parking space close to the front door from a potential paying customer". We'd sign in at the customer service desk – "you never want to give the store manager an easy reason to say 'no', by circumventing store policy and not signing in - even though he's known you for years". Tricks to the trade. I made mental notes. To this day, I don't park near the front of a grocery store. Old habits die slow.

We'd wander through the store to check out P&G products on the shelves, taking note of which products were in stock, which ones were priced incorrectly, which of the products were on display, what competitors were doing. We'd take meticulous notes, and prepare a quick analysis with two copies: one for the P&G sales report, and one for the store manager with suggestions on what to order from the warehouse to keep his shelves fully stocked with P&G products. Bob would greet the aisle clerk, usually by name — "if the aisle clerk doesn't like you, your shelves will never be kept right. Make him your friend."

More tricks to the trade. More mental notes. I was learning and liking this.

When we completed our in-store preliminaries, we'd wait patiently and silently for the store manager to complete his current task — "people usually don't say 'yes' to anything you want if you've interrupted them". When a suitable pause came up, Bob would greet the store manager with a firm handshake, introduce me, update the store manager on the state of our products in the store, and give him the suggested order sheet.

And THEN, the real selling began.

On this trip, we were selling a new fragrance of Secret Deodorant ("Strong enough for a man, but made for a woman"). Bob had prepared a detailed, two-page pitch for the store manager, connecting all the product features into the key benefits to the consumer and to the retailer, along with all the pertinent details like sizes, target pricing, special discounts and profit per unit to the retailer. Bob presented this with such elegance, it sounded like an aria. And before I knew it, we had hit five stores, and had generated five sales of the new Secret Deodorant fragrance.

Now I really believed Bob's billing was no hype. His title was not undeserved. He truly was the Greatest Sales Rep in the Carolinas. And I was truly honored to bear witness to him in action.

As we approached the lunch hour, the sixth call of the day was at the Piggly Wiggly store in the quaint little town of Denmark, SC. Denmark had a four block main street, with small stores lining each side. There was Daniels' Pharmacy, Brooker's Hardware, Ness's Dry Goods, The Dane movie theater, and even a small Coca Cola bottler. You could stand outside the plate glass window and watch the equipment fill 6oz glass bottles of Coca Cola. Denmark had not one, but two, traffic signals.

Beyond Daniels' pharmacy was the Piggly Wiggly store. As we pulled into the farthest parking space from the front door, Bob told me to wait before getting out. He looked at me and said, "OK, it's your turn to step up to the plate. You lead this call. You conduct all the in-store preliminaries. You make the pitch. Are you ready?"

"Do you think I am?"

"Absolutely. We'll go in together, but you lead. I'll be right behind you." I loved his confidence. I loved his confidence *in me*.

"OK, Bob, I'm fired up. Let's go."

And we did. I followed all Bob's prescribed procedures. I signed in, did all the shelf work, prepared the reports, smiled nicely and greeted the aisle clerks, while Bob followed me dutifully, giving me winks now and then to assure me I was on the right track.

Then it was time to meet the store manager. I waited until he gave me a nod, and I stepped forward to introduce myself and Bob.

"Pleased to meet you, Michael" said Mr. Hankel, the store manager. "Bob, it's always good to see you."

And I proceeded to take Mr. Hankel through all the work we had done, presented the proposed order from the warehouse and then began my pitch for the new Secret Deodorant item. Mr. Hankel listened patiently to my pitch, but the vibe was definitely a bit different than when Bob presented to the other store managers. I got the sense Mr. Hankel wasn't going to bite. I was starting to get a bit nervous; I was going to fail my first time out – and in front of the Greatest Sales Rep in the Carolinas, no less. After I completed my pitch, Mr. Hankel framed a grim look at me.

"Thank you kindly for all the work you've done for me, son. I really do appreciate it. But I gotta tell you, I don't believe we need any more Secret deodorant on the shelf than we have already. Just like I told Bob the last two times he tried to sell me these very same items. Thank you just the same, but I'm quite sure we've got all the Secret Deodorant we need."

I thought "'the last two times' – what was that about?" Before I could even complete the thought, we were startled by a high pitched voice coming from across the store.

"Michael Elliot, is that you? I declare, it is. My Lord, but don't you look handsome, with your coat and tie on. Mr. Hankel, do you know who this is? Michael here, is the son of my husband Harvey's sister Rona, who lives in Charleston. You remember Rona don't you? We all call her Monkey, but you probably remember her as Rona. Not Dutch, that's Harvey's older sister Sonya. You know, as in the 'Dutchess of Denmark'? Isn't that *just precious*? I love that. No, this is Rona, his younger sister. She has three boys and Michael here is the youngest. He's best friends with my boy Paul and his cousin Robert, you know, Judge Knoll's son. They used to run these streets all summer long when Michael would come to visit. I'm surprised you don't remember him. But he's grown so, you probably don't recognize him. I barely do myself. Isn't he handsome? Looks just like his grandfather, may he rest in peace. What a lovely man, Mr. Knoll was. Oh, Paul's going to be so sorry he missed you, Michael. Why, have y'all had lunch? I'll have some chicken frying at home, you simply must stop by...."

We were all speechless (or rather not able to get a word in edgewise) at the presence of my Aunt Amy Knoll, who happen to wander into the Piggly Wiggly while I was making my pitch. Speechless and wide-eyed we were, as she completed her soliloquy and insisted that all three of us come to her house for lunch, and then wandered off to complete her shopping.

The three of us just stared at each other for a moment, wondering what just hit us. *Hurricane Amy* we guessed.

Mr. Hankel broke the silence. "Well, Michael, I didn't realize who you were, and I'm sorry for not remembering you. I certainly had great respect for your grandfather. What a fine man he was. Made this town a lot of what it is today. Made sure people had what they needed from his dry goods store, even if they couldn't pay. A fine man for sure. And your uncle Judge Knoll was a deeply respected man around these parts, too. Tell you what, why don't you just go back over to that shelf and set it with whatever items of Secret Deodorant you think we need. I'm sure you'll take care of us just fine. Like your Grandfather would. And please tell Miss Amy that I said thanks for the lunch offer, but I can't rightly leave the store midday."

AFTER COMPLETING THE shelf tags for the seven new items of Secret Deodorant the store was missing and leaving the order with Mr. Hankel, Bob and I walked silently out of the store and got back in the car.

Bob stuck the keys in the ignition and, without a word, turned the car on. He got ready to put the car in reverse, but stopped, took a sudden interest in the floor of the car, and shook his head.

He looked at me, and said, somewhat miffed, "Why didn't you tell me before we went in the store that you had not only been to Denmark before, but you also had kin here?"

I looked him squarely in the eye. I anticipated the possibility of this question coming while we silently attended to Mr. Hankel's request. I figured a good offense is the best defense.

"Why didn't *you tell me* before we went in the store that you'd pitched Mr. Hankel on Secret and he'd already said no -- *twice?*"

It was a tense moment between the two of us. The air was thick. It wasn't due to the humidity of the deep South.

The Greatest Sales Rep in the Carolinas looked at me and issued me a wry smile. It was at that moment that he called the match even with his eyes and smile. A respect, and dare I say, friendship, was cemented at that very moment.

"I think you're gonna do fine, Mr. Elliot. My work here is done."

So we went to eat fried chicken together at Aunt Amy's.

5

CONSUMERS, NOT CUSTOMERS

MY FATHER ALWAYS wanted to be an accountant. He has a gift for dealing with numbers, remembering dates, doing math quickly in his head. He also has a very orderly way about him; neat, organized. Everything in its time and place.

Unfortunately, he never got the opportunity to an accountant. He would have been a good one.

He turned 18 in 1943 at the height of World War II and was called on to serve his country as an infantryman in the US Army. He was trained at a military camp in Indiana and boarded a naval vessel headed to England, in advance of Operation Overlord -- more commonly known as the Normandy Invasion.

It's quite possible that I owe my presence here on Earth to an intestinal flu. On his way over to England where the Allies were amassing the troops, equipment and ships necessary to launch the Allied Invasion to retake Europe from the Third Reich, my dad contracted an intestinal flu. The ship's medical staff couldn't figure out how to cure him and he became quite ill. He was immediately hospitalized when he arrived in England. He struggled in the hospital for three weeks and lost a lot of weight. Confounded, the doctors decided, subsequently, to ship him home.

By the grace of the intestinal flu, he avoided the probability of a bloody death on the beaches of Normandy.

Fortunately, once back stateside, my father recovered. After celebrating the Allied victory in World War II and receiving his honorable discharge from the US Army, my father looked forward to attending college to pursue that degree in Accounting.

However, this time my grandfather fell ill, and Dad's help was needed to fill in for him at our family's furniture store. Dad would end up spending the next 40 years *filling in* at the furniture store. And never getting the chance to earn that accounting degree.

———

I WAS BARELY 25 years old when I was promoted to Brand Manager at Procter & Gamble. It was my first real managerial-level job and my second promotion in my short three and a half year tenure at P&G. As one of the few who entered the Brand Management program as an undergraduate and survived until Brand Manager, I was fortunate. But I was also very *green* and I don't mean environmentally conscious. I was more naïve than I would have believed at the time. My managers shrewdly recognized this but wanted to continue to challenge me. So P&G gave me a Brand Manager's role, yet it was on the smallest brand in the shop – Lilt homeperms.

When people think of Procter & Gamble, they think of iconic brands like Pampers diapers, Tide detergent, Ivory soap, and Crest toothpaste. Not Lilt homeperms. In fact, most people did not know what a homeperm was, much less that P&G made one.

But I didn't care. It didn't matter what business they gave me; I was determined to build it. So I undertook my new assignment with zest (not the soap, the attitude). Lilt had been in a multi-year decline which had been accelerating in the previous two years. I had to stem the losses quickly and then find a way to turn the brand's fortunes around. No easy task. Especially when you're the youngest person in the shop, managing the smallest brand, to which few P&G'ers paid much attention.

So I ended up taking a lot of people out for beer (I couldn't get their time in the office) and asking what they suggest I do. And I got plenty of advice (I found out free beer forms a powerful motivator). "You need a new advertising campaign". "More creative promotions." "New products are what this brand needs." These were all reasonable suggestions, but all these things had also been tried in the past few years, led by people smarter than me. Despite doing them all, the brand's fortunes were still declining.

To compound matters, Lilt's consumer demographics were different than the normal P&G brand. Its users tended to be older, live in more rural locations, and have lower income than the average P&G consumer. The Lilt consumer was clearly not the dazzling housewife with the gleaming teeth portrayed in so many P&G commercials at the time.

I felt I needed something else, something different, but had no idea what that might be.

One Sunday I was speaking with my dad on the phone, as I did each weekend. "Michael, you sound down. You just got promoted! I would have thought you'd be excited. What's going on?"

So I explained my problem and asked him a question. "Dad, when your business at the store was off, when you were in one of those housing downturns and you needed to generate some cash flow, how did you go about doing it?"

"You know, son, the furniture business is very different than the homeperm business."

"Yes, it is. But I'm totally stumped. I need some ideas."

"Well, as you may recall, many of our customers at the store were rather poor. They couldn't afford big outlays of cash and didn't have much access to credit. So if we sold them a washing machine, we'd get as much of a down payment from them as they could pull together, and then allow them to pay the rest on weekly payment plans. Sometimes only a few dollars a week. But if they paid regularly, and most did, we'd make out OK. And it would surely help them out."

"So what did you do when business was slow?" I asked.

"I'd glance through the books, looking for two things. First, I'd look to see who had been paying both regularly and on-time. Second, I'd look to see who was nearing the end of payments on their latest purchase. The people that fit in both categories, well, I'd go pay them a visit."

"A visit? Why?" I asked, bewildered by what good that would do.

"When I got to their house, I'd spend a little time with 'em, see how they were getting along. I'd keep my eyes open, see what they might be needing. But mostly, I'd just listen to them. Maybe a fan, a rocking chair, a new mattress. There was usually something on their list. So I'd find a way to offer them the new item in a structure that they could just continue to pay the same weekly payment they were making now. That usually worked."

You know, as he described it, I could see my dad doing just that. Sitting on his customer's front porch, maybe sipping a little iced tea in the South Carolina heat, patiently listening to whatever the customer wanted to talk about. But listening intently to their needs. Because he is the type of person who genuinely cares.

While I enjoyed hearing him tell the story, it really seemed irrelevant to my business. My customers weren't on payment plans – we delivered and they paid. It was fairly routine. Plus, it's not like snooping around a Lilt consumer's house to see if they needed any Tide would help the Lilt business problems. I just wasn't getting any answers that really addressed my problems.

Or was I?

———

ABOUT THREE DAYS later, it hit me.

My dad was talking about customers. I was thinking about consumers. They were one and the same to him – the customer to whom he sold a rocking chair was also the *consumer* of that product. Whereas, in Lilt's case the customer was a retailer and the consumer was the end user. Different people. I knew a lot about Lilt's best consumers, but I couldn't answer squat when it came to questions about Lilt's customers. In fact, I couldn't even tell you who the top ten were.

So I asked my brand assistant to run an analysis for me. I wanted to know: a) who Lilt's top 100 customers were; b) how much did they purchase from us in the past twelve months; c) what percent of the total Lilt business that customer comprised; and d) how all that compared to the same analysis conducted for P&G's overall Beauty Care business – just to see if Lilt was truly different.

Believe it or not, this was such a rarely performed analysis, we had to get a special computer program written to extract the data from P&G's computers.

What I discovered from the analysis astounded me.

First, Lilt had a much bigger concentration of customers than our division. Only 40 customers generated 80% of Lilt's total revenue. And only 10 customers comprised 33%.

Second, the list of Lilt's top customers was very different than the Division's top customers. Whereas the division's top customers tended to be grocery accounts in large metropolitan areas (like Kroger, Pathmark, Von's, and Stop 'n Shop), Lilt's top customers weren't grocery accounts at all. They were customer names you didn't hear a lot about at P&G back then – Dollar General Stores, Family Dollar Stores, Walgreens, and a little account in Arkansas that no one paid much attention at the time – Wal-Mart stores. While Wal-Mart had over $1 billion in revenue in the early 1980's (compared to roughly $600 billion thirty years later), it was only starting to show up on P&G's radar. Lilt's customers were retailers that tended to skew more rural, or were more specialty in their nature, like drug stores.

Third, business with our largest customers was declining at a faster rate than the smaller customers. And that was a bad sign, because it said your business is really sick when you're declining more rapidly with your *best* customers.

Now I had a few leads, a few clues, a few notions of what a different solution might be. But I didn't have answers yet. The next challenge was figuring how I could get on these customers' *porches* and listen to them like my Dad.

It was funny, but of all the market research P&G did in the 1980's, very little of it at the time was *customer* research. It was all consumer research. So I could find no existing information on customer preferences, especially THIS list of customers. I was going to have to find a different way to *get on their porch*.

———

IN THE 1980's, United Airlines ran a TV ad that showed an advertising agency executive sitting at a board room table surrounded by his senior staff.

"I just got a call from our largest client. Told me he was taking his business to a different ad agency. When I asked why, he said he didn't *know us* anymore." The agency executive began handing out airline tickets to each of the executives, urging them to get out of the office, go meet with their clients, and do something of which they hadn't done enough: listen to them.

And that's exactly what I did. I went out to visit personally the hair care buyers at each of the top customers to see what they thought of the home perm business, and more importantly, what they thought of Lilt. It wasn't a scientific poll. I was just trying to get on their porch.

Amazingly, I didn't need much other than a lead question to get them talking: "what are we doing right and what are we doing wrong?" These customers were very happy to tell us what we had done wrong and not many felt we were doing much right. And the interesting part – the answers were very consistent.

We took the responses and reworked our product offering in ways that now met the needs of not only consumers, but our core customers, too. We reallocated and changed our marketing spending and cost structure so that we could afford the changes and still do so profitably. And we put all of this into a regional test to see if it might work. Not surprisingly, this test included that little account in Arkansas, Wal-Mart.

Literally, within weeks, we saw a response in the business — with both revenue and profit up. So we rolled out the program to all customers nationally and began tracking performance by *Top 40 customers*, playing off the name of a popular radio show at the time, "Kasey Kasum's America's Top 40" which played the forty most popular songs in America at the time.

Lilt revenue and profit for the next year was up double-digits. We discovered that if you can grow your top customers' business, it will drive your *entire* business. Lilt's business was back on track. It may have had just a miniscule impact on the overall financials of Procter & Gamble, but it was a small victory for my team. And an important and formative managerial experience for me.

As I LATER took on other brand assignments after Lilt -- with Pantene and Head & Shoulders -- regular customer visits and tracking became a staple within my marketing programs. Sometimes, marketing practices catch fire at P&G and you start to see the same ones showing up on brands across the company. This, however, was not one of marketing practices. This stayed somewhat local, in my own bag of tricks. Not because I kept it that way; more likely because few in marketing at the time really saw listening to customers as important. The P&G marketer's domain was consumers, not customers. That was OK with me; it worked to build the businesses I was running and I intended to stick with it.

About two years later, I received a company-wide award for the Top 40 Program as an "innovative marketing program." I admit, I had to smile when realizing the source of innovation at the world's largest and best known consumer products company came from a small furniture retailer on King Street in Charleston, SC. A guy just trying to feed his family.

About six months later, my phone rang innocently at the office. A sterile voice insisted, "Please hold for Mr. Pepper."

This was an important and unexpected call. *Mr. Pepper* was P&G's President and CEO, John Pepper. He did not make a habit of routinely calling Brand Managers to *check in*. At least, not in my limited experience. Requests from the CEO usually came down the chain of command, and there were five *commanders* between the CEO and me. Brand Managers usually created a written answer to the CEO's question, and it made its way back up the chain of command – and usually was heavily edited en route. I had spoken directly to Mr. Pepper once in my career before this call.

"What can I do for you Mr. Pepper?" I asked casually as my stomach tightened. I felt like I should be putting my suit jacket on to speak with him -- by phone!

"Michael, what kind of promotion have you been running with retailers that I've been hearing about?" he asked. I quickly explained that it was less a *promotion* and more a strategy of getting retailer needs reflected in marketing plans, like we did with consumers, and then monthly tracking of shipment performance at individual retailers (this was all before retail scanner data became available).

"And what kind of results are you getting?" he inquired, a little softer. I explained the double digit increases we had sustained now for quarters, even years in some cases. And the fact that we had implemented it across multiple brands, suggesting it wasn't an anomaly.

"And what kind of results have you been getting at some customer in Arkansas called Wal-Mart?"

"The best of all of them. Our business was up by one-third over the last twelve months alone," I responded, thankful that I had the data carefully ordered in my fact book, right in my top right drawer, of course. I made a mental note to reward my Administrative Assistant for keeping the fact book updated. "My perception is these Wal-Mart guys are on top of their numbers," I continued, "and they sure know their customers. When I focus on where our strategies overlap with theirs, we seem to grow our combined businesses and we both make more money."

"Hmmmmm," he mulled.

"Is there something else, sir?" I had no idea where this was going, but you don't just hang up on the CEO when the line goes quiet.

"Well, yes, there is something else. I got this call from this fairly friendly but pushy guy, Sam Walton, who apparently owns Wal-Mart. Says that he could knock out 20% of the cost of doing business between our two companies, and that he thought that was a conservative estimate. Wants me to come to Arkansas and go duck hunting with him for a weekend. He'll tell me more about how to do it then."

"So what's the concern, sir?" I still had no idea why he was calling *me* to decide if he was going duck hunting in Arkansas.

"Well, I haven't made a habit of visiting customers and I certainly don't go duck hunting much. But the results of your program are making me wonder why I don't."

—ooo—

TODAY, MOST CONSUMER products companies' sales departments are organized into "customer teams". Rather than regional structures that call on all stores in a geography, the traditional organizational structure, most companies now have individual teams assigned to each major customer — comprised of multiple job functions including, sales, finance, marketing, IT, supply chain, etc. The focus of the customer team is to maximize the synergy between the consumer products company and the customer through seamless integration of operations and marketing. This approach lowers the cost of doing business, increases competition and curbs inflation by helping to keep consumer prices low.

This concept was pioneered by P&G and Wal-Mart, ostensibly as a brainchild that resulted from a meeting at a duck hunt by John Pepper and Sam Walton. P&G and Wal-Mart spent a number of years creating and optimizing the model, and many other companies followed suit, first at Wal-Mart, and then with a variety of other large retailers.

To be clear, there was absolutely nothing in the Top 40 Program that contemplated any of the elements that modern customer teams have embedded in their structure or practices. Except perhaps, listening to customers and beginning to see them as a partner. If the results of the Top 40 Program encouraged John Pepper to do something no other P&G CEO had done before — to take a weekend, visit with a customer, sacrifice a few ducks, and ponder a different way of thinking.....I wonder how really different that is from the way my dad spoke of sitting on his customer's front porch, drinking iced tea, and, as they say in the South, *chewing the fat?*

6

P&G vs. Fashion Models

SHORTLY BEFORE I joined P&G in 1982, there was a big event in which one division was split into two: Beauty Care and Health & Personal Care. This was an unusual event in P&G history because new divisions were not formed every day ...or even every decade. The Hair Care Brands and Deodorant Brands became part of the Beauty Care Division while the Toothpaste and Mouthwash brands went into the Health & Personal Care Division. While this may not seem like a major event to the average person, it was at P&G, especially when you consider what the division was called before the split: Toilet Goods.

I kid you not. Toilet Goods.

It's truly hard to imagine words that elicit thoughts of beauty, engender visions of sophistication, and embody imagery of high end products more than the moniker "Toilet Goods". I'd say creating "Beauty Care" was a good call.

So when Bob Carmichael became the new Division Vice President of Beauty Care, he really challenged the Brand Groups to "think beauty". And he went out of his way to staff the business properly. For example, there were more female brand managers in Beauty Care than anywhere else in P&G. And the first time in P&G history, all three General Managers in a Division were female -- and were in Beauty Care. In fact, I only had one male boss in the three plus years before I became a Brand Manager at P&G. And in the early 1980's, that was a rarity. Remember the "3M's" in laundry, and one of those "M's" stood for "male".

Carmichael's inspired charge to "think beauty" challenged Beauty Care employees to explore taking our brands to beauty places not seen before. While a good idea in concept, the only problem was that the brands were Head & Shoulders, Prell, Lilt, Pert, and Ivory Shampoo. These were not the "haute couture" brands of those times. Or *any* times. The brand imagery was more of soap company products than of Parisian High Fashion.

I recall getting my new assignment when I returned from Sales Training -- I was assigned to the Prell Brand as the junior ABM. When I joined the brand, the senior ABM and the Brand Manager were working on a new advertising campaign with Prell's Advertising Agency, Wells Rich Greene, with its famed Chief Executive, Mary Wells. Mary had seen to it that the campaign had been enthusiastically endorsed up the management chain all the way to Carmichael, who had "green-lighted" it for production.

Which pretty much meant that no junior ABM just back from sales training with reservations about whether it would work could stop this train. So I didn't try.

The Agency was putting the basic touches on the $250,000 contract with Christie Brinkley to become the spokesperson for Prell. And in 1984, $250k was no small figure for commercial talent. Historically, P&G did not use celebrities in advertising; if you look at the historical reel of P&G advertising, you'll see more celebrities in P&G ads *before* they became celebrities than after. More often, P&G created its own fictional characters and made stars out of the actors. Witness what Charmin's Mr. Whipple character did for actor Dick Wilson and Bounty's Rosie character did for Nancy Walker. I'll bet you recognized the character's names, but not the actor's names! So signing Christie Brinkley was quite a departure for P&G, and an expensive one at that.

Fresh off her role aside Chevy Chase in National Lampoon's Hollywood hit *Vacation*, Christie Brinkley had adorned the cover of every major fashion magazine in America. She was America's new fresh face. She was the California blonde that would soon capture the hearts of America, in addition to one particular New Yorker, Billy Joel.

The Prell brand considered this contract quite a coup, and it was going to be key in transforming the brand from its dowdy 1950's image to trendy 1980's. Many in the Ad media wondered how Wells Rich Greene had pulled off this off, how they convinced P&G to take this risk, how they convinced Christie. It was later found out that, to secure the sponsorship, one of the things the Agency promised Christie was that she could actually write and produce a Prell commercial herself.

Oy.

The Prell business had been in a multi-year market share decline, and the first Christie Brinkley ad was considered such a success upon completion, that the Brand immediately changed the national advertising campaign to get Christie on the air as soon as possible. This was an unusual move at the time, as most new campaigns went into regional test markets first to quantify its impact on the business — positive or negative. But everyone in Beauty Care was so confident of what Christie would do for Prell that the move "to go national" was immediately executed.

Pictures of Christie Brinkley were popping up on shampoo displays in grocery stores, drug stores, note pads, posters, you name it. Big Hair was in, and Christie was the be-all and end-all of Big Hair. The Prell-Christie Brinkley lip-lock was all over *Advertising Age* magazine, the industry "rag" at the time, and the Brand Group had fulfilled Carmichael's command to "think beauty".

I was glad I didn't express my reservations because I would have been dead wrong.

Then the market share reports came in. The problem was the Christie campaign did not really stem the long term market share declines. Rather, it was exacerbating it as market share actually declined *faster*. When challenged by then-CEO John Smale as to whether the Christie Campaign was actually working, the Brand Group implored him to give it more time. So Smale relented. But he watched the data carefully.

After two more bi-monthly periods of share declines — six months in total - Smale put a hold on all Prell ad spending and personally called Mary Wells and told her that he would not spend another dime on Christie advertising for Prell. If the Agency wanted to see *any* media spending for Prell at all, then they better find other advertising. At the time, P&G Ad Agencies were compensated on a percentage of the brand's advertising spending. If the Brand didn't run advertising, the Agency didn't get paid. The Agency understood what this meant and the old advertising went back on air lickety split.

So P&G's first experiment with "thinking beauty" failed. And the experiment with fashion models was equally unsuccessful. As a result, no more fashion model advertising was proposed for some time — on *any* P&G brand. P&G Brand Managers watch what's going on in the internal political realm, and learn fast.

P&G ACTUALLY BEGAN its fascination with Hollywood and fashion a while before the dubious practice of hiring fashion models for commercials. P&G had a unit entitled *P&G Productions* for quite some time. It developed radio shows and later television shows, primarily as content to carry P&G commercials. Famous daytime television shows like *Days of Our Lives* and *As The World Turns* were from P&G Productions. It's actually the origin of the term "Soap Opera", as they were created to entertain, but primarily to sell P&G soap.

And so there were a number of P&G people that actually considered themselves *part* of Hollywood. Just nestled on the shore of the Ohio River instead of the Pacific Ocean, I guess.

The lights and stars of Hollywood always attract an interesting crowd. And P&G was no exception to this. Among those who imagined themselves as part of Hollywood was Beauty Care's Commercial Production Supervisor, Laura Sachay. Laura's job was primarily to control the cost of producing P&G commercials. It was Laura's job to ensure some crafty agency type or savvy Hollywood director wasn't incurring unnecessary cost to get the job done. And that happened a lot more often than one would think. Commercial Production Supervisors could generally save P&G many times their salaries annually in unnecessary expense.

And Laura fit the bill. She loved hobnobbing with the Hollywood types. Laura was only about 5 feet tall, almost sickly thin, long brown hair, bright blue eyes, eternally tanned (back when you had to do it naturally), and always just coming out of a hot relationship that "just wasn't destined to work out".

And she was quite full of what I called "Hollywood Self-Importance". The sun rose and set over Hollywood in Laura's mind.

Once I had left her a voice message, and she returned the call the next day. "I'm sorry I couldn't take your call earlier, Michael. I had Los Angeles on the other line," she sighed dramatically.

"The whole city?" I asked sarcastically. "That's incredible! Does the Mayor know this? Did AT&T help?" I detest self-importance. Did it show in my sarcasm?

"Oh, Michael, you're always joking," she demurred. I once saw a poster that said "Tact is the ability to tell someone to go to hell and make them feel happy to be on their way". I had hoped that was a tactful comment. Laura seemed unoffended.

The purpose of my call to Laura was to nail down our travel plans for an upcoming commercial shoot for P&G brand Lilt Homeperms. I was very excited because this would be the first commercial I had ever shot from storyboard to finished film.

It was to be Lilt's highest fashion commercial yet – without fashion models. And after all, Carmichael wanted us to "think beauty".

Lilt's advertising agency, Leo Burnett, had sold P&G management on using a very high end fashion *director* in Hollywood, who was known for shooting films, not commercials. So we'd try fashion directors instead of fashion models. See how that goes. And Laura was as excited as she could be to hobnob with the gliteratti.

Laura made all the travel plans. When we arrived at LAX – Laura, Scott LaRue, my boss on the Lilt Brand, and me – Laura had picked up our rental car: a convertible of course. This was already off to a bad start – any type of *showy* expense was frowned upon through the eyes of midwestern P&G sensibilities.

"Totally within policy for rental car per diem," she said, as if she were reading my mind. I made a mental note not to think negative thoughts in front of her anymore.

As we drove down La Cienega toward Sunset Boulevard – the heart of Hollywood – Laura pulled off on a quiet side street and stopped the car outside a boutique hotel, the Sunset Marquis.

"Within the hotel per diem, too" she quipped, again reading my mind. Damn, how did she do that?

As we waited in line to check in, a balding fellow stepped in front of us and walked right up to the counter. I bristled a bit as he cut in line, but used those Midwestern sensibilities not to make a scene.

"Can you tell me if Ms. Sarandon has gotten to her usual room yet?" he asked the clerk. With the clerk's discreet nod to this not-so-discreet question, the balding man brushed right by us as quickly as he arrived.

"Do you know who that was?" Laura murmured in a low voice, all aflutter.

"No, should I?" Scott asked, echoing my thoughts.

"Peter Boyle. Didn't you recognize him?" Laura shot back, underscoring how Hollywood un-savvy we were. Today, most people would recognize Peter Boyle as the Emmy award winning actor who famously played Ray Romano's father on the TV show *Everybody Loves Raymond*. But this was before the first line of *Raymond* was ever written. I recognized the name only because, as an avid Mel Brooks fan, I knew him as the monster in *Young Frankenstein* who grunted and danced to *Puttin' On the Ritz* with Gene Wilder. I could hear the horses whinny when anyone said "Frau Bleucher". It was years later when I found out a 'bleucher" was a glue factory. Gotta love Mel Brooks.

But I digress.

Peter Boyle looked a little different without the monster make up on, so I didn't recognize him.

"So he's having an affair with Susan Sarandon?" whispered Laura, all excited about what she had just discovered. Too bad there was neither Twitter nor TMZ at the time. She would have been scandalous and loved it.

I thought this presumption of an affair was a bit premature. Not much information on which to draw that conclusion. Witness my good P&G training – it ain't real if it doesn't have data supporting it.

"Is this something you remotely give a crap about?" Scott asked me quietly. Scott was ex-military and "100% I don't give a damn" about stuff like this.

"Not really. But it seems to have made Laura's day. Look how excited she is. Let's let her have her moment."

After checking in, we headed over to the Director's bungalow studio a few blocks away for the pre-production meeting. In this meeting, we would give final approvals to all sets, wardrobe, shooting plans, lighting and, most importantly, casting for the commercial that would be shot the next day. After grinding through three hours of nuanced debate over the myriad issues, we finally got to casting.

The Director and Agency Creatives had narrowed down the casting for the lead role in the commercial to five models. It was less the models and more the process that actually jarred me.

One at a time, each of the models was brought into the room, standing in front of a group of about a dozen people. The model was not introduced, nor was there any conversation with her. She could have been a mannequin. I was later told that the role did not require speaking, so why did we need to hear her voice? Practical, I guess, if not rude for sure. As she stood at the front of the room, a make-up stylist and hair stylist stood astride her and began to literally rip her apart.

Touching her face, the first stylist said, "Her cheekbones are not very high, but it's possible to make up her cheeks with shadow that will create a desirable hollowness that will give the appearance of raising her cheekbones."

The second stylist pawed at her hair, "Terribly stringy. No body at all. I could texturize to add fullness and maybe do something with it. But it will take all my creative powers to do anything with this rat's nest."

My gosh – did they really say these things about her? While she was standing right there? The first model was summarily dismissed and the next model was brought in. Similar criticisms, similar dissection of every possible visible flaw.

As I watched this, I got this disturbing feeling in my stomach. I was sure it was embarrassment. I couldn't believe we were treating these women — these human beings — this way. No one even spoke to them. They were just brought in like life-less meat on hooks, with the butchers beginning to chop away at various cuts. My stomach literally hurt from embarrassment at this treatment of a person. My mother would have scolded me for sure. "That is not the way I raised you to treat another person," she would have said. And she would have been right.

And I suddenly realized that this was normal for Hollywood. Everyone in the room, save for Scott and me, saw this as simply what they did every day. People "in the biz" talked this way all the time. According to some of the production crew, the models didn't seem to mind; rather they somewhat expected it. The get called in; they get picked over. Maybe they get the job. Maybe they don't. More often they don't.

It's the way it *worked*. The strange thing in the room was not how they behaved; rather it was how Scott and I reacted to it. We were clearly the outliers. So despite the messages I was getting from my stomach, I went with the flow and helped make the decisions necessary to complete the pre-production meeting about 3pm.

With the day's work done, it was agreed that everyone would meet at the pool at the Sunset Marquis for drinks. As we got back to the hotel, I couldn't shake the bad feeling I had in my stomach, which had surprisingly grown stronger.

"I'm not feeling too well," I said to Scott and Laura. "I'm just going to lie down in my room. Y'all have fun at the pool. Have a drink for me."

"Are you sure you're OK?" they inquired. Laura was astounded that I'd miss the hob-nob session at the Sunset Marquis pool. Think of all the celebrity sightings I'd miss!

"I'm sure I'll be OK," and I retired to my room.

Over the course of the next two hours, the pain in my stomach grew. The mount-ing pressure was enormous, such that I couldn't even lie stretched out on the bed. About 5pm, Scott knocked on my door. I struggled to the door to open it for him, and then retreated to the fetal position on my bed.

"You don't look good," Scott said.

"Yeah, my cheekbones are not high enough and my hair is too stringy," I replied, eliciting a smile from Scott.

"No, I'm serious, Michael. I think we should call a doctor."

Despite my protests, Scott called the front desk and they agreed to call the Hotel Doctor. Yes, back in those days, they still had "hotel doctors" that actually made house calls. I wondered at what some of the calls he made to the Sunset Marquis were about.

The doctor arrived about a half hour later and examined me. After a few questions and some painful compressions on my abdomen, he said, "I'm not sure exactly what's going on – it could be a number of things – but I think it would be best to get you over to Cedars Sinai Hospital for further examination."

"The hospital?" I asked. "Is that really necessary?"

Scott jumped in, with a concerned look on his face. "Michael, I think you should go. You really don't look good."

"At this time of day, it would take an ambulance too long to get here through traffic, so I'm just going to arrange to have the hotel car take you to the hospital. The front desk will call you in a few moments when the car is ready and I'll meet you there," the doctor said with a surety that both concerned me and gave me comfort. For some reason, I did not pick up on the mention of the "ambulance", which should have tipped me off to his seriousness.

Only a few moments after the doctor departed, the phone rang. "We'll be down in a moment," Scott said and then hung up the phone. "Let's go, Michael. Can I give you a hand?"

As I went to rise, I felt a sharp pain in my stomach and realized that I couldn't straighten up. We walked carefully to the front of the hotel; in my tee shirt, shorts and tennis shoes, people gazed ruefully at me. I couldn't tell if they felt sorry for me at my physical condition or the poor quality of my wardrobe. After all, I was at the Sunset Marquis.

At the front of the hotel, we were met by what had to be the longest crème-colored limousine I had ever seen. "Here's the hotel car, ready to take you to the hospital," the gracious doorman said as he opened the door.

"You gotta be kidding me," I said to Scott. This was Hollywood ridiculousness taken to the extreme. Little did I know that I hadn't seen anything yet.

I crawled in the backseat and stretched out. Scott sat across from me, next to a full wet bar, as we began to take off for the hospital. The limo driver was moving with some haste. It didn't take us long before we pulled into Cedars Sinai Hospital. The only way I knew we had arrived was that I could see the Star of David on the top of the building through one of the three sunroofs in the limo. Another strange sign of comfort.

As we got in the admitting area, Scott took over. "You just lay down; I'll give them all the info they need and get things moving here."

I appreciated it, because the pressure in my abdomen was getting more intense and my breathing hastening. Scott used every one of his command skills from the military to get things moving. I was quickly moved by wheelchair to a private hospital room, where I was elevated into a bed by medical attendants and covered up by blankets. I was quickly connected to an IV and by wire to some machines. Scott and the nurses were speaking out in the hall.

All of a sudden while I was alone in the room for a moment, the pressure gave way, like the air going out of a balloon. All the pain I was feeling dissipated quickly. I felt an instant sense of relief.

The nurse came back in the room and asked, "How are we feeling?"

"Rather embarrassed, actually" I responded. "I got everybody all inconvenienced, and as soon as you get me into the hospital bed, all the pain seems to have gone away. I'm awfully sorry for troubling you." I expected to get up and leave.

The nurse put her hand on my forehead, and to my surprise, this set off a further flurry of activity. A bevy of nurses flooded the room with two doctors. One set of nurses was removing my clothing while another started asking me questions from a clipboard. What medications had I taken that day? Did I have any allergies? When was the last time I went to the bathroom?

The bed started rolling out of the room and down the hall as the IV/Equipment stand was being dragged along.

One of the doctors started informing me that I was being taken into the operating room for exploratory abdominal surgery. "Why? The pain went away?" I asked, noticing that my head was somewhat heavier and my body felt weirdly lighter.

"The pain going away might actually be a bad sign," the doctor said. "We need your permission to perform surgery now." The word *now* had a degree of emphasis that did not give me comfort. I signed whatever it was he put in front of me.

They rolled me down the hall, through multiple sets of doors, with haste. I was transferred from the gurney onto a table with a collection of bright lights above me. My arms were spread and the doctor said, "I'm going to put you to sleep now. Can you please start counting aloud down from ten?"

"Sure," I replied. "Ten, nine..." I don't recall hitting eight.

"Don't worry, I gave you a bikini scar."

My eyes fluttered. I was trying to get a fix on who was talking to me, where I might be. It was a brightly lit room, with a nice window with sun beaming in. There was a man with silver hair in a white coat standing in front of me, with a friendly smile on his face.

"I said, 'don't worry, I gave you a bikini scar'," the man repeated with a gentle voice. "In fact, I did the same procedure on Chevy Chase just last week. So you're in good company."

The only thing that registered was bikini, which says a little bit about how my mind works, even when coming out of anesthesia. And what was that about Chevy Chase?

"But I don't wear bikini's," was all I could think to respond. My mouth was very dry and I wasn't on a beach.

The white-coated man let out a belly laugh, which I thought was odd. But perhaps no more odd than his telling me he gave me a bikini scar and he operates on Chevy Chase.

"Who are you, where am I, and what am I doing here? And why would I want a bikini scar?" I asked, now a little more awake and a lot more confused.

"I am Dr. Cohen, you are in Cedars Sinai Hospital in Los Angeles, California. You just came out of surgery, and you're going to be here for a while."

News like that will wake you up.

I was somewhat relieved to see Scott LaRue come into view.

"Hey man, you OK?" Scott said with a smile. "You gave me a bit of a scare."

"What's going on? I'm really confused," I responded.

"Do you remember us coming to the hospital in the hotel limo? You were in a lot of pain?" Scott asked.

"Sort of. Yeah, I think so. But the pain went away." It was all starting to come back to me.

"Yes, but the pain going away was a bad thing, not a good thing," Dr. Cohen said. "Essentially, the pain was an inflamed appendix. And the pressure relief occurred because the appendix burst, and spewed nasty stuff all through your abdomen, starting an infection. Your temperature shot up, and we needed to get you into surgery immediately or you could have died. Fortunately, the problem was what we thought it was and we were able to get to it and fix it fast. But you'll be here for a week or so, on heavy anti-biotics, until we can be sure all the infection has cleared up."

"Well, thank you, Doctor Cohen." I was stunned, so I resorted to being polite. Southern upbringing and all. "I really appreciate all you did for me, especially for a guy who just came in off the street."

"No problem. Happy to help. We're gonna get you fixed up." Dr. Cohen winked at me as he left the room.

I looked at Scott. "Hey, please tell Laura I don't think I want to go on any more commercial shoots. I've had enough of Hollywood."

EVEN THOUGH P&G's early experiments with *thinking beauty* and fashion models were less than successful, P&G is not an easily deterred company. P&G was determined to get into Beauty business, either organically or through acquisition.

And that happened in 1985, when P&G bought Richardson-Vicks. The RVI acquisition really put P&G on the map in three areas. First, it was P&G's first foray into over-the-counter drugs, particularly through RVI's namesake Vicks medicines. Second, it really put P&G into the Skin Care business with the Olay brand. P&G had introduced, unsuccessfully, the Wondra body lotion brand in the 70's which ultimately failed. Olay was a time honored brand with a proven track record. A little dowdy perhaps at the time, but proven nonetheless. Finally, and perhaps most importantly of the three areas, the RVI acquisition is really what made P&G a global company. RVI had operations on the ground in over 80 countries around the world. This became the channel for P&G to begin distributing many of its primarily US brands overseas.

Despite the Christie fiasco, Bob Carmichael had not given up on *thinking beauty*. He was a determined man, and he would find a way. For the Hair Care business, and for Carmichael specifically, the RVI acquisition was a real coup. With RVI came the Vidal Sassoon brand. With Sassoon, P&G really could *think beauty* at a whole new level because Sassoon was an authentic Salon brand with cutting edge imagery. Sassoon's signature geometric cut brought a contemporary, high fashion image to P&G that it likely could have not developed on its own at the time. It even came with real salons under the Sassoon brand, including its signature salon on Madison Avenue in New York, to continue to support that image!

P&G was so excited about Sassoon — and so concerned about possibly sullying Sassoon's image — that it decided to create a separate business unit apart from the other Hair Care brands just for Sassoon, reporting to Carmichael. This made a huge organizational statement and was probably a very smart move.

What P&G was *less excited* about were some of the lesser brands that came with the RVI acquisition, including a small $4 million *boutique* brand called Pantene, which was sold predominantly in high end Department Stores. P&G did not do business in department store channels. Department Stores didn't sell soap, they didn't buy in bulk, and they were notorious at the time for not paying their invoices on time. That made them *persona non grata* at P&G. Pantene was sold in relatively small 7 ounce bottles with dramatic, gold domed caps and was priced at retail at $9 a bottle. Department Stores could order them in *each's* – meaning as little as one bottle at a time – and they would be shipped via UPS to the Department Store's front door. P&G didn't like to sell anything in *each's*; P&G sold in *carloads,* as in train car loads. If a retailer didn't pay its invoice when it was due, the retailer didn't get shipped product again until it did. It's amazing that Macy's, among the largest department store chains in the US, and P&G are headquartered just a few short blocks from each other in Cincinnati. Because based on their customer/supplier strategies at the time, they operated in different universes.

RVI had spent a lot of time cultivating Pantene's high end image. You would see advertisements for Pantene alongside Rolex, Cartier, and Rolls Royce at, of all places, Polo Matches. There were no Tide or Charmin ads at Polo Matches. Pantene print ads - featuring trendy fashion models at the time such as Paulina Porizkova and Iman, David Bowie's striking wife - were found in high end fashion magazines Pantene had also just begun television advertising using another new model and actress, Kelly LeBrock. Kelly would begin the TV ad dressed elegantly and looking fabulous, cooing "Don't Hate Me Because I'm Beautiful." The commercial would then cut to black and white film of Kelly without make-up and hair styling, and proceed through the steps of shampooing, conditioning, styling and make up, transforming hers from frumpy to glittering, all in 30 seconds. It was a controversial commercial at the time. Some women loved it, because it was the first time anyone dared to show a fashion model unmade and they could relate to all the steps required to make themselves beautiful that few, especially males, could appreciate. The line was also criticized by feminists and became a catchphrase for narcissistic behavior. Either way, it was eliciting public response, and that's how brands get built.

Despite being a forty year old European brand, Pantene was still new to most in the US. Generating only $4 million in annual revenue coupled with spending millions in expensive image creation, Pantene was racking up huge losses. And that's not a way to win positive attention from P&G management. With all P&G's high level of interest in Sassoon, which was nearly a $150 million brand, Pantene was a step-child at best, an annoyance at worst. While Sassoon was allocated more than 10 marketing people in multiple brand groups, P&G decided Pantene wasn't even worth having a single dedicated Brand Group. So they gave it to a young Brand Manager who had turned around the Lilt homeperm business, and asked him if he could make these problems go away.

Guess who?

PANTENE WAS HEADACHES from the start. First, it was a financial disaster losing in excess of $10 million that year alone. It's generally considered *problematic* to be racking up nearly three times your annual revenue in losses, unless you could show a clear path to profitability. Second, Pantene was complex and costly - with expensive model contracts, expensive packaging, and many sku's (items in the product line) which made it complex to manufacture and warehouse. Finally, when Pantene was inte-grated into P&G, and now under P&G retailer terms (e.g., paying bills on time), into its corporate all business immediately stopped. Yes, stopped. All the department store customers were past due on their bills and therefore, there was not a single customer order that P&G was willing to ship. It's hard to make your annual plan when you can't sell anything.

This wasn't just *headaches*. This was an *unmitigated disaster*.

But I didn't really see it that way. The more I looked at Pantene, the more I would think there really was something there to build upon. Something lasting and different. While some brands were starting to promise *healthy* hair, Pantene really delivered it. It had vitamins in its formula, and consumers would swear how it helped their hair – which was interesting, since hair follicles are actually dead and that made it hard to prove. While the biggest brands were locked into retail pricing at roughly 10 cents or less per ounce, Pantene was selling at well over $1 an ounce. And while many brands were trying to take their images from frumpy to fabulous (witness the Christie Brinkley fiasco for Prell), Pantene had already established an upscale image. So while it had all these good things going for it, the problem was that it lacked suf-ficient scale to support all the expensive marketing, and was therefore losing millions of dollars. It just needed to be a bigger business. We believed it had the potential to be "Class for the Mass".

So we thought maybe we should give Pantene a business make-over pretty enough to match its image. But my team and I had a lot of convincing to do with P&G management as they fawned over the newly acquired Sassoon business.

Pantene's brand image and advertising were fine. In fact, it was better than anything P&G likely could have done on its own at the time. However, it would simply never achieve a mass appeal being sold through Department Stores. Too niched. People shopped for cosmetics and fragrances in Department Stores; but they didn't shop for shampoo and conditioner there. So the raging debate in P&G was whether to kill Pantene or follow a more traditional P&G-marketing model – move its distribution through grocery stores and price it more popularly.

The answer proved to be *neither*.

Essentially, we reduced the price, but kept it at a significant price premium to most shampoos -- it would retail for a mere *five times* the market price (50 cents per ounce vs. 10 cents per ounce). We also changed the distribution from through department stores, but we didn't go to grocery stores – at least not initially. We sold it through drug stores – with a promise to retailers that you could *really* make money on this product. And they did. After establishing it in drug stores, we then sought distribution in mass merchants (like Wal-Mart) in the next wave, and then took it to grocers after Pantene was clearly successful and they demanded it – at *any* price.

Pantene went from $4 million in sales to $100 million in roughly 18 months, defying all predictions. Within a few years, it actually eclipsed Sassoon. Today, twenty-five years later, Pantene is one of P&G's largest hair care franchises with over $3 billion in global sales.

———

INTERESTINGLY, IT WASN'T the big things on Pantene that were tough to make work – selling the vision to P&G management, generating the consumer data to suggest a high priced product could sell successfully, or even utilizing non-conventional distribution practices to introduce a brand. Rather, the tough stuff on Pantene was really getting the *little* things done right.

And not surprisingly, most of those little things revolved around managing fashion models.

When Kelly LeBrock was featured in the first "Don't Hate Me" commercial, she had been a moderately successful Hollywood actress, starring alongside Gene Wilder in *The Woman in Red* and Anthony Michael Hall in *Weird Science*. But it was the "Don't Hate Me" commercials that made her broadly recognizable. RVI, and then P&G, spent a lot money advertising Pantene; the "Don't Hate Me" commercials were quite talked about, and P&G was quite pleased with the buzz they had created – both positive and controversial.

That led to a $450,000 annual contract for Kelly, the largest P&G had ever completed with an actress at the time, dwarfing the Christie Brinkley deal. For perspective, Michael Jordan had just signed the largest endorsement contract for an athlete at that time – for $500,000 a year from Nike. So Kelly's contract was a big deal. And it was for ten days' work a year. Just ten days. At least we had proof the advertising worked *before* we inked this expensive contract, unlike Christie Brinkley's. We learned.

The problems were not with Kelly herself, at least not initially. The problems were with her boyfriend - and eventual father of her child. The boyfriend had been a martial arts expert, who had made his way into a handful of action films, also with moderate Hollywood success. Kelly's contract stipulated that P&G would have to pay for a "companion" to come to all commercial shoots, to "support her emotionally".

Oy.

OK, so what's a few extra first class airline tickets in the context of a $450,000 contract?

Ha! Little did we know.

Kelly's first commercial shoot under the new contract was for a print ad that would be placed in top fashion magazines. With all the newfound excitement around Pantene, Grey Advertising, Pantene's advertising agency, had convinced P&G management that we should use top fashion photographers for ads. So they had contracted with Francesco Scavullo, who had shot the majority of the *Cosmopolitan* magazine covers from its inception until his death in 2004. In the mid-1980's, Scavullo's daily rate was $80,000. Yes, he was paid $80,000. A day. In the mid-1980's. No, I have not been smoking anything. But apparently, Grey Advertising was, and perhaps those of us at P&G too, because we agreed to it.

Needless to say we wanted to have this shoot go well.

Upon their arrival at the studio for the shoot, Kelly was immediately whisked into two hours of hair styling and make-up. The boyfriend spent an inordinate amount of time flirting with one of the young, female production assistants while Kelly was being attended to. Classy.

I was just worried about how much all this cost and making sure everything went right.

When models are prepped for commercial shoots, they are usually over-made-up to account for the lighting and other necessities of shooting. Once you see final film, the model doesn't look like she has so much make up on. Most people who are familiar with fashion photography are aware of this abundance of make-up. We soon found out that the boyfriend was not.

"You look like shit," he said to Kelly as she came out of the two hours of hair styling and make-up. At which point, Kelly immediately burst into tears. It only took 15 seconds to ruin two hours of work. Or, as I was calculating, $20,000 of Mr. Scavullo's time.

"Please do something about *the boyfriend*," I quietly appealed to the producer. "I'm not sure what, but I don't think we can afford to have him on the set. Any ideas?"

"I got this covered," the producer responded.

The crafty producer responded gave a young and attractive production assistant a wad of cash and she invited the boyfriend to go out and see Chicago — ostensibly so he wouldn't be bored. After all, he would just be sitting around while Kelly was back in make-up for extended periods of time. The boyfriend thought this was an excellent idea — and so did I. I have no idea where they went or what they did, and did not see them for the rest of the day. Nor did I care. The operative word there was *out* and that enabled Mr. Scavullo to focus on getting the beautiful photos of Kelly that appeared the following month in one of the inaugural issues of *Elle* magazine. Apparently, contrary to the boyfriend's judgment, Kelly did NOT look like shit. Hardly. Kelly looked great and she felt great and it showed in the results. Mr. Scavullo earned his fee.

Kelly's second *event* was following the delivery of her out-of-wedlock child with the boyfriend. While that is quite common today in Hollywood, perhaps even the norm, it was a reasonably big issue at the time. I recall having multiple discussions with P&G and Agency lawyers about whether it violated the morals clause in her contract. After all, my job was to protect the Pantene Brand. So Kelly's pregnancy was an awkward matter, and, unfortunately, one that could not be overlooked. Except, perhaps, when the business is growing like a weed. It was decided that we would wait to see if we got any level of objection from consumers via consumer call-in 800 line, which we did not. Consumers were often quite vociferous in how they felt and called us with frequency. We liked that. But consumers did not seem to care about Kelly's pregnancy or lack of a husband. As such, it was deemed a *non-issue*. Maybe it was being in Hollywood that helped me to *channel* Jeff Goldblum and he brought me that power, once again, to rationalize. Kelly and the boyfriend were all over the Hollywood press, and as they say in Hollywood, all publicity is good publicity.

At times, I beg to differ. But this was *not* one of those times.

Kelly agreed to shoot one commercial during her first trimester of pregnancy, after which she would no longer appear on camera. "I'm too fat," she would lament. So we had to make do for a while, continuing to run the commercials we had already shot.

Many months later, she was 12 weeks post-partum and we had not shot a commercial in what seemed like an eternity for a fashion brand, which must have a high frequency of new advertising to say fresh. When we inquired, as gently as possible, as to when Kelly might be ready to shoot again, we were told that she "still felt fat" and couldn't say when she'd be ready. Mind you, this was during the second $450,000 contract year; we only got one print ad and one television commercial out of the first year.

So we inquired as to whether there might be something supportive we could do to help her feel *better*. I thought that was rather sensitively asked. The answer we got was a proposal for a Pantene-paid trip to the Golden Door for a week, a spa in Southern California, which cost approximately $5,000 at the time. Outrageous, but another small investment relative to the $450,000 contract.

It was a successful week, and Kelly returned from the Golden Door rejuvenated, cleansed, and feeling ready to shoot. I think the Golden Door fee was booked as a production cost on the next shoot, because I can assure you that P&G had no accounting entry for "Spa Fees". Regardless, we got her shooting, and all was good again in Pantene land.

Or so we thought.

The final *event* for Kelly, which led to her ultimate demise as the face of Pantene, was a call I received one afternoon from her agent. We were approaching another cycle for a commercial shoot, and her agent decided maybe he and I should speak.

"Ah, Michael, I wanted to let you know that Kelly is considering cutting her hair," the Agent sheepishly informed me on the phone.

Me thinks me smells a rat.

"As you know, the fullness and length of Kelly's hair are really key to the communication of Pantene's core hair health benefit in the commercials," I communicated with as much equanimity as possible.

"Of course it is. That's why I thought we should speak," the Agent replied, meaninglessly. This response added nothing to the conversation, which was something I was used to in speaking with agents.

"Then why would she think cutting her hair would be a good idea?" I inquired, somewhat incredulously. I didn't quite grasp how incredulous the conversation was yet.

"Well, it would only be a trim."

"How much of a trim?"

"Two inches."

"Two inches in length?"

"No, to within two inches all around her head."

It was with every element of self-control that I could muster to reply in an even voice, "I could check with our Legal Department, but I'm pretty sure that would be in violation of her contract. You might ask her to reconsider that choice." I thought that was graciously put. Southern upbringing and all.

"I shall speak with her on the matter then. That's why I wanted to check with you before doing so."

"Please let me know what she decides. I will be most interested." I shook my head. Models. Jeeeesh. This didn't feel good.

It was two days later that I was informed that Kelly cut her hair to within not two inches, but to within one inch, of her scalp. A single inch of hair. All that beautiful hair was gone.

And so was her relationship with Pantene. It was two days and two minutes after my call with her agent that I took great pleasure in ripping up her contract.

Models. Jeeeesh.

7

BUDGET SEASON

I FEEL SO left out when I go to a cocktail party and people discuss skiing. They talk about the powder in Vail, the better runs in Aspen, snowboarding in Vermont, even the *après ski* drinks around the fireplace at the lodge. I feel the same as when my wife is watching *The View* – I have nothing to add to this conversation.

So you might be thinking "what is his problem with skiing?"

In truth, I don't have anything against skiing. It looks like a pretty cool sport. Neat equipment. Cool gear. Exciting destinations. My problem is that I just never got the chance to ski. Never even got the chance to *try* it. I guess I could fly to Colorado now if I wanted. I could get on the bunny slopes and learn to ski just like anyone else and dream about conquering those double diamonds. But at 50+, I'd probably just be worried about how sore I'm going to be that night, or what happens if I skied slap into a tree or how much I really don't appreciate cold weather anymore.

Yes, I got old.

But when I was younger, I could have done all of it – and I would have loved it. I just never got the chance. Why not, might you ask? For a simple reason: ski season coincided with a different season. *Budget Season*. And what, might you ask, is Budget Season? A good question indeed.

Budget Season was the period of time in the Procter & Gamble world that roughly coincided with January to Mid-April. As P&G operated on an odd fiscal year -- July to June. While most companies did next year's planning at the end of the summer or during the back to school time frame, Procter & Gamble's third quarter planning season began in January. This was the period in which all the Brand Groups developed and proposed their budgets for the next fiscal year. Thus the name, Budget Season. Catchy, huh?

And one would NEVER, EVER think of taking vacation during Budget Season. In fact, one didn't think of taking even a weekend off during Budget Season. The days, as measured by sunlight, were short. The days, as measured by work hours, were long. It's a good thing *Proctoids* don't generate energy through photosynthesis. They'd be an extinct species. Galapagos & Gamble.

BUDGET SEASON WAS Procter discipline in its most evolved form. It was, in short, a rigorous process of business evaluation. *Stepping back*, in Procter parlance, and evaluating the business from the bottom up, from the top down, and every other way one could think. There were no levels of rigor that were considered out of bounds. It was almost a test of character to see how objective (read: critical) the Brand Group could be of their own business. Turn the business upside down and divine its strengths and vulnerabilities.

In addition to analyzing the business itself, the Brand Group would also analyze the marketplace and competition. What had changed, which segments had grown, which had declined, how consumption patterns varied by region, how consumer preferences were evolving, and how effective the competition was at building their businesses and at whose expense.

And all this analysis was turned into a summary with a deceptively simple title — *Lessons Learned*. Sometimes, if your business was up, there were lessons learned via victory; other times, there were lessons learned in the woodshed. And whether victor or vanquished, the lessons that were learned became the basis for next year's marketing plan. What you learned had to be reflected in what you would propose for the following year.

It seemed the only time it was acceptable for a Brand Manager to admit vulnerability - to show a shred of humanity in that a mistake may have been made — was only if it could be quickly followed up with a corrective action. You only admitted error in the context of selling the fix! For some P&G Brand Managers, admitting error was a very difficult human experience. After all, it is a well-known fact that the only thing more arrogant than a P&G Brand Manager is one who is also a Harvard MBA. An annual victor in the *Know it All* Olympics.

This annual compendium of business knowledge was collected in the Budget Book, a proposal to management for the following fiscal year's financial targets, volume objectives and marketing budget. Like all P&G communication, it was rigid and regimented: Four Pages of prose maximum. Four pages of data exhibits. Never more, never less.

One might think that once the Budget Books were developed, typed, bound and delivered, that the 90 days of preparation, the sleepless nights and weekend-less work weeks had come to an end and the Brand Team could take a breather. Rest. Recover.

But one would be wrong.

With the coaching of the Associate Advertising Manager, the Brand Manager would bind the Budget Book and deliver it to the Division's Advertising Manager -- and the next phase of torture would begin. The Advertising Manager would play the role of Devil's Advocate to the proposal. And of course, this was an upper level equivalent of the Brand Manager's test of objectivity.

The Devil's Advocate would develop a two page document, a listing of questions that should be asked and addressed about the business proposal. This question list would become the script for what would be called the Budget Meeting – a two hour session, where the Advertising Manager sat on one side of the room and the Brand Group sat on the other side of the room. The Advertising Manager went through the script, question by question, sometimes in order, sometimes not. Sometimes all questions would be asked; sometimes only select ones. It was at the Advertising Manager's discretion. And the spectators watched the Matador and the Bull go at it. For two hours. Mano a mano – or whatever the female equivalent of that is.

An intriguing match for sure. At a high level, the questions attacked the basic assumptions of the proposal; at a detailed level the questions might ask why the marketing spending rate was $5.00 per case in Dallas, but $2.50 per case in New York. And you never knew whether the Advertising Manager thought $5.00 in Dallas was too expensive or $2.50 in New York was too cheap. Thus, the basis for the intrigue.

So the astute Brand Group prepared a detailed, numerically-based response to every single question – and even some that weren't asked but might logically come up. The Brand Manager then *memorized* the answers. Yes, memorized the answer to every single question. You did not go into a gun fight with a knife. You went in with a .44 Magnum. "Do you feel lucky, Punk? Well do you???"

Every Brand Manager worth his or her salt became *Dirty Harry*.

Make no mistake, the budget meeting *was* a test of mettle. Brand Manger performances in Budget Meetings were legendary – both positive and negative. I knew Brand Managers that didn't sleep for two days before a Budget Meeting; some who went into the bathroom and literally threw up due to nervousness before the Budget Meeting began.

As a Brand Manager, I actually savored the Budget Meeting – I'm weird in that way. The preparation sucked, don't get me wrong. I didn't like it. And the cultural dynamics were certainly quirky! But it also prepared me to be absolutely *expert* in my business. Like some marathoners say about marathon race preparation: it's hellish training, but it feels great to be in the best shape possible! Beyond becoming expert, the meeting was a stage, a performance, a proof point of how well you really knew your business. Perhaps dating back to my high school basketball and tennis matches, I relished the challenge and the competition. I didn't see it as an opportunity to fail, though it certainly was; rather, it was an opportunity to sparkle, to demonstrate mastery. And if I wasn't up to the challenge, well, simply put, I shouldn't be there. *Machismo*!

That, however, didn't mean I was without nervousness. My wife tells the story of me bolting up in bed during the middle of the night before my first budget meeting and exclaiming at the top of my lungs, "I'm sorry, Mr. Johnson, but there is no definitive answer to that question." And then collapsing back into deep sleep. She claims my eyes were not open, but my voice was certainly clear.

I have no recollection of that event. I also plead the Fifth. Clearly, though, I was nervous about not having a definitive answer to some question about my business, at least at a subconscious level. Every game plan has a soft underbelly, the space where an astute competitor can land a killer blow. A winner knows where that space is -- on his competitor and on himself. Knows how to attack it and how to defend against it. But knowing it's there doesn't reduce the vulnerability. Apparently, my subconscious knew it and it worked its way through my affected sleep.

But as staged as this Budget Meeting battle was, it was hardly a farce. There were still wild cards in the audience. Prior to the Budget Meetings, the Budget Book and the Questions would be paper clipped together (using a large square owl clip, of course), and forwarded to the Senior Management of P&G. At that point, it was hoped for, but not required, that Senior Managers considering attending the meeting might provide some advance notice to the Brand Group of their own questions.

Often, the Division's General Manager (known as a President today) would attend and add a few questions of his or her own. Sometimes, the CEO of the Company showed up -- or the Chief Marketing Officer. On occasion, you'd get some advance notice of their questions. But that practice was inconsistent. And thus, a wild card....

Sometimes the Wild Cards came from unexpected places. Sometimes, the Brand Groups and the Advertising Management created their own unintended wild cards. In their zeal to prepare, they didn't need Senior Managers to throw wild cards at them. Sometimes they were self-inflicted.

I recall one Budget Meeting on Hawaiian Punch (do you remember the little guy singing "Fruit Juicy, How about a nice Hawaiian Punch?" Maybe you're not that old). Hawaiian Punch had been acquired by P&G in 1990 and was headquartered for some reason in Mt. Dora, Florida, adjacent to a Sunny Delight packaging plant. Sunny Delight was headquartered in Cincinnati, but Hawaiian Punch was located in Florida. Go figure. I was sent down there to start a P&G marketing department for Hawaiian Punch, and a few other acquired brands. So I did what all good P&G soldiers do — I packed my family up and moved where I was told.

For this Hawaiian Punch Budget Meeting, I was the Associate Advertising Manager, playing the coaching role for the Brand Team, which had done an awesome job preparing their Budget Book. They had gotten the questions from the Advertising Manager and had completed their answers — and completely, too. There were no "I'm sorry, Mr. Johnson, there is no definitive answer to that question" responses.

The Brand Manager, Fred Stallone, had studied up, memorized his answers. I had done two dry runs with him to prepare him for his test. Fred was a United States Naval Academy graduate, an officer in the Military, and had spent time on submarines. He once told me that the saddest day on a six month submarine mission was about two weeks into the mission when the real eggs ran out. Powdered eggs apparently were more demoralizing to Fred than not seeing the sun for six months. I guess that's why Budget Season never bothered Fred. He didn't need sun. Even in Florida. For a guy who could handle submarine missions, four years at Annapolis, and powdered eggs, there wasn't much P&G could throw at him that he couldn't handle. Fred was ready.

Or so he thought.

The day before the Budget Meeting, the Group Vice President of P&G decided he was going to attend the Hawaiian Punch Budget Meeting. We discovered this because his administrative assistant called Chip Sharp, the Advertising Manager and my boss, and indicated the GVP was planning to attend. In a perplexing move, the GVP faxed over his copy of the Budget Book and Questions. On it, he wrote only a single word – *Margins*.

"Cryptic, but clear," Sharp declared to the gathered group after informing us that the GVP was going to be the guest of honor at the Budget Meeting. "The Group Vice President believes the profit we are promising for next year is insufficient. We'll need to develop a new plan that generates more profit."

The teams' eyes went wide. "A new plan....from scratch?" asked Fred. "In less than 24 hours?" Even the Navy hadn't prepared him for that eventuality.

"Absolutely" declared Chip, with triumph. Nothing is difficult for those who don't have to actually *do the work*.

Finding myself squarely in the middle, between the Brand Group and the Advertising Manager, I offered a bit of diplomacy. "Perhaps we might give the GVP a call and get him to give us a little more color on his thinking, find out what's on his mind," I offered, hoping to avoid having my team jump off the top floor of the building.

"How much more color do you need?" Chip retorted quickly and somewhat angrily. Like I was an idiot. "You can see we've already failed. He's screaming at us with just one word. I don't know about you, but I don't want to be further humiliated by a conversation on this matter. Get to it."

I was not easily intimidated. "Well, for example, how much does he believe we're off from a profit perspective? Is the profit margin off by two points or ten points? He must have some figure in mind that he thinks is sufficient. Why don't we save ourselves a lot of trouble, find out what he wants, and then we'll work all night if we have to and give him options." I thought this was a rational suggestion; apparently it wasn't.

"Five more points of profit margin. That's what we need. Get to it. End of discussion," Chip ordered us to work and then walked out. So it is said, so it shall be done. The Pharaoh has spoken.

And so that is exactly what we did. I had pushed it as far as I could.

We spent the next twenty-four hours straight finding five margin points. We cut back on price promotion, display materials, advertising spending, the extra sales promotion we needed to deliver the extra volume promised, advertising production costs, test market ideas. No line item in the budget was spared. It took us all night and into the early hours after sunrise, but we got it done. We weren't nearly as confident we could deliver the plan without the marketing support we just deducted to increase profit, but hesitancy was not a luxury we could afford a few hours before the budget meeting.

At 8:00am, Chip stopped by. "Did you get me the five points?" he inquired.

Yes, and a pleasant good morning to you, too. We had a sleepless and stress-filled night, at your behest. How did you sleep?

"As requested," Fred responded, his Navy chest puffed out with his clipped Military lingo kicking back in. He briefly described where the marketing support was cut and the profit improvement was created.

"How confident do you now feel about delivering the plan?" Chip asked.

"Not very," I interrupted. I wanted to save Fred from either lying or admitting vulnerability before the meeting. "Last minute changes to the plan without sufficient thought and consideration present more risk than I think we'd normally want to take."

"Doesn't appear we have much choice, do we?" Chip quipped. "I'll see you all on the plane to Cincinnati at 10:30am for the Budget Meeting. Go home and get showered. You guys look a mess."

Of course we had a choice. We could have simply asked the GVP what he really expected from us. I guess we'll find out soon enough.

———

THE BUDGET MEETING began promptly that afternoon at 4:00pm after the flight to Cincinnati. Chip Sharp -- clad in his crisp white shirt, dark paisley tie and gray suit — sat in the middle seat at the table to the left of the room. Fred Stallone, similarly clad, sat at a table on the right, girded for battle. The spectators all gathered on the sides — six representatives from the Advertising Agency, the entire Brand Group, the Division Sales Manager and assorted others. And of course, the Group Vice President, Sam Deauville.

Chip welcomed the attendees to the meeting. And cut right to the chase. Chip was going to give Sam exactly what Sam asked for, and he wasn't going to make Sam wait. Chip had big career aspirations at P&G, and he wasn't going to make management wait one second longer than necessary for what they wanted.

"Sam, it came to our attention yesterday that you felt the profit margins on the Hawaiian Punch business were insufficient. So I'd suggest we start out the meeting with Fred presenting the revised proposed financials for next fiscal year. Fred?"

Chip did not notice that Sam had a furrowed brow in response to this introduction. But Sam was a smart guy; rather than interrupting, he let the team proceed.

And Fred did a masterful job. He handed out a new set of neatly typed financials, starting with Sam. Fred walked the group through the changes carefully, emphasizing the right points, and logically explaining it all. Well done, Captain.

Chip watched Sam carefully as Fred presented, eyes never veering. Sam's prodigious eyebrows were arched as he listened intently. His expression demonstrated pleasure, but also appeared to have elements of surprise in it.

When Frank finished, Chip looked at Sam and said, "Does this achieve what you were looking for when you sent the Budget Book back with 'margins' written on it, Sam?"

"Well," Sam said expressionless, "to be honest, I liked the original plan very much. When I wrote 'margins' on the Budget Book, I was trying to tell you that to fit your plan on four typed pages, you didn't leave me any room in the margins of the document to jot down any comments or thoughts like I usually do. But I'll happily take the extra profit you're offering up for next year's plan. This will build a nice cushion in the overall Division profit plan. I was only planning to stay for the first 15 minutes of this morning's meetings as I have other commitments, so let me just say 'nice work to all'." And with that, Sam got up and left the meeting.

It's a good thing there were no flies in the room. They would have had a lot of places to land with all the jaws dropped to the floor.

—✿—

THERE HAVE ONLY been a few times in my life when I actually regretted not being able to ski. That moment was one of them. It was not, however, the first time I regretted working for Chip. Nor would it be the last.

8

YA AIN'T GOTS TO LIKE IT; YA JUST GOTS TO DO IT

GROWING UP IN the South often feels like you're part of one big family. Even if you're not *blood relatives* with someone, the familiar nature of southern communities breeds the presence of more Aunts and Uncles than normal blood lines would allow. If that certain person is close enough to your family or is present often enough in your house, over time, that person just becomes "Uncle So & So".

Growing up, I had so many Aunts and Uncles that it wasn't until later in life that I actually figured out who was blood and who wasn't. Truth be told, it really didn't matter whether they were blood or not. Unless of course, you were planning to marry; then that would be another issue entirely. All that mattered was they were part of the community that raised you. Hillary Clinton was certainly right – it takes a village to raise a child. And my village sure raised me.

One of my non-blood uncles was a man we all called Uncle Happy. Maybe he could be considered *almost* blood because Uncle Happy's sister was married to my dad's brother. I'm not sure what that makes us, other than perhaps inbred. But that's another story altogether.

Uncle Happy was one of my dad's best friends – and also one of my dad's poker buddies. My dad, Uncle Happy and about 8 other friends played in a Thursday Night poker game. The game rotated from house to house alphabetically. I remember vividly when the game would be at our house. The men all ate dinner at home and showed up promptly at 8pm. That was usually my cue to perform my ritual: shut off the TV in the family room, come into the kitchen where the men were gathered, greet them cheerfully, get a glass of coca cola (I knew I could get away with it when we had "company"!), and then retreat into my bedroom to do anything other than watch or listen to them playing poker. I didn't come out of the room for the rest of the night, in order not to disturb them. It was their "bro-time" and my dad deserved some time with his "bro's". He worked hard six days a week.

Now, mind you, this was not a very high stakes poker game. The tri-colors of the poker chips corresponded to pennies, nickels and dimes. And despite the rise in inflation over the *fifty-plus* years these gentlemen have been spending Thursday nights together, the tri-colors have only inflated to nickels, dimes and quarters. If you lost the maximum $20 in a single night, you were allowed to continue playing for free. Every person had the others' back. They were truly "bro's."

While this was obviously a friendly poker game, there were still those in the deep south in the 1960's who thought of ANY card game as gambling, and therefore, the *devil's work*. So in public discussions, the Thursday Night Poker Game became affectionately referred to as *Choir Practice*. The origins of this moniker come from Uncle Happy's assistant at his dental office.

One time the game had to be moved from one house to another at the last minute, outside the appointed alphabetical order. So calls were made along the phone chain. Uncle Happy had to be called at his dental office rather than his home given the late change. His assistant, Ms. Maudlin, had tried to give him the message, but Uncle Happy's schedule was packed with patients that day and she didn't get a chance to tell him until it was time for her to leave. She didn't want to interrupt him with a patient; yet at the same time she needed to give him the message before she left.

So Ms. Maudlin gently opened the door to the Operatory and started to give Uncle Happy the message. As she started to pass along the change in plan, she realized that Reverend Winthrop, the Minister at the First Baptist Church, was in Uncle Happy's dental chair. And it certainly would upset the Minister to know that his dentist engaged in the devil's work.

So she developed her own code.

"I just wanted to let you know that 'Choir Practice' has been moved tonight to the Elliot's House," she said to Uncle Happy with a wink.

Uncle Happy, a little puzzled at first, put two and two together quickly with the mention of the Elliot House, and it being Thursday.

"That's a fine thing that you do – participating in the Jewish Choir like that," said Reverend Winthrop. "I'm sure the Rabbi appreciates your participation."

"I'm sure he does," Uncle Happy replied hesitantly, shooting a thankful wink at Ms. Maudlin.

And so the Poker Game became known thereafter as *Thursday Night Choir Practice*. And it was with some frequency that charitable donations were made or raffle tickets were purchased in the name of *Thursday Night Choir Practice*-- with the winnings of the poker game.

———

BEING A DENTIST was a perfect job for Uncle Happy. Actually, "Happy" was a bit of an ironic name for him. Because he really was more of a tough guy than a happy-go-lucky fellow. Perhaps he earned the name in large part due to its irony. Perhaps Uncle Happy should have been known as Uncle Disciplinarian. OK, not a very good name, and not very catchy, but a more apt description.

Uncle Happy lived up to his reputation as a disciplinarian, by striking fear into the hearts of kids en route to the dentist office. I recall riding my bike to Uncle Happy's office for my semi-annual dental appointments. The wood paneled waiting room had an antiseptic smell, naugahyde furniture that made your sweaty palms stick to it, and plastic plants due to the limited natural light. Said room didn't even have windows – just opaque glass brick. In later years, I remember glass brick gaining a stylish use in bathrooms, allowing some light in, but obscuring view. It's the one design element of any house we've ever had that my wife proposed that I had to veto – glass block reminded me too much of going to the dentist.

The only *good* thing in Uncle Happy's office was the recent issue of *Highlights* that sat on the waiting room coffee table, with its brain teasers and puzzles. ANYTHING to keep your mind off the pain that was about to be inflicted in Uncle Happy's operatory.

When the cheerful Ms. Maudlin called your name – she was as inaptly named as Uncle Happy – you froze. It was paradoxical. How could someone so nice escort you to the evil bunker? It made you wonder if someone as cheerful as her stood outside the gates of hell. I hope to never find out.

Before I knew it, I was in that dental chair with a paper towel chained around my neck and Uncle Happy's hairy hands in my mouth. And I knew it wouldn't be long before he scolded me for eating too much candy and not brushing my teeth frequently enough.

"But I don't like brushing my teeth," I would complain.

Uncle Happy would calmly, but firmly reply, with a line I will never forget. With a gravelly voice resembling that of Louis Armstrong, and a southern intonation that sounded like Mammy in *Gone With the Wind*, Uncle Happy would simply reply, "No one said ya gonna like ev'rythin' in life. With some thin's, ya ain't gots to like it, ya just gots to do it."

A simpler message of self-discipline was never better worded or delivered.

———

IT WAS A little more than a year after I had been promoted to Associate Advertising Manager at P&G - and eight years into my tenure there - that I first started wondering if I should work somewhere else. I had certainly been contacted before by executive recruiters and tempted with similar jobs at other companies. I even went on a few interviews. But each time, I concluded, rightly or wrongly, that if I wanted to be in Brand Management, P&G was the best place.

In retrospect, my unrest was probably less related to P&G and more related to the challenges of being in Middle Management – it just wasn't *fun*. You really weren't high enough in the management pecking order to really call shots; and you were too high up to have fun running the business like you did in Brand Groups. If you tried to get involved the Brand's fun stuff, you were labeled a micromanager, a manager who crowded his people.

I always thought that business was the most fun at 80,000 feet and 8 feet – with the former number referring to managing at a very high strategic level and the latter managing right on the ground. And it was clear to me I was stuck at about 8,000 feet, in *no man's land*. A middle manager is just stuck between people who like to tell people what to do -- and people who have to do it and don't want to be told how. It's nearly impossible to make *anyone* happy – especially yourself.

It was the first time I gave serious consideration to doing something else entirely. The thought of a new business start-up with like-minded friends seemed very appealing. But I wasn't ready yet to toss in the towel on my P&G career.

So I decided to go hunting for other jobs in P&G that might give me a little more freedom to operate, where the rules were less rigid and history was less confining.

I thought it might be best to have a conversation with a mentor of mine at P&G, Al Harmann. Al was a military man through and through, having come to P&G after serving in the Korean War. The dedication that he showed in serving his country embodied the same dedication he showed in serving P&G. Al had risen up through the Brand Management ranks, ultimately becoming an Associate Advertising Manager on P&G's Deodorant Brands in Beauty Care when I met him. I was just a baby brand assistant at the time.

I took an instant liking to Al, and he to me. Al had great people instincts and later assumed the position as the Director of Advertising Personnel, with responsibility for talent management of P&G's marketing personnel. This was a pretty big job, given at the time that the majority of P&G's top management came from the Advertising Department, which included Brand Managers. Also, given that Brand Management was an "up or out" organization – meaning that they rarely hired from the outside and they fired more people than they promoted – Al's job was to identify and develop the next CEO's of P&G; and alternatively, to weed out others. A daunting task which required great human insight and great discipline.

I shared the frustration of my current assignment with Al. He understood my frustration; he had lived it himself. Al suggested that maybe it was time for me to take an assignment *off the coast*, like he did when he took an early P&G International assignment, before P&G really became a global company.

"Maybe we need to get you out of P&G headquarters for a little while, and see what you learn," Al offered. "I'll think about it some more and let you know if I can come up with something. In the meantime, keep your nose clean and don't do anything stupid." That was Al's way of saying "don't go talking to headhunters about jobs outside the company." I was cool with that, especially since I had already decided to stay.

About two weeks later, Al summoned me to his office on the 8th floor.

"I've got two opportunities for you; each will get you off the coast for a little while," Al declared. "The first will take you to our offices in Connecticut, where you would become the Associate Advertising Manager on a new brand of analgesic we're creating, taking a product from prescription to over-the-counter. The next level of pain management. The FDA hasn't approved it yet, so it will be a lot of planning. But you'd be building a brand from the ground up." This sounded interesting. It was the brand that would ultimately come market as Aleve.

"The other opportunity will take you to Florida, where you would become the Associate Advertising Manager for a new company we acquired in the Juice Business,

Sundor Brands. We also just bought the Hawaiian Punch brand, plus a whole collection of regional fruit juices to manage, all under the Sundor umbrella. We have just a few junior marketing people on the ground there; so you'd have to build a department pretty much from scratch." This also sounded interesting. Wow, what opportunities you can find, just for asking!

"I want you to get your butt out to both places in the next two weeks – take your wife with you – and come back and tell me: a) which opportunity you want; or b) that you're recommitting yourself to working in the Beauty Care role. I'll take no other answers. And by the way, get them to like you. I can't jam you down anyone's throat."

"Sir, yes sir," I replied with a mock salute. He was, after all, a military man and I was a mockery. Perfect complement of complete opposites. I have never been dismissed so excited.

The Connecticut opportunity was near Trumbull, a beautiful and charming bedroom community with marvelous neighborhoods and wooded yards on shady streets. A perfect place to raise our now expanding family with our 1 ½ year old son. P&G had built a brand new office building in nearby Shelton. Great homes, great office space, great business opportunity.

The Florida opportunity was in a little town northwest of Orlando called Mt. Dora. The offices were in two double-wide trailers between a juice packaging plant and orange groves, next to the dusty construction site of a new low-rise office building. Most of the P&G employees lived in Orlando and commuted the 45 minutes to Mt. Dora daily. Mt. Dora itself was a great place to live – if you were about 75 years old. But not so great at the time to raise small children.

Most people would have loved the civility of Connecticut. Most people would have loved the opportunity to shape a new brand, launch a new business with a megabucks marketing budget in the ever-growing health care field.

But I was not *most people*. I really wanted what Al called *off the coast*. I wanted more entrepreneurship, not more bureaucracy. I wanted the "roll up your sleeves, go figure it out, go move some serious volume, go make some serious money for the Company business", not the "plan, wait years for the FDA to approve it, plan some more, wait some more, see what happens" business.

I wanted that dingy office in the double wide trailer before the new office building got completed. I wanted to drive my Ford Bronco through the back country roads with the warm Florida breeze blowing, not freezing along the Merritt Parkway in Connecticut between traffic jams. No offense to Connecticut.

So I packed up my family and moved to Florida.

It took less than six months for me to understand the depths of the mistake I had made.

⸺

I WAS AN optimist, a *believer*. So I dismissed the early signs. I wanted this to be my next great adventure, so I didn't acknowledge the warnings and flashing red lights that were all around me. As always, I was determined to make this a success.

As if determination alone was all that was necessary.....

The first big sign was a subtle one, but a warning sign nonetheless. Those who have studied P&G have heard of the famed P&G One-Page Memo. The Reco. To keep things efficient and the thinking clarified, the Reco was limited to a single page, unless they were Budget Books or National Expansion Reco's. Brand Assistants were schooled in the thinking and writing skills to compose the one page Reco. It was not uncommon to get the first submission of the Reco back from your manager loaded with comments on how to make the language more economical or more focused. It was actually a very good thinking discipline to learn, and it has served me well in life. To be able to boil down complex issues to a simple analysis with a limited set of options – limited enough to fit on a single page. Truly, it was one of the best thinking skills I learned at P&G and have applied it often in business and life since.

That said, it was a skill one learned as a Brand Assistant, not three levels higher as an Associate Advertising Manager. And like boot camp, one assumed that once you got promoted from Brand Assistant to Assistant Brand Manager, one was also freed of seeing Reco's come back asking to be rewritten. Much less as a Brand Manager. And certainly NOT as an Associate Advertising Manager.

But I had not met anyone like Chip Sharp before.

My first Reco came back from Chip, well.... *shredded* would be an accurate description. Not literally, but certainly figuratively. There was not a single sentence on the page that didn't have words changed, phrases added, ideas sliced into pieces. And to make matters worse, he made all these comments in red, felt tip ink. The page looked like it had spent the day on the floor of an emergency room or a M*A*S*H unit. Clearly, patients had bled to death to part with this much red fluid.

When I was able to calm myself, rewrite the Reco to Chip's modifications, and then discuss the Reco with Chip, I was astounded to find out that he agreed with my original recommendation completely. Yet he took more than an hour of his own time to write all the comments and had me spend another three hours re-writing the Reco – all to say *yes* to the original request! What a colossal waste of time and effort!

Unless, of course, the objective was not to change the Reco in the first place.

If the objective was to demonstrate who was in control, who was superior, who was the boss, and who *owned* you -- then it was a very productive use of time.

And Chip was a man who used his time well.

The second big sign of concern came through my review of the Reco that P&G senior management approved to acquire the Hawaiian Punch business and fold it into Sundor Brands. This was more than one page. The Reco amounted to the promises made by Chip and his boss as to how quickly we would grow the business if we were successful in acquiring it. The term used for these types of financial promises is *acquisition economics*.

Hey, I went to college in the 70's. Believe me, I experimented in college like most others at the time. But I had never smoked the dope Chip and his boss did to develop these acquisition economics. I'm not sure who smoked more – the guys who put the economics together, or the guys who said "yes, we'll give you the hundreds of millions of dollars required to buy the Hawaiian Punch business based on this plan." *Caveat Emptor*. Buyer Beware.

This was an undeliverable plan, based on unachievable assumptions. And the five extra profit margin points that we gave Sam Deauville in the Plan was merely a drop in the bucket as to how far the business was behind the acquisition economics.

That almost immediately became evident as we reported repeated monthly profit & loss statements (mostly *loss* statements) that widely deviated from the acquisition economics and the annual plan. And by *deviation*, I mean *negative deviation*. Like leaving LA, heading for Vegas and ending up in Des Moines. This was embarrassing – I had never missed "Plan" in my eight years with P&G.

So about six months into my Florida expedition, I chose to call my mentor, Al Harmann. "Al, this is a total *Charlie Foxtrot* down here," I lamented. Al was a military man. He knew that *Charlie Foxtrot* was code for two words that began with *Cluster* and the second....well, you can figure it out. Just to be sure he understood how deep a *Charlie Foxtrot* it was, I gave him some of the details.

"Wow, I didn't realize how messed up things were there," Al empathized.

"And that's only a fraction of what I see every day. You gotta get me out of here, Al. I don't think I can take much more of this," said the Mouse.

Al was silent on the other end. I let the silence settle on the conversation like the wet blanket that it was. It dampened not only the conversation, but also my hopes.

"That's just not gonna happen, Michael," Al finally spoke. There was an eerie calm in his voice. A calm that said I was about to be *schooled*. And I was.

"I know you don't want to hear this, but P&G spent $50,000 to take you to Florida. Bought your house in Cincinnati; paid for all your closing costs in Florida; moved your family. All at *your* request. The Company needs to get a return on that investment before it takes you anywhere else. You can't just pull out because it's messy. You have one option, and *only* one option – you have to stay there, deal with it, and find a way – ANY way – to make that business successful. You do that inside the next two years, and you'll not only get out of Florida, you'll get *promoted* out of Florida -- and out of Chip's hair."

As much as I didn't want to hear it, Al was right. And all I could think of was Uncle Happy saying, "Ya ain't gots to like it; ya just gots to do it."

9

LIFE CHANGING REVELATIONS

AL WAS RIGHT. My only option was to take this situation and turn it into a success. Even if that meant it was Chip's success. I guess I really did have another option – I could have quit and taken a job elsewhere. Lord knows there were plenty of executive recruiters calling P&G management every day. But quitting P&G just because the going was tough didn't feel to me to be the right thing to do.

To move things in a positive direction, I determined I needed to do a couple of things. First, I had to change my attitude about Chip. I had to acknowledge that my problem with Chip was, in fact, *my problem*, not Chip's. Chip was who he was, and I wasn't going to change him. And once it's decided that you won't change another person, you can adjust both your behavior and attitude to *change yourself* instead. Or at least change how I choose to react to Chip.

The second thing was something we had to do, as a team. We had to re-craft the plan. We had to reset management expectations. If we couldn't deliver the acquisition economics – for whatever reason - then what *could* we deliver? So we rolled up our sleeves and rebuilt the plan from the ground up. We reconstructed the economics based on reality, not hopes and dreams. And we flew to Cincinnati and shared that "reality".

While it wasn't enthusiastically received by P&G Management, this was apparently not their first *ro-day-o* (OK, "rodeo" for those less Southernly inclined). We were not the first ones to have to reset lofty expectations. And while that put us in the dog house, we knew the only way out of the dog house was to make some new promises, and to deliver on the new promises we made.

And that is precisely what we did. We knew we were being watched carefully by P&G Management, and they would not give us much room for error. We spent more time in Cincinnati than we did in Florida, so we could be under the proverbial P&G management thumb. I would drive to the Orlando airport each Monday morning and fly to Cincinnati, only to return to Orlando on Friday evening. The rental car and hotel people knew me so well, they called me by first name. It got to the point where I'd walk by the National Car Rental counter in Cincinnati's airport and they would just toss me the keys to the same white Pontiac Bonneville that I would rent from them every week. "See ya Friday, Michael," Debbie would cheerfully say from behind the rental counter. I'd get to the Hyatt Regency in Cincinnati, and Carl would take my keys and park the car. Larry would grab my suitcase and would escort me, having already grabbed my key from the desk, to my upgraded room. They knew I was coming and when I'd get there. Like clockwork. People back then really knew how to take care of regular customers.

It was tough on my family with me gone all week. But my wife was a very good sport about it. We discussed the situation. I shared with her the conversation with Al. She knew what we had to do — and what her part was. So she made the best of it. We joked, "How many people at P&G's headquarters in Cincinnati get to go to Florida every weekend — at company expense?" It was our way of coping.

Chip and I spent the next year retooling Hawaiian Punch — new packaging, new sizes, new pricing, new promotions, new products, new advertising. We even brought back the little cartoon "Punchy" character that was in advertising in the 60's.

And it worked. Within 15 months, the business was up over 30%. We over-delivered that year's annual plan, we built momentum and excitement around the business, and we re-established our credibility.

Importantly, for my relationship with Chip, we did it *together*. It was a joint effort, of which we could be proud. Not only for Chip and me, but for the whole team that we worked with — Marketing, Sales, Manufacturing, Finance, Product Development. It was a "win" for everyone.

One day, Chip called me into his office. "Close the door," he said ominously. "P&G's has decided to close the Florida operations. We're moving back to Cincinnati."

Surprised, I said, "But we just built offices down here, just got rid of the double-wide trailers." I still had an affinity for the double-wide.

"Small change, financially, compared to what it's worth to P&G to consolidate offices," he replied. It was clear to me that this was a done deal. It was happening. I could tell by the tone it was not to be questioned.

"So what's going to happen to all the people here?" I asked.

"The manufacturing people will stay here and continue to operate the plant. That's not closing. But we're going to lose much of the office staff, except for the managers in Sales, Marketing and Product Development. They'll all be offered moving packages back to Cincinnati," Chip told me, seeming somewhat melancholy. He viewed this as his operation and he was clearly sad to have to give it up.

"Well, that's mostly the P&G people that were moved down here post-acquisition. What happens to the original Sundor Brands and Hawaiian Punch employees?" asked the Mouse.

Chip stared at me blankly. "Do I have to spell it out?"

OK, I got where this was going. "How are we going to take care of them?" I asked, with the faces of my soon-to-be-ex-teammates flashing through my mind.

"P&G doesn't have much experience with layoffs. It's not something they've had to do often. So the lawyers are especially nervous, which is actually good news for those going to be let go. The terms seem fairly generous. Original Sundor Brands or Hawaiian Punch employees will be given one month of salary for every year worked for P&G, Sundor Brands or Hawaiian Punch — with at least one year of severance minimum. They'll also be given outplacement counseling to help them search for new jobs. They'll have to sign wavers of liability and agreements not to compete for a period of time. But one catch: if you came to Sundor as a P&G employee, like you did, Michael, you're *not* eligible for the package. So any of the original P&G employees who want to stay in Florida does so without any package. It would be just like they quit on their own. No benefits at all."

Ouch. The lawyers were serious here. If you were an original Sundor or Hawaiian Punch employee, it's clear what your option was — and it was reasonably generous, for someone losing his job. If you were an original P&G employee, you had to make a choice: back to Cincinnati or leave the company. And the penalties for picking a non-P&G side were significant. Here today, gone tomorrow.

"At least the Sundor people will have a year of a safety net. That's pretty good, I guess." What did I know about severance packages? What else could I say? This was serious and I had never faced anything like this before. "So what's the next step?"

"Well, it won't be announced for two months, so you've got to keep it totally confidential. Since you and I won't have a lot of time to transition, I want you to go to Cincinnati and start house-hunting as soon as possible. The Company will buy your house in Florida, so you won't have to put a sign in the yard until after you've left. That won't tip off anyone locally to what's happening. The Company wants you and me settled in Cincinnati when the announcement is made so we can affect the transition as cleanly as possible."

"So how should I house-hunt without people knowing?"

"You and Toni go on the weekend. Find a place quickly. Plan the move quietly – work confidentially with P&G's HR department. No one can know."

I felt like the Baltimore Colts plotting the midnight departure to Indianapolis. Nothing but dust and an extension cord on the floor Monday morning.

I was a Proctoid; I followed orders. We found a new house under construction in a new neighborhood. All we had to do was pick the finishing touches – paint, fixtures, carpeting - and it would be done in about 4 weeks. I remember having to check on the house in the evenings after work so no one would know about it in the Cincinnati offices. One guy who worked on my floor actually lived in the neighborhood. I had to duck down when I drove through. Good thing I had a rental car so he wouldn't recognize me; he didn't know about my regular white Bonneville.

The two months of waiting, knowing that the guillotine would fall, was excruciating. I busied myself staying on the road so I didn't have to face the unknowing people each day that I was going to have to fire. Some of that travel included being away over the weekend, so I suggested to my wife that she take the kids – we had a second son while in Florida who was now four months old – and go visit her parents for 10 days or so while I was travelling. At least she'd have help with the kids while I was gone.

So she did. I recall that I was to get home on a Friday afternoon after two weeks of travel, and she would return on Saturday morning. I arrived the Orlando airport that Friday afternoon and got home about 6pm. Long week. Quiet house. Maybe I should enjoy the amenities of my *Florida Vacation Home* while I still had it. So I turned on some music, grabbed a beer and jumped in our hot tub by the pool.

Ahhhh.....I was pretty proud of myself. Just 31 years old and look at what I had amassed already – a 3,000 square foot, 4 bedroom, 3 ½ bath home with a screened-in pool, hot tub – all overlooking a golf course. As this was before the Florida golf course building craze of the 90's, these houses weren't quite as prevalent yet.

I told myself that I had *earned* this. That I deserved it. The rewards of hard work. I surveyed my manor, lazily eying the golfers as they plopped their tee shots into the water surrounding the island green.

I took my first sip of the beer, and something felt wrong. I started feeling nauseated, queasy, as if I was going to throw up. "Must be a bad beer," I said aloud as I stared at the beer, looking for floating nasties in it. I got out of the hot tub, dried off and went to lay down in the bedroom. I was dizzy. I flopped on the bed. I closed my eyes....

... And didn't open them for 13 hours. I awoke at 7am the next morning feeling fine. Curious as to what happened, but feeling fine. So I showered, ate breakfast, read the newspaper and prepared for my family to come home.

I heard the garage door open and saw my oldest son, Jason, come running into the house. "Daddy, daddy," he yelled as he ran across the kitchen floor and jumped into my arms. It is the best feeling in the world to gaze upon your child.

My wife came in next, holding the baby, and handed him to me. I kissed and hugged her and turned my attention to the baby. I cradled Jordan in my arms and looked down at him.

And then it hit me.

I got this feeling that Jordan didn't really know who was holding him. There was a bit of a blank stare in his eyes. People say that babies don't know who's holding them; just that they're being held. Jordan didn't cry. He didn't fidget. But I could just tell he didn't know me from Adam. I wasn't his dad. I was just a warm body holding him.

And then it hit me again.

That queasy, nauseous feeling I had last night, came upon me again, only this time without the beer, and this time with greater ferocity. My knees buckled. I almost fell to the floor. My wife came to my aid, took the baby, propped me up.

"Are you OK?" she asked with concern in her voice.

"Yeah, fine," I replied as I struggled for composure. But another wave hit me and I ran to the bathroom and wrenched my guts into the toilet.

"Must have been that bad beer last night," I thought as I rinsed my mouth with cold water. But then I looked at myself in the mirror.

And I knew.

It wasn't bad beer. If it was bad beer, why would the breakfast I ate this morning go down with no problems? Why would bad beer make me sleep 13 hours straight?

Why did all this happen the way it did? Why did I get the feeling last night? And why did it come back this morning at the moment I held Jordan?

In my heart, I knew it wasn't bad beer. This must be the feeling you get when you haven't been the person you know you should be. This must be the feeling you get when you ignore your family, your values, or who you really are. This must be the feeling you get when you feel self-satisfied at your material accomplishments, even while staring in the face of good people who are about to lose their jobs. This must be the feeling you get when you come to grips with your own shameful behavior. This must be the feeling you get — and deserve — when you're so focused on your career that your child doesn't even know who you are.

I was going to have to do something about this, but what?

I never discussed the incident or the revelation with Toni — or anyone for that matter. In fact, I tried to do what most normal human beings would do when your soul is opened up and exposed — and you don't like what you see.

Try to repress it. Try to forget it happened. Try to move on. Rationalize it. "Jeff Goldblum" it.

I FOCUSED ON more pressing matters. Like our pending move back to Cincinnati. While the P&G movers would do all the packing, I felt the need to use this as an opportunity to do some *inventory reduction*, going through our belongings and tossing the irrelevant things that had accumulated over time.

As I was going through the storage area, I found a familiar sight that made me smile. My old footlocker. My mother had purchased the footlocker for me from the Army/Navy Surplus store on King Street in Charleston before I went to summer camp when I was 11 years old. The Trailways bus shipping sticker was still on it. I had used that footlocker for a few summers of camp, four years of college, eight years in Cincinnati, and now in Florida. It had served me in many capacities — as luggage, as a coffee table in college (with a light blanket as a table cloth), and now as a holder of keepsakes. The footlocker had certainly served me well.

I had not opened it since I had lived in Florida. The moving stickers from the previous move were still on it. As I peered inside, the memories of my life came flooding back in waves of joy. In this treasure chest were the pieces of my collective life experience thus far. As I gently picked up each item, I saw faces, heard music, and remembered laughter from the many places the footlocker had travelled and the treasures it held.

Among them was a blue binder that took me a moment to place. It was from the summer of 1977, when I was 17 years old. I belonged to a teen youth group called BBYO, and I had gotten a scholarship to attend a 3 week summer leadership program in the mountains of Pennsylvania. As I looked through the binder, I was reminded of some of the details of the leadership curriculum. I laughed out loud, remembering my first year at P&G, when I attended management training, only to find it was the same exact curriculum that BBYO's International Leadership Training Conference had used. Little did I know at the time how advanced that BBYO's training was and still is.

Leafing through the binder, I came across an exercise I had to complete as part of the summer leadership training program. The exercise required me to write my own obituary. I remembered when I got the assignment how morbid it seemed to me. The purpose of the exercise – to envision what you wanted to be remembered for, and therefore to crystallize what was important to you to accomplish in life – only came clear to me after completing the exercise.

While I vaguely recalled the exercise, I didn't recall specifically how my obituary read. So I delved right in. And as I read it, I got that sick feeling in my stomach again. But I couldn't tear myself away from the blue binder. I was astounded at what I was reading.

At 17 I had written down all the accomplishments in life for which I wanted to be remembered. The community work that I had done, the contributions I had made, the kids' teams that I had coached, the children I had helped to raise, the way I had lived my life.

The *nauseating* part was that, 14 years later, I had accomplished *none* of it. Not one single thing that was written on the page. I had been so wrapped up in climbing the corporate ladder, adding the notches of accomplishment to my belt, that I had ignored *what mattered most* to me.

And the *scary* part was that, according to my obituary, I had died at age 38. Oh my gosh! What if this was right? What if this was predictive? What if I really only had seven years left to live? Was I going to die with nothing of value to say in my obituary? Only that I had turned around Hawaiian Punch and Lilt? That I helped to make Pantene into a big brand? That I had fired Kelly LeBrock?

Was this all my life had amounted to? Was this the sum total of my accomplishments on Planet Earth?

How sad would that be?

No, it was clear to me that I needed to seriously change my life. I was certainly succeeding; but it was a success measured by standards that didn't really match my values. I was focused on all the wrong things. And these events, this nausea, those little four month old eyes — they were all telling me the same thing: if *you* don't get your life going where you want it, *who will?*

Wait, wait wait. Now just hold on a moment. That all seems noble. A quaint notion. Maybe worthy of a quote from a poster from the 70's.

But I had to make a living. I had a family to feed and a mortgage to pay. I had to live in the *real world*. Sure, a great obituary is wonderful; but it's an obituary — that means I'll be dead! What's the difference? I had practical realities: like what would I do besides work at P&G? I mean, really? The Plan was history. How could I be guaranteed that if I worked somewhere else I'd actually get to spend more time with my family? Even if I did decide to leave P&G, how could I really leave now while they were buying my house in Florida and moving us to Cincinnati? You can't just quit in the middle of all that....

This was simply too much to process. Too overwhelming. And it wasn't *practical* thinking. It was *wishful* thinking, dreams. It was for someone who had the luxury of wishful thinking in their lives. I didn't have that luxury.

So I did the same thing I did before. Try to repress the feelings. Try to forget this happened. This feeling will pass. As sure as it came is as sure as it will pass.

Or so I thought....

10

I've Got (The Knife In) Your Back

P&G REALLY DIDN'T believe in having fun at work. For example, one never, ever, played golf with customers. That was for companies who didn't have substance to sell – they needed to rely on relationship. Industry conferences? Nope. We had real work to do; no time for standing around, lamenting the state of the industry. At P&G, we created substance. We did *real* work, day in and day out. We come from Cincinnati, with its Germanic history and culture. You don't have fun. You work. That's what you do.

So it came to me as quite a surprise when Chip called me to let me know that I was to attend the Industry Meeting of the Association of Apple Processors at the Turnberry Isle Golf Resort in South Florida. When P&G bought Sundor Brands, the acquisition included a number of regional apple juice brands that were managed under my group. We had been trying to aggregate them into a single brand called Parents' Choice, which would be a "super" apple juice that contained calcium. When you aggregated all the regional apple juice businesses, plus Parents' Choice, P&G had become the second largest apple juice seller in the US. As such, we got a seat on the executive committee of the Association of Apple Processors. So I was going to a meeting.

"What happens at these meetings?" asked the Mouse. "I've never been to one before."

"Not a lot, generally. But this one may be important. The US Food and Drug Administration is considering making significant changes to juice labeling. For better or for worse, our interests are being represented by the AAP and you need to be there to ensure our interests are well represented. I'll have the lawyers brief you on the issues."

"OK, so when do I go?"

"This Friday. Take Toni and the boys. Drive down. Have fun." Chip loved being magnanimous…when he could.

TURNBERRY ISLE WAS beautiful. Toni perched with the boys at the pool. They played, ate snacks, napped in the sun. I went to "plenary sessions" in golf shirts and shorts. Played golf in the obligatory golf scramble tournament. Attended more sessions. Didn't get that much done, but I had a good time. Now I know why P&G discouraged attendance at these things.

At the small Executive Committee Meeting, we discussed juice labeling issues and came to agreement as to how we'd approach the FDA. All good. As we finished business, the Chairman looked at me and said, "Michael, we have a customary Executive Committee dinner tomorrow night to finish off the annual meeting – just us and the wives – if you'd like to join us."

"That's very kind of you to offer," I replied, and I meant it. It would be nice to build good relationships here. "But we brought our kids, and I suspect you wouldn't want them to join us. I'm not sure *I* would want them to join us," I quipped.

Everybody chuckled. One of the other Executive Committee members said, "I know that Toni and your kids have been hanging out at the pool with my wife and kids. And we brought two nannies with us. If you wouldn't mind, we'd be happy to ask one of the nannies watch your kids while you joined us for dinner."

"Wow, that would be great. Let me just check with Toni and be sure she's comfortable. If so, we're in!" replied the Mouse enthusiastically.

Toni was OK. We were "in".

On Sunday evening, our table of 10 was having a fine time at dinner. Five executive committee members of the AAP and five spouses. A few drinks. A nice dinner. A bit of wine. A lot of fun.

The other members of the committee asked Toni and me lots of questions. First about our family. Then about us. Then about P&G. It was clear to me that we were getting *checked out*; but that's OK. I understood what was happening.

Or so I thought.

We had just finished ordering dinner, when one of the executive committee members asked me a question. "So Michael, if you'll forgive me delving into business a little more, how long do you expect to keep your retail pricing on three-pack apple juice drink boxes at 99 cents in the Northeast?"

On the outside, I was staring at my bread plate, and with every ounce of self control I slowly lifted my eyes to meet his. I was doing everything I could to appear calm on the outside. Because on the inside, bells, whistles, sirens, and emergency flashers were all going off at once.

While that might seem like a simple and somewhat innocuous question, it was the first time in my life I had actually seen a Federal law flagrantly broken in public. Collectively, the five gentlemen around the table represented nearly 90% of the United States production of apple juice. While that may not seem quite like the cast of *Wall Street* or even qualify for *Barbarians at the Gate*, there are certain things a group like this is legally allowed to discuss and certain things they are not.

Pricing, without a shadow of a legal doubt, was one of those things that could not be discussed. It is clearly spelled out by the Federal Trade Commission that such discussions are patently illegal. And I was being asked point blank about P&G's pricing by a competitor. In front of other competitors. To participate in such a discussion was to commit a federal crime. Yes, even for something as basic as apple juice.

It was at that point that I noticed this was the first meeting of the weekend where the Association's legal counsel wasn't present. Even worse.

As I looked around the table, it wasn't like the other three gentlemen were surprised by the question. It was as if we were discussing NFL teams or the weather. It struck me that this was *normal* conversation for them. That was when I realized that the reason they wanted me at dinner was specifically to discuss pricing. This was a planned, and possibly annual, price fixing meeting.

And I was the guest of honor.

With as much calm in my voice as I could muster, I did the only thing I could think of doing in this awkward situation. I lied. I *bold face lied*, to buy a little time to think.

"You know, I didn't even know that 99 cents was our price on that size in the Northeast. You see, at P&G, The Sales Department sets the pricing." Not true at all." Now if you'll excuse me for a moment, I have to go to the restroom."

I walked slowly, at a measured pace, to the men's room. I got inside and stood at the sink. I splashed water on my face. I gathered myself. I couldn't believe what I had gotten myself into. I had heard that stuff like this went on sometimes; but I never thought it happened in businesses I was in. That was the stuff of Mafioso, Oil Cartels, and People that Play for Keeps. Not guys who crush apples to make juice for little kids to drink.

I needed an exit from this dinner and I needed one fast.

And then it hit me. An idea quickly turned into a plan. But could I pull it off?

When I returned to the table, I looked at Toni and said, "While at the restroom, I called back to the hotel to check on the kids. It seems Jordan hasn't stopped crying since we left. Perhaps we should excuse ourselves and relieve the nanny."

"But your dinner hasn't even arrived yet," protested one of the Executive Committee members. I couldn't tell if they sensed my panic.

"Please accept our apologies, but we best get back to attend to Jordan. I hope you all have a great evening, and once again, sorry to have to run out."

And with that we simply left. Dinner hadn't even arrived yet, and we just left. I suspect the abrupt departure sent the message that P&G would not be a willing player in their game of price fixing. Nor would Michael Elliot.

As we got in the cab, I explained to Toni that Jordan was fine, as far as I knew, but that we had to exit that conversation as soon as possible. I was too thin to look good in an orange prison jumpsuit.

When we got back to the hotel, I immediately opened my laptop computer and typed out a file memorandum, chronicling the event, the attendees, the manner in which the legally prohibited conversation came up, and how I handled the matter. I stayed up late, worked over the details in my head, edited the memo carefully to be sure it covered the matter thoroughly. I was still wired when my head hit the pillow.

The next morning we drove back to Orlando. I dropped off Toni, the kids and the bags, and headed straight to the Mt. Dora office. Upon arrival, I printed out a copy of the memo and took it directly to Chip's office.

"How was the meeting?" Chip asked, quite *chipper* in fact.

"Not so good. I'm not sure these are good guys. You better read this."

"What's this?" he asked, a little less *chipper*.

"Just read it. Call me when you're done. Then let's talk next steps." And I left his office.

Fifteen minutes later, Chip rang my phone. "Michael, you better come up here." Now he really didn't sound very *chipper*.

When I arrived at his office, I was instructed to close the door and sit down. I followed instruction.

"I just faxed this to Chuck Motley, our division counsel. He and I discussed it. I want you to go home, unpack your bags from the weekend, and repack your bags because you're flying to Cincinnati this afternoon. You have a 9:00am meeting tomorrow with John Jamison, P&G's General Counsel."

"Why, what's there to discuss? It's all spelled out in the memo."

"You'll need to discuss that with the General Counsel."

"So why do I need to fly to Cincinnati? At the last minute, that will probably cost $2,000 or more. Why can't I talk to him on the phone?"

"Because they want to discuss it in person."

"'They'?" Red flags were flying all around my head. "Chip, what the hell's going on here?"

"Michael, I want you to understand clearly what's happening: Motley's calling for your job. He wants you fired for your involvement in this."

"Fired? Calling for my job? Why?"

"Motley says that if the FTC ever got word that this conversation took place, P&G could be more protected from prosecution if it can say it discovered the issue immediately and terminated the employee involved with due haste."

OK. So now I knew what this was really all about. And now I knew whose ass was being covered. I had become the Legal Department's sacrificial lamb. There was nothing more to say. Silently, I got up and headed for the door. As I opened the door, I paused, turned and looked Chip straight in the eye. There was one more thing I needed to know.

"Chip, you read the file memo. It was written exactly how it happened. Do you believe I did something wrong here?"

Chip looked at me, coldly. "That's not for me to decide."

And that answer told me exactly whose ass was really being covered.

"WHAT ARE YOU doing back home so early?" Toni asked.

I was not about to tell my wife, playing on the floor with my two young children, that I was headed to Cincinnati to get fired.

"Something's come up while we were gone. You know P&G — everything is an emergency. I've got to grab a plane this afternoon to Cincinnati for a meeting tomorrow morning. So I'm just gonna go repack quickly."

That was not a surprise to my wife. What would have been a surprise was to know I was withholding from her something very important, something that would affect both us deeply. Withholding information was not the way our marriage worked.

It was a long drive to the airport. It was a long flight to Cincinnati. I didn't smile so much when Debbie threw me the keys to the National Car Rental white Bonneville or when Carl greeted me at the front door of the Hyatt Regency Hotel. Actually, it was quite a long and sleepless night.

How could this happen? I thought I had been a pretty good employee. How many businesses had I turned around for P&G? How many people had I trained and promoted? How loyal had I been for the previous ten years? Was I not the quintessential "Ya ain't gots to like it, ya just gots to do it" kind of guy? How could they allow a lawyer to just toss away like wastepaper someone who had delivered for the shareholders? And for what? Walking into a sticky situation that he didn't ask to be put in? And finding a clever way to keep the Company from harm? I just didn't *get* what was happening. And moreover, couldn't believe it was happening to me. Couldn't believe Chip was *letting* it happen to me.

And that part really burned me up. Chip. He ran for the hills at the first sign of trouble. As soon as Motley called for my job, did Chip even make an attempt to defend me? To challenge the Legal Department? Absolutely not. He immediately tried to distance himself from me, from something that might have blowback on him. Did he care about me at all? No, he was squarely focused on personal damage control.

I tossed and turned all night. P&G was going to fire a very tired guy the next morning. At least I would look reasonably close to how I felt.

AT PRECISELY FIVE minutes before 9:00 the next morning, I pressed the button in the elevator for the 11th floor at P&G's downtown Cincinnati headquarters. I checked my tie and suit lapel in the metallic reflection of the door as the elevator moved toward the heavens. When the door opened, I walked onto the crushed velvet green carpeting and strode down the mahogany paneled walls, eyeing the framed oil paintings of P&G's founders, William Procter and James Gamble, and the handful of CEO's that had stood at the helm of this American institution over the previous 150 years. The 11th floor was quiet. Quiet as a morgue. What a fitting analogy to the situation I faced. And the way I felt.

"Come right in," John Jamison, General Counsel of P&G, said. John greeted me with a smile, which felt somewhat surprising. Was he really going to smile as he fired me? How cruel is this place? His round tortoise shell spectacles complemented his red hair and ruddy complexion. Seemed like a nice guy. What a paradox. "Just have a seat right here in this chair," he offered.

I looked down to see if the chair was electrified. Needless to say, I was ill at ease and more than a little paranoid.

"Why don't you tell me what happened, in your own words," he began.

"It's really all right there in the document sitting in front of you," I quietly replied, pointing to the fax copy of my typed memo on the table.

"I know and I've read it. A couple of times. I'd just like to hear you tell it to me."

Man, they really aimed to torture me, didn't they? Why couldn't they just shoot me and get it over with. So I told him what happened. Nearly exactly as I wrote it in the memo. When I finished, John Jamison just looked me. Exhaled. Here it comes.

"You know, the possibility of something like this happening is one of the reasons P&G frowns on participation in such industry organizations. It puts our corporation at risk. Do you think we should resign our membership in the AAP?" he asked.

Aw c'mon. Don't draw it out. If you're gonna fire me, just do it already. Let's don't discuss the details of my funeral.

But it was clear he was interested in my response. "Normally, I'd say we should resign our membership, because it's now clear that they don't operate within the law, at least when the Association's counsel isn't looking. That said, they will represent P&G to the US Food & Drug Administration on matters of importance to us, and could work against us to make it difficult to introduce new technology, like our calcium-fortified apple juice. Few industries welcome P&G into it. Maybe we should stay in the AAP, but not attend any meetings where the Association's counsel isn't present. You know, like in *The Godfather*: 'Keep your friends close, but your enemies closer.'"

"You may be right. That might strike the balance of best protecting the Company's varied interests in this matter. I'll give it some thought and let you know."

That seemed curious. Let me know? Let me know what? I'll be gone.

"OK, well thanks for coming up to my office to speak with me," and he offered his hand.

If I wasn't mistaken, it appeared the meeting was over.

"Is that it?" I asked.

"Were you expecting something else?"

"Yes, as a matter of fact, I was led to believe that we'd discuss another matter."

"And what matter would that be?"

"That my employment with P&G would be terminated."

"What? Who led you to believe that?"

"My boss, Chip Sharp, and division counsel, Chuck Motley."

"And why would we terminate your employment?"

"I was told that if the if the FTC ever got word that this conversation took place, P&G could be more protected from prosecution if it can say it discovered the issue on its own and terminated the employee involved immediately."

"I guess it's possibly true that P&G might be better protected. But that would also be an incredibly stupid thing for us to do, in my view. Michael, let me explain something to you. As General Counsel of a global company the size of P&G, I worry every day that somewhere around the world, one of our employees is getting put in the awkward situation that you were put in, handling it wrong, and putting the corporation at risk.

"But if every employee," he continued, "handled the situation with the diplomacy and propriety that you handled it; well, I could get a lot more sleep. From my perspective, the way you handled it – immediately exiting the conversation, documenting it, and then sharing it right away with your management and the Legal Department – is the textbook way to do it. And you, not being a trained lawyer, did it reflexively. So let me say - as an officer of Procter & Gamble, and as a shareholder - thank you for the way you handled this. Seriously, thank you." He smiled and stuck out his hand to shake mine.

I was dumbfounded. I couldn't even speak. I just shook his hand.

"Now go get back to building the business," he said as he smiled and patted me on the shoulder.

As I departed John's office and strolled back down the plush carpeting, my mind was in a netherworld. I had no idea what just happened.

But out of the vagaries of the moment, the confusion, the swirling miasma of my consciousness as that very moment, two distinct thoughts formed in my mind.

The first was, "That rotten son of a bitch." And I wasn't thinking about John Jamison.

The second was, "No more delays. No more rationalizations. It's time."

11

UP AND OUT

I took the elevator down to the lobby. Walked right of the building. Headed to the airport. Didn't speak to a soul.

On the flight home, with the assistance of an *adult beverage* or two, I worked over various options in my mind of exactly how I was going to tell Chip Sharp to "take this job and shove it." The more boring option was the simple letter of resignation that I would deliver the next morning. The less boring one involved me detailing in the letter of resignation all my grievances with Chip, and faxing that letter to John Pepper, the President of P&G, instead of giving it to Chip. I would love to be a fly on the wall when Mr. Pepper called Chip to ask about why he received it. Probably the most interesting option was simply to walk into Chip's office, deliver a round house punch that would deck him -- and then ask him how he liked *that* Hawaiian Punch?!

After a while, I realized that while these were ideas, none was actually a *good* idea and I was just engaging in unproductive, negative thinking. This exercise was serving only to make me angrier and, thus, less clear headed. But it *was* entertaining, and somewhat cathartic. I reminded myself that at this point in time, with all the transition going on, was not the time to take action. It was the time to step back and consider options. Which I would most certainly do. But I still smiled at the thought of the Hawaiian Punch for Chip.

I chose to shift my mind to more positive thoughts, one of which was something on my "to do" list when I got back from Turnberry Isle, which was to promote one of our Assistant Brand Managers to Brand Manager.

This was a huge step for her — only about one-third of the people that start as Brand Assistants make it to Brand Manager. Less than 10% make it to Associate Advertising Manager, and less than 2% to Advertising Manager and General Manager. People are so conscious of these numbers that they track their progress very carefully — to the point of establishing norms, measured in months between roles. Since Brand Management was an *up or out* culture at P&G at the time, one watched the month-count carefully, in order to assess whether one was going to make it. Better to pull the rip cord on your parachute for yourself than get thrown out of the proverbial plane. Which many did.

Because of this dynamic, promotions were not really surprises to people. It was more like *relief*. When someone would get within two months of *generally accepted promotion timing*, people looked for any sign that today was possibly THE day. A late Friday afternoon meeting with the Advertising Manager. Someone in a role above you leaving the company. ANYTHING!

To generate some sense of excitement when promoting someone, the more inventive managers tried to create diversions, circumstances that the "to be promoted" person might not pick up that today was THE day.

I could tell the Assistant Brand Manager was on edge. Every time I walked by her desk, she eyed me as if I was going to steal something off her desk. Is now the time? Is today the day? I needed to think of something clever to do as a distraction to her from my real purpose.

As I was thinking though promotion options, I was reminded that even the best laid plans of mice and men are often disrupted by the forces of the universe. I chuckled as I thought about how I was informed of my promotion to Associate Advertising Manager, three year prior.

My wife's nursing school roommate, MaryAnne, married a guy named Tim O'Malley, a union electrician in Cincinnati. Tim had achieved a certain level of security clearance that allowed him to work at P&G for the electrician's union. While the Union generally had the right to send whichever electrician they wanted to any company requiring electrical work, P&G would only accept a select group of electricians who were pre-cleared through P&G's security. Evidently, you never sure who might be secretly working for Unilever.

Toni and I hung out with Tim and MaryAnne O'Malley with some frequency before we moved to Florida. They were a lot of fun and I rather enjoyed having friends who didn't talk Brand Management. Given that P&G had lots of needs for electricians

— like every time they rearranged a bullpen — and the limited number of security-cleared electricians, Tim pretty much worked at P&G full time. So I would regularly see him around the office.

I was actually seeing him *daily* when Tim was working on a large office remodel on my floor. One Tuesday I ran into him and I asked if they were almost finished with the redesign work, which had been going on for quite a while.

"Yup," he said. "It will be completed Friday. I'm off to the seventh floor starting next Monday. Hey, by the way, MaryAnne tells me you guys are coming over to watch the Bengals game at our house this Sunday."

"We are? I haven't gotten my weekend orders yet. But that sounds great! Looking forward to it." We slapped five casually. "Catch you later."

When we got to Tim and MaryAnne's on Sunday, our kids took off to the basement to play with the O'Malley boys, about the same ages.

"It's Miller Time," Tim beamed as he brought out four cold beers for us. As he popped the caps on each and handed them around, he proposed a toast.

"Here's to the Bengals still being in the game at halftime!" he shouted. After just losing the Superbowl to the San Francisco 49'ers on a last minute Joe Montana drive in January 1989, the Bengals had gone on to put up one of the most dismal records in the 1990's. "And oh yeah, congratulations on your promotion!"

"Thanks," I said as we clinked bottles all around. "But, *promotion*? What are you talking about?"

"I assumed you got promoted this week," he said, cautiously, wondering if he'd misstepped. "The larger office on the end of your floor that I finished this week had your name on the work orders. It's definitely an Associate Advertising Manager-sized office. You know how structured P&G is — only that level gets the 12 x 12 office — measured by the ceiling tiles!"

"Well, you're right about P&G's structure for sure, but nobody said anything to me about a promotion," I replied. "Hmmm, yet we *are* supposed to move offices tomorrow. I packed my office up Friday as instructed before I left work. I guess we'll see what happens."

And, wouldn't you know it? Tim was right. The next morning I got promoted to Associate Advertising Manager and moved into the new office that Tim had wired. I suspect that it was the first time in P&G history that someone was promoted by the floor's electrician. With Tim as a good friend and a cold beer between us, I couldn't think of a better way!

———∞———

WHEN I GOT back to Orlando from the meeting with the General Counsel in Cincinnati, I noticed the delivery of a number of box flats that would be used by the packers when they arrived the following week. This dose of reality made me realize that quitting immediately would create a number of pragmatic issues. As nice as Orlando is, it was not where Toni and I wanted to be – Cincinnati was. As such, I had no really viable option but to suck it up and complete the move. Once we got back to Cincinnati, then we could assess the appropriate next steps. So that killed all my elaborate and dramatic *take this job and shove it* scenarios. Or at least delayed them.

What I also realized was that I was in the process of making a lot of choices about *us* – Toni and me -- that I really hadn't discussed with the other half of *us*. Due to all the confused feelings I was having, I had decided not to talk to Toni about them until I had some clarity on how I really felt. I needed to lay out all of this to Toni and get her input. After all, it affected her tremendously.

"Honey, I think we have to talk." And so it began that evening when I got home. I laid the whole thing out for her – the nausea, the obituary, the meeting in Cincinnati, the *faux firing*, all of it. How I felt. What I thought I wanted to do. How complex the issue was, especially regarding the move. A waterfall of my *emotional stuff* cascaded all over her.

She took it all in stride.

To her credit, she said only two things: "I'd rather be in Cincinnati than Orlando." And "Whatever you want to do, I'll support it." When God created spouses, I think he broke the mold after he made Toni. Yet another reason I had considered myself for quite some time to be way *over-chicked*. She was truly much better than I deserved.

———∞———

A FEW MONTHS had passed – a few hectic months. We moved back to Cincinnati, got settled, dealt with the displeasure of closing the Mt. Dora offices, took care of people, got the business moved to P&G's Cincinnati headquarters, and generally got back to work.

Chip never spoke again of the Turnberry Isle Incident, nor of my meeting with the General Counsel. He knew the outcome, but never asked me about it. To maintain civility – and my composure -- I chose not to bring the subject up. I was afraid the Hawaiian Punch scenario might erupt. Nonetheless, my general feeling that it was time to leave P&G had not changed. I just had to figure out when and how.

Sitting in my new office in Cincinnati one day contemplating that exact topic, I was surprised to see Chip standing at my door. I was normally *summoned* to his office. He rarely deigned to pay a personal visit. It wasn't his way.

"Got a minute?" he asked sheepishly. I sensed trouble immediately, and it must have been reflected in my expression. He picked up on it right away as he closed the door.

"Don't worry, this isn't bad news, just something I need to cover with you," he began. That typically meant it was an inconsequential topic; yet this didn't *feel* inconsequential. That comment felt like a head fake. I had hoped it wasn't as obvious to him as it was to me that my trust level with him had gone to, yeah, *zero*.

"If you recall, when we shut down the Mt. Dora offices, departure packages were only offered to original Sundor Brands employees. The P&G employees were not eligible. Right? Well, the Legal Department has reviewed that decision and decided that the Company is obliged to offer the same package to P&G employees, retroactively."

"Retroactively?" I inquired. "How do you do that? The Company has already moved everyone up here."

"It's just a legal procedure we have to go through. So I'm informing you – *officially*. You're being offered a separation package."

"OK, you can consider me *officially informed*." I acted like it didn't matter, as if I were allowing him to perform his perfunctory duty. Yet, the wheels were turning in my mind.

"Officially, yes, but it really doesn't matter," he commented, now with a grin resembling the Cheshire Cat.

"Why not?" This was getting weird.

"You wouldn't *need* a separation package, because today we're promoting you to Advertising Manager of P&G's Snacks Business. Congratulations," Chip beamed.

"I'm what?" I was floored. I was speechless.

"Yep. You'll be reporting to Bob Graybeal, the General Manager of the Snacks Business."

"Bob's a great guy," I replied, not knowing what else to say. And Bob *was* a great guy. I had known Bob and a number of people who worked for him. People raved about working for him, in fact. What I wanted to say was "Bob is a great guy, especially compared to you!" But discretion is the greater part of valor.

Instead I said, "But I don't get it. Three months ago, I was going to be fired to *protect* the Company. Ninety days later, I'm *promoted*? Really? Is that the way it works?"

Chip shifted uncomfortably in his chair. "Well that was all just a big misunderstanding. What you've done with Hawaiian Punch is amazing, and has not gone unnoticed by P&G's Senior Management. And as you know, making it to Advertising Manager is really just a holding position until the next General Manager spot opens up. Normally, a year or less. This is the management level where the real money kicks in, too. Additional bonuses. Stock Options. Enhanced retirement. Once you've made it to this level, you can count on being worth millions in ten years or less." Chip clearly wanted to move off the Turnberry Isle topic and I sensed him moving into selling mode.

"Well, thank you, I guess," replied the Mouse.

And then something occurred to me. More wheels turning in my mind. It wasn't a totally coherent thought yet, but certainly a forming one.

"When do you and Bob intend to announce this?" I asked.

"This afternoon."

"Can it wait until tomorrow morning to be announced?" I inquired.

"Why?" Chip was immediately suspicious. Perhaps that trust thing went both ways.

"Well, clearly, this is a huge move for me. Life-changing perhaps. I'm thinking I should talk about it with Toni. After all, she's my wife - my life partner - and it will affect her as much as me." That felt like a request to which it was hard to say no.

"Well, I guess so. I'll call Bob and let him know. Tomorrow morning it is. Congratulations again." Chip said, brandishing his best polished smile.

He shook my hand vigorously. I wanted to wash it afterwards.

———

"They did what?" Toni asked incredulously.

"You heard me. *They offered me a separation package and a promotion in the same conversation.* I even went up to HR to confirm that the package is really an option. I didn't believe it myself."

"So wait. You mean to say that even after they bought our house in Florida, moved us up here, paid for all the closing costs for our new house, and gave us two months' salary as a moving bonus – just 60 days later, they would then pay us, on top of all that, a year's salary *to leave*?"Toni summed up the craziness of the whole situation pretty well.

"Yes. But I don't think they *intended* to do that. It just happened that way. I think the lawyers felt they need to reassess the risk in their decision and if that would cost the Company some money, so be it. I guess they think it's cheaper than potential law suits. But, as it relates to me, I suspect they think of the separation package as only *potential* cost, because why would someone turn down a promotion to Ad Manager? And history would likely be on their side. There's a lot of money and prestige associated with the Ad Manager role. It's worth a lot more than a year's salary."

"So you think you want to take the Ad Manager job? That would get you out from under Chip. And even I've heard what a great guy Bob is." Toni said, supportively.

'I don't know. It is tempting though. The promotion's a real game changer. What do you think?" asked the Mouse.

"I think it looks like this: For a lot of good reasons, you were going to leave P&G — and that was for *free*. So what's changed so much that you wouldn't leave P&G for a year's salary?"

That's my wife. She cut right through to the most salient point. I am totally *overchicked*.

———

"WHAT DO YOU mean, you're 'taking the package'?" Chip was furious as we spoke in my office the next morning. No, he was incensed. That vein in his rather voluminous forehead throbbed as he screamed at me. "No one, I mean NO one, has ever turned down a promotion to Ad Manager. Have you gone absolutely nuts?"

"I appreciate the promotion. I really do. But it's just time for me to go, Chip." I responded calmly, hoping my tone of voice would calm him some, too.

"This is unprecedented. Unheard of. No one does this. NO one!" he repeated, now nearly screaming. No hope of keeping this matter private. His voice reverberated within my office walls, and no doubt *through* them. My calm voice was having no contagious effect.

"Well, you've always heard of P&G having an *up or out* culture. Today, we're pioneering *up AND out*," I quipped, trying to lighten up the conversation.

It didn't work.

"Do you realize how this will look for me?" Chip screamed. Ah, now it became clear what the *real* issue was. He wasn't mad that I quit; he was mad that I quit *on his watch*. Losing an employee the Company wanted to promote does not reflect well on the employee's manager. Once again, Chip was just looking after his own self-interest. And my resignation at this moment was not in his self-interest.

Just an added benefit, I thought. I was rather enjoying this now.

"Chip, this isn't about you. It's about me. It's just time for me to go. That's all."

"We'll see about that," he retorted, with forehead vein throbbing as he stormed out of my office.

⸙

THIRTY MINUTES LATER, Chip was back in my office. In the meantime, I had spoken to HR to get the process moving -- and to try to blunt Chip's ability to maneuver. No telling what he was up to.

"Sam Deauville is expecting you in his office in ten minutes," Chip commanded, his voice much more calm and controlled. Sam Deauville was the Group Vice President of P&G's Food & Beverage business. He reported to the President & CEO. It was clear Chip had regrouped and had assembled a plan to change my mind. Or, more likely, to cover his butt. He was right to be concerned that my departure would reflect poorly on him. In P&G parlance, given that I was being offered a promotion, I would be classified as a *regretted loss* if I left, and that doesn't reflect well on the manager.

I was prepared for this. This was Page One in the standard P&G playbook for turning around the resignation of a regretted loss. Call in the Big Guns. Tell the employee how much he is loved, how bright a future he has ahead of him at P&G, how important he is to the Big Gun making the statement. And lay it on thick enough in hopes that it doesn't make the employee stop and wonder why he hadn't heard this from the Big Gun in the ten years he had been there – why it happened only when he resigned. Makes it ring a little hollow. Nonetheless, it's generally effective. It works. Otherwise, it wouldn't continue to be Page One.

I took the elevator up the 11th floor. Trudged right past John Jamison's office, reminding me of my last trip to the 11th floor, and girding me to stick to my decision to leave. I would soon find out that wouldn't be too difficult.

THE ELECTRONIC DOOR to Sam Deauville's office opened mechanically. His assistant nodded toward the office, signaling that it was now safe for me to enter. Sam was sitting behind his desk with his back to me, looking at something on a messaging screen. Without turning around, he simply said, ostensibly to the screen and not to me, "You do realize that your resignation is really messing up our plans."

When I determined that he was actually speaking to me and not the machine, I thought he was trying to lightly start the conversation with a bit of humor. It was when I saw the look on his face as he swung around in his chair that I realized he was not trying to be funny. He was mad. I really had messed up his plans. He was being brutally honest. And he wasn't happy with me.

"I assure you, my resignation was not intended to mess up the Company's plans. And I apologize if it has," said the Mouse. The resolute Mouse.

"You are the perfect fit for this spot in Snacks. The Pringles business is just starting to light a fire under Frito-Lay and there's nothing they can do to beat us," he said, figuratively beating his chest. Frito-Lay is about as serious as you can get in the Snacks business. I don't suspect they roll over easily nor were they quaking in their boots over Pringles. "You were a key cog in our plans for carving out a significant position in Snacks. How can you do this to us?"

This was a strange tack to take. I had not anticipated the guilt route, despite having a Jewish mother. Mistake on my part.

"Again, I assure you, I'm not trying to do the Company any harm. It's just time for me to leave," I replied trying to redirect the conversation to ground on which I felt more comfortable.

"Why is it 'time for you to go'? What's so bad here that you feel you have to leave?" he demanded, still no warmth in his voice.

I was not going to be led down the path of bad-mouthing anyone or anything as I headed out the door, as much as I might have enjoyed the fleeting pleasure of doing so. I had already decided there was nothing to be gained by that approach.

"There's no problem. My ten years here have been great. It's just time for me to do something else, and I'm pleased to be able to leave while I still have such a pleasant regard for my time here." OK, maybe a little thick, but I was up against a tough adversary here.

"Not buying it," he snorted, shaking his head slowly, eyes bearing down on me. "No one resigns on the day he's promoted to Ad Manager. No one. You have worked ten years here *just for this day*. How can you walk out at the exact moment that you've achieved your goal?"

Man, this guy was good. He posed a compelling question.

"Because it's just time for me to go." I stood my ground. Keep reiterating the position.

"Still not buying it." I guess he knew how to stand ground and reiterate a position, too. It was an old fashioned stand off. He was standing his ground and I was standing mine.

Then he took yet another turn I didn't expect. He was good at this.

"My conclusion is that you have another job you've already accepted. It's probably with a competitor, and that's why you don't want to tell us. So who's your job with? You owe it to us to tell us. Who is it?"

"I have no job offer from a competitor. In fact, I have no other job at all, Sam. I only have the time the Company has allotted me in which to find one, which I greatly appreciate." Stick to the facts, be gracious.

"You're lying. Lying, lying, lying." Wow, I've never been accused of that so directly. But now Sam was losing his cool.

"Sam, I'm not sure where you're from, but where I come from, people don't generally take well to being called liars." To try to lighten things up, I added, "And if you're trying to talk me OUT of resigning, I don't think this approach is working."

And with that, his features softened a bit.

So I added with equal softness, trying to draw the tension down a notch, "Honestly, Sam, I don't have another job. I'm not going to work for a competitor. I'm not trying to purposely mess up your plans. I'm not here to bad-mouth anyone or anything. I'm leaving because I don't want to be one of those guys that stays here too long and starts to resent the place, wondering what I might have been if I hadn't tried anything else. I will walk out of here with many fond memories of P&G, many friends, and positive feelings of real accomplishment. The best way I can say it is as I've said it already, it's *just time for me to go*. Each person knows when the time is right for them, and the time is right for me now. Let's not spoil it by making it ugly. How about it?"

With that he reached under his desk, pressed the button for the electronic door to swing open, and said with the even tone of Star Trek's Mr. Spock, "Then be well and prosper." No handshake, nothing else. I was dismissed; he just turned around and went back to business.

———

AFTER LUNCH WITH Bob Graybeal, who also made a friendly and noble attempt to *save* me, I was sitting at my desk when Chip showed up at my door. Crap, what next?

"Mr. Pepper will see you in his office in 10 minutes," Chip beamed. Man, he was calling in the Cavalry. John Pepper was the Company's President & CEO.

"I'm not going to see Mr. Pepper," I replied flatly.

"What do you mean, 'not going'? He's the CEO; he wants to see you; you're still an employee of this company; when the CEO calls, you go!" Chip retorted, incredulous at my response.

"Still not going," replied a somewhat invigorated Mouse.

"And may I ask, why not? Don't you think he deserves that respect?"

"He absolutely deserves that respect. And it's precisely *because* I respect him so deeply that I won't sit in front of him and tell him I'm quitting his team. I'd run through walls for him. That's how much I respect him. So I won't tell him I'm quitting."

"And that's the *exact* reason why I want you to go," Chip said with a smug smile.

"I understand what you want. That does not mean I'm going, though."

And this incensed Chip. His soft demeanor melted, his face flushed, and he quite thoroughly lost it. He started yelling at me, "Don't you think John Pepper's smart enough to determine what he thinks is a valuable use of his time and what isn't? He's decided he wants to see you and that's how he wants to spend his time. He's the CEO! So get going, you'll be late!" he commanded me, *willing* me to obey.

There are moments in life where your mind goes into overdrive and you have to consider your options at supersonic speed -- and then just *act*. In this case, I calculated I had two choices -- retreat or attack. I had considered what a retreat option would look like, and it was to pay a visit to Al Harmann in HR. Al had been unusually quiet during this entire episode and I was absolutely sure he knew of my promotion (he had to have approved it) and about my inquiry yesterday in HR about the separation package. I quickly calculated that if Al wanted to intervene, he would have already. He was staying quiet for a reason, one I'd only find out years later after he retired from P&G and did some great consulting projects for me. He knew that if I didn't take the promotion, it meant there was no saving me. And I knew if I had to talk with

Al, he'd believe this was largely, but not entirely, about Chip, due to our previous conversations. That's not how I wanted to leave. That's not what I wanted to make this resignation about.

So if the call wasn't to retreat, the only other option was to attack.

I steeled myself with a deep breath, an extended exhale, and lowered my voice an octave. I looked Chip right in the eyes.

"Chip, you've got two choices. You can either go back to your office, call Mr. Pepper's assistant and convey that I won't be coming because we don't want to waste his time. Or, I will do exactly as you ask, and I will go to Mr. Pepper's office. I'll sit down right in front of him. And when he asks me why I am leaving, I'm going to tell him every rotten thing you've done to me while I've worked for you. *Everything*. It'll take longer than you'd like. And it will not be pretty. So this is no longer about *my* P&G career, Chip, it's now about *your* P&G career. Therefore, it's really not my choice anymore, Chip, it's now yours: I can go quietly as I've been trying to do, or I can go noisily. I think *quietly* would be in everyone's best interest. Especially yours. What do you think, Chip?"

Chip's eyes were wide as he fathomed what I was saying, imagining what I might possibly say to Mr. Pepper, and envisioning the possible negative consequences. I could see his considerable brain matter traversing a sizable decision tree, all boiling down to a single concept, the concept Chip understood better than any other — what was best for Chip.

"So are you gonna make that call now, Chip?"

One could accuse Chip of being many things, but a fool he was not.

⌘

HUMAN RESOURCES SET my final day of work at the end of the month, tied to the end of the pay period. Ten days of tactfully avoiding Chip, which wasn't very hard. Chip didn't want to see my face; he didn't want to hear my voice. He didn't want to be in the same universe with me. I hoped the time would pass without incident. Hoped...

I spent my time transferring the business to my successor and taking care of my people. Word of my resignation spread quickly, as it usually does in the hallowed halls of Procter. And word of the failed promotion was buried quickly and didn't get out publicly. It was not desirable for anyone else in P&G to know of it, and I respected that. So I spent time visiting with the many good friends I had accumulated over the past ten years and generally laying low.

My last day of work was a Monday. It was the day of the Division's bi-weekly management meeting, when the senior leadership met to work through the various issues facing the business. It began after lunch, promptly at 1:30pm, and often went well into the evening. As such, I packed up my office, so that all I would have to do is pick up the box of personal items that sat on my desk and depart when the leadership team meeting was over.

At 1:25pm, I strolled into the Leadership Team meeting. The team was largely assembled, mulling around. Lots of handshakes and well wishes on my departure. Good people. Lots of smiles. I couldn't tell if they felt sorry for me or envied me.

Chip strolled in at 1:30pm exactly. He stopped dead in his tracks and stared at me.

"What are you doing here?" he snarled.

"Well, I'm employed through the end of the day," I responded, admittedly caught off-guard. For some reason, I had naively not expected this reaction. Although as soon as he asked the question, I knew I should have expected he would want to have the last word.

"I noticed there were a number of topics on the agenda that fall into my area of responsibility. I thought I might be able to help before I left," said the Mouse.

This was my peace offering, my way of saying no hard feelings – the business should always be more important than the personalities involved.

"Your *former* area of responsibility," Chip replied, in a clipped tone.

"After today, you're absolutely right," I responded. Trying to keep things on an even bearing through the last few hours. But the air was thick with animosity.

"Your insight is no longer necessary -- nor welcome," Chip stated quite clearly, not even looking at me, as he turned to make his way to his usual seat at the head of the table.

It was pretty clear I was being summarily dismissed.

"Then I guess I'll be going now." I gathered my notebook. I looked to say goodbye to the team, but everybody in the room had taken a keen interest in their shoes. I felt bad that they had to witness that. I felt guilty leaving them to Chip. For the first time, I even felt like perhaps I was abandoning my teammates. But time for sentimentality was way past. I gently closed the door as I left the room, eyes down.

When I got back to my office, I sat down in my chair. Nothing on the walls. All the artifacts of my ten years with P&G packed in the box. Awards, pictures, memento's. I looked out of the window and realized it was over. I was done at P&G. There was nothing more for me to do.....but to leave.

And that's when it occurred to me how big companies become self-sustaining. The machine had just lost one of its cogs, and a new one was in place right away. The same size. The same shape. The same function. Honed for just that purpose. To sustain itself, big companies must regenerate – with similar cogs, performing similar functions, thinking in similar ways. Life went on for P&G, whether Michael Elliot was one of those cogs or not. It never looks back. Only forward.

And that's the way it was...and that's the way it *needs to be*. Sentimentality is a luxury a big company simply cannot afford.

So I did something I had never done in my previous 10 years working at P&G. I left the office early. I picked up my box, wandered down the hall, drifted down the escalator, passed the security guards unnoticed, and simply left the building. I had become invisible. The membrane sealed behind me.

12

THE NEXT ADVENTURE

I'M ALWAYS AMAZED at people who can magically recall quotes from films or song lyrics seemingly out of thin air. Sometimes, it's from a song we heard in our teenage years whose lyrics captured a particularly stressful, fun or celebratory moment. The music we grew up with seems to stay with us, or perhaps lifts us out of the grind of our daily lives and takes us back to a time that seemed better, simpler, perhaps even more romantic. It could be called *the soundtrack of our lives*.

As my good friend Larry Kuhlman says, "life is better with a soundtrack." I couldn't agree more. I guess that's why Larry always brings music – no matter where we go, even when we play golf. Stuffy blowhards at the golf club may not feel music is appropriate when one is playing golf; but that's why they're stuffy blowhards.

In addition to music, I have found there are lines from films that magically appear to me at certain moments in time. Films that capture that *certain moment* are perhaps epic, not only in a cinematographic sense, but also in a timeless sense. "That film just spoke to me," people often say.

These are the films that win the Academy Awards, that blaze new trails in cinema, that have performances that make an actor's career. Peter Finch opening the window and screaming "I'm mad as hell and I won't take it anymore" in *Network*. Shirley MacLain's Best Actress Performance in *Terms of Endearment*. Jack Nicholson's haunting "Honey, I'm Home" in *The Shining,* as he chopped his way through the bathroom door. Robert De Niro's eerie portrayal of Max Cady in Martin Scorcese's *Cape Fear*:

"Everyman….everyman has to go through hell to reach paradise." Oooh, I get chills just thinking of it.

Yup. Great films. They capture special places in our hearts and minds. Everyone's got one of them. That great film that *just speaks to me.*

Mine is *Animal House.* OK, maybe there were no academy award performances involved here. Maybe there was no exceptional cinematography, eye-popping special effects, or catchy dialogue either. But, in my view, John Landis knocked this one out of the park and it certainly had many memorable moments.

Are you not buying this?

C'mon. Remember when Bluto and the Boys get hauled into Dean Wormer's office to be told they're failing in school? Am I really the only one of you who would want to hang pencils out of your nose like Bluto did when the Dean dressed you down? Am I the only one of you who agrees that the *most appropriate response* to getting put on double secret probation is to have a toga party? Am I alone in this world in thinking that the best thing to do when a pledge brings his brother's brand new Lincoln Continental (with suicide doors no less!) to the fraternity house is to grab multiple cases of beer and road-trip to a nearby women's college? I mean, really, I can't imagine what *else* you would do!

There are answers to life's most pressing philosophical questions in these scenes, if only we can step back and realize it. C'mon, I'll show you.

———

As I WALKED silently out of P&G's headquarters for the last time as an employee, the only response that seemed adequate to me was ROAD-TRIP! I felt like Eric Stratton, Rush Chairman, and I was damn glad to meet you. I only needed a Lincoln Continental with suicide doors.

I knew Toni was home wondering how my last day went, and I was determined not to walk in the house in a somber mood, despite Chip's best efforts to get the last word – which, by the way, he did quite effectively. I had to admit it.

So on the way home, I stopped by Wal-Mart, bought something for Toni, and wrapped it in bright paper and a bow. Do I know how to *buy nice* for a girl or what? Nothing but Wal-Mart's top of the line stuff for my sweetheart! When I got home, I kissed Toni and handed her the wrapped box.

"What's this? How did your last day go?" I clearly caught her off guard.

"The last day is over. The next chapter begins. Open the box," I prodded.

"What? What are you doing?" She was still caught off guard. Excellent.

"Don't worry. Just open the box. You've got a decision to make," I prodded again. I knew that would get her – she hates to make decisions.

Now when a man opens a gift, he tears at the paper like a kid on Christmas morning. When a woman opens a gift, she admires the bow, handles it as if it were a vase from the Ming Dynasty, and gently lifts at the flap of the wrapping paper like she's doing surgery. Protecting the wrapping. For what? I have no idea. It's not like the wrapping is THE gift.

But I digress....

"It's from Wal-Mart – don't get too excited. I really went all-out for you," I stoked her curiosity yet again.

"What is it?" she asked with her eyes alit.

OK, whenever you've gotten a present in your life – think every birthday, every Christmas (or Hanukkah) - have you ever had anyone actually tell you what it is before you opened it? If so, they should be drawn and quartered. I think the point of a surprise is, well, *surprise*, isn't it?

"Well, go crazy, even tear the paper if you can get that wild, and you'll find out." I was now having fun watching her eyes, her endearing blue eyes.

After she disrobed the box, she stared at it in wonderment, with a puzzled look on her face. She looked at me again, "OK, I'll ask the question a second time: what is it?"

"The way this concept works is that first you take off the paper, then you open the box to find out what's inside. That's how these things work. Go figure."

She ignored my sarcasm as she usually does and proceeded to open the box, gently lifting out the globe that was inside. It wasn't a decorative globe, or even an artistic one. Just a normal world globe. It looked just like the globe that was sitting in your fifth grade classroom. Even looked like it had some of the same dust and finger smudges on it. After all, it was from Wal-Mart, the most practical purveyor of goods on Earth.

"Oooh. Just what I always wanted," she cooed, matching my sarcasm, fighting fire with fire. Game on! "Whew, I'm so glad it wasn't jewelry or anything I wouldn't want like that! I was worried there for a second. OK, I may regret asking this, but not that I don't appreciate your effort here, but why did you get me a globe?" She was genuinely curious now. Perfect.

"Read the tag hanging down from the South Pole," I said smugly, knowing I had her by the nose ring (not that she had a nose ring – that's just a figure of speech).

"It says, 'Pick the Place'," Toni said with genuine confusion. Again, just where I wanted her.

"Yes, as in 'pick the place you want to go'. Let's roadtrip!" I blurted as I watched the realization of what I meant dawn on her.

"Really? You just lost your job. Did you lose your mind, too?" Ever the practical one.

"Nope. I just got 12 months' pay deposited in our checking account. It won't take me 12 months to find another job. Let's use some of that money to go somewhere. Somewhere you've never been and always wanted to go. Just you and me."

"But what about the kids?"

"We'll get your mom and dad to come stay with them."

"Don't you want to bring them?"

"No, I'd prefer to leave the your mom and dad at home for this trip. We can take them on a trip this summer," I quipped.

"I meant the kids."

"Nope. If just the two of us go away together, I don't know who'll be happier – the kids, your parents or us. Everyone wins! It'll take a week to deprogram the kids when we get back. Your parents, too. But it will be worth it. And when we get home, the kids will see more of their dad than they've ever seen before! C'mon, it's second honeymoon time! The kids are definitely staying with your parents. Just you and me."

It was a very nice kiss. Really.

———— ⁂ ————

UNCLE TAD AND Aunt Estelle. My father's older sister and brother-in-law had moved to Hawaii in the mid-1950's, before statehood. Uncle Tad had been editor of his high school newspaper and had greater gifts in telling stories than shooting guns. Good old Uncle Sam had figured this out and when drafting him into World War II, they assigned him to work on *Stars and Stripes*, the military newspaper. His area of coverage was the Pacific Theater after the bombing of Pearl Harbor, and was stationed in Honolulu, Hawaii. It was there he fell in love not only with newspaper work, but also with the people and beauty of Hawaii (he had already fallen in love with Aunt Estelle). After a stint at the *New Orleans Times-Pacayune* after the war, Uncle Tad accepted a job as the editor of the *Honolulu Advertiser*. Picked up Aunt Estelle, and their young son and daughter, and made their way halfway across the world. My father's family thought they had gone nuts.

Uncle Tad knew what he was doing. He proceeded to spend much of the next half century in Hawaii. And during that time, he got as *dug in* as any Hawaiian Native. He watched Hawaii become a state, and then develop both economically and culturally. In fact, in his role as editor of the newspaper, he not only watched it, he chronicled it. And in doing so, Uncle Tad became a fixture in the community.

So it was not only appropriate, but impossible NOT to visit with Uncle Tad and Aunt Estelle when Toni selected Hawaii as the place on the globe that she wanted to visit. Maybe it was the way I positioned it as a second honeymoon that prompted her to choose Hawaii. I don't know. But it didn't matter; we were going wherever she wanted. And Hawaii was her choice.

After spending a week on Maui and the Big Island of Hawaii, we made time to stop in Honolulu on our way home. Uncle Tad picked us up at the airport and quickly whisked us away to meet Aunt Estelle for lunch at the Hilton Hawaiian Village Waikiki Beach Resort. Uncle Tad's celebrity in Hawaii became readily apparent. You would have thought he was King Kamehameha himself by the way he was treated – and the way we were treated by extension.

Through the course of the day, Uncle Tad showed us Honolulu like no tour guide could. He was as worldly as I remembered him as a child. He used to come to the mainland once a year for the annual newspaper editors' convention. He and Aunt Estelle would come to Charleston for a week after the convention and stay across the street from my parents' house at my Uncle Ike and Aunt Diedre's home. Diedre and Estelle were two of my dad's sisters and they were very close. Over the many years and visits while I was a young boy, I got to know Uncle Tad and Aunt Estelle.

Which reminded me of something I needed to ask Uncle Tad.

As we were driving through the neighborhoods of Honolulu – Uncle Tad and me sitting in the front seats of the car, and Aunt Estelle and Toni in the back -- I decided to broach the subject with Uncle Tad.

"Uncle Tad, there's been something I've been meaning to ask you ever since I was a little boy," I opened.

"Sounds important. What's on your mind?" Uncle Tad responded, ever the serious one.

"I remember when I was a little boy, Uncle Ike used to tell me that he unmasked the Lone Ranger and you used to tell me that you knew Steve McGarrett of Hawaii Five-O." I paused for a little dramatic emphasis.

"Yes, and...." Uncle Tad urged me on, despite the upturn at the corner of his mouth, belying a smile.

"Well, as I've gotten somewhat older and reflected on that, I'm wondering whether or not you and Uncle Ike were *really* telling me the truth?" My question was, admittedly, a bit tongue-in-cheek, so I anticipated this would engender an interesting response.

But I got something that was totally unexpected.

"That's a very fair question. Given that Uncle Ike has passed away, I guess there's no way to truly prove the veracity of his story." Uncle Tad even spoke like a newspaper editor. "But I would tend to believe him."

Sure. They all stick together.

Uncle Tad continued, "And as for *my* story regarding Mr. McGarrett, I submit that it was, and still is, not only tue, but I can also offer verifiable proof -- *at this very moment*." And with that, Uncle Tad pulled the car over to the side of the road. I had no idea what he was doing.

Walking along the sidewalk was an elderly man with a walker, escorted by a nurse. The man looked somewhat shaky, but still moving along in his 70's — which was OLD back then. Today, for some reason, as I get ever closer to it, 70 doesn't seem very old!

Uncle Tad put the car in park and rolled down my window electronically. Through the window, he yelled, "Hey Jack, my nephew here doesn't believe you and I are friends!"

And as God is my witness, even though I, not Uncle Tad, brought up the subject, there was Jack Lord — right there in the flesh. A little older and a few more miles on him for sure, but it was the actor who played Steve McGarrett on the famous CBS television show of the 70's, Hawaii Five-O. Angled jaw and all.

He looked into the car to verify its occupants. He looked a little puzzled when he peered into my face, but smiled with recognition when he saw Uncle Tad. "Tad, how are you? You need me to book this criminal?" Jack quipped, pointing at me and leaning over with a big smile. I liked Jack Lord calling me a criminal for some odd reason.

"Where's Danno when you need him?" I asked somewhat sheepishly, holding out my wrists for the handcuffs.

"Can I say it?" Tad asked Jack with anticipation. Jack winked back.

And we all said in unison, "Book 'em, Danno!" rendering McGarrett's's famous catchphrase that ended each show when they caught the criminal. A hearty laugh followed.

As Tad put the car in gear and got us back on the road, he heard my voice come from my shaking head in the passenger seat, still in utter disbelief. "I will never question your word, again, Uncle Tad. I promise."

AFTER WE RETURNED from the grand trip to Hawaii, I determined it was time to get down to some serious unemployment. Yup, I was going to do all the things I never had time for when I was working 70 hours a week. And it all started with being a better dad. Pre-school carpool. Playdates for our nearly 4 year old. Reading books. Watching videos. Changing diapers.

And it didn't stop there. We had a new house that needed lots of little things done – or what my brother likes to call *honey-do's*, as in "honey, will you do this?" I found out that it was possible to organize the kitchen the *right way*. Maybe even two or three *right ways*.

I had also become a *regular* at Home Depot. I never knew there were so many possible ways to hang yard tools in the garage. Watering the new sod was one of my chief responsibilities, even though we installed an irrigation system. Swings to be hung under the elevated deck. Crushed stone to be placed under the deck to keep from stepping in mud. Numbers affixed to the new mailbox. Fall flowers to be planted. The driveway basketball goal to be installed. Speakers to be added to the back deck. A life to discover.

I also used this as my opportunity to perform some service to the community, given that I had done very little (read: nothing) in my ten years at P&G. Who had time? No, I didn't volunteer to be a crossing guard. I did, however, get myself on two not-for-profit Boards, which started taking time in the afternoon and evenings.

I was busy, but these are exactly the things my obituary said I should be busy with. It's what I wanted. *It's your destiny, Young Skywalker.*

After completing all my projects and activities, I came to realize two things: 1) how expensive it was to be home full time (when you're working, you're making money; when you're home full time, you're spending money) and 2) how much the house was my wife's domain and how much I had encroached upon it. In some ways, I'm sure she felt it was helpful to have me there. In other ways, she found it frustrating for me to be home, but not always doing what *she* wanted done. I was doing *my* honey-do list, not hers.

It all came home to roost when one day, about eight weeks into my sabbatical, she walked into my office, crossed her arms and looked me in the eye: "I love you. And for it to stay that way, you definitely need to go back to work." With that she turned on her heels, and walked back to the kitchen.

Message received. She was right. Time to start thinking about employment options.

As I was wrapping my mind around going back to work, I got a call to have lunch with an old friend, Charlie MacAvoy. I met Charlie the first month I started at P&G, ten years prior, and over time we became good friends. Charlie worked in Sales, and I was in Brand Management. In the old P&G days, Sales people often viewed *Brand Management Types* as overpaid academics who didn't really know how to get their hands dirty and do the *real* work that drove the business (which of course, was *Selling*). In many cases, they were right. But Charlie and I never struggled with at issue and hit it off from my very first day -- he was running a key test market and I was working on the new brand being tested. And that test was quite successful. Nothing like collective success to cement a working relationship.

Charlie was the ultimate networker. He believed in the concept of *six degrees of separation* — that everyone is only six steps or less away, by way of conncection, from any other person in the world. Six Degree of Separation concept was first established by Frigyes Karinthy and popularized in a play by John Guare. And while theatre wasn't quite Charlie's currency of life, he could work those six degrees like no one I had ever seen. As such, Charlie was perhaps the best networker — and salesperson -- I have ever met in my life. And I've met more than a few.

Frequently, while we were at P&G, Charlie would bring me sales ideas for my brand. He had a major customer that he thought was open to a big idea. All it required was a little money and a little legwork. Charlie could provide the legwork; the Brand had the money. More often than not, Charlie was right. Over time, I learned it was generally good to bet on Charlie. If he had a good idea, I wanted to fund it. We both won.

Over time, Charlie and I worked together in a variety of capacities at P&G, and became friends outside of work, too. We lived around the corner from each other, and we shared Cincinnati Reds season tickets as part of a group he coordinated. Charlie would get the tickets – usually through his elaborate network -- and I would help him put the group together, divide up the tickets, collect the money, help him with the legwork. I had even introduced Charlie to his wife, attended their wedding, and watched them raise their kids. We were tight.

Over lunch, Charlie inquired as to my post-P&G plans. He was very adept at getting the *potential target* to talk, looking for the right opening for the proposal he always had in his back pocket. And when he saw the opening, Charlie carefully probed my interest in small business as opposed to another big company.

Working for another big consumer products company was the last thing I wanted at the time. I wanted to join in a business where: 1) I trusted the people I'd be working with, unlike my experiences with Chip; 2) I could learn something new and grow; and 3) the opportunity was big and personally meaningful. With these criteria established, Charlie set about telling me of a business that he and a few other former-P&G friends had started, a company called On Target Media. They had successfully launched the company and were ready to begin expanding it.

That's when I realized that, today, I was Charlie's *potential target*.

I knew, and had great respect for, a number of Charlie's partners at On Target, including its CEO/ managing partner, George Howerleigh. I had spent time in training with George when he was Brand Manager on Gleem Toothpaste – and George and I instantly became friends, having a common love for music, among other things. On Target's other partner was Mitch "Monk" Christie, another ex-P&G'er who I had known quite well. I had the responsibility of taking Monk out to dinner on his final recruiting visit to P&G. My charge from above was to get Monk to accept our offer to join P&G that night. A little alcohol was involved, I must admit. Monk and I had become friends over the years and the more Charlie discussed the idea of me joining them at On Target, the more I liked it.

It didn't take long for us to come to an amenable arrangement and I happily became Vice President of Client Services and a Partner at On Target Media.

—◦◦◦—

ON TARGET MEDIA pioneered a marketing concept which George dubbed *aperture marketing*. Allow me to explain. At the time, there were essentially four types of media: television, print (newspapers and magazines), radio and billboards. Of course, this was all before Al Gore invented the internet. So advertising was essentially designed to *interrupt* whatever program or article you were enjoying. How nice....

Aperture Marketing sought to target people with advertising messages at times when they would find the message interesting rather than interruptive – perhaps even at times when they were not only receptive to the ad message, but *actually looking for it*. When might that be, you ask? Does anyone *ever* want to hear a commercial message?

Well, actually, yes. When your lease is due to expire on your car and you have to get a new one, you're interested in hearing about certain cars in your consideration set. When you get diagnosed by your doctor with a medical condition, you're interested in information that helps you better understand the condition along with the medication or procedure that will help you treat it. When you're pregnant with your first child, you have interest in products that will help you care for that squirmy little thing in your belly. These were all times that people actually *invited* commercial messages, because at the time, there wasn't an internet to go query information that would be at their fingertips in a moment's notice. Back then, people actually had to do research – work – to find information that was relevant to them. And the public library was hardly the most user-friendly avenue.

So this concept became the basis of new media properties that On Target sought to create, specifically to carry the advertising message of a client. If Pampers wanted to create a medium that would reach ONLY women who were in their third trimester of their first pregnancy – quite a narrowly targeted audience – On Target created a free teaching curriculum that Childbirth Educators would receive free of charge from Pampers, as long as the Educators would allow the curriculum to carry a Pampers Coupon and Product Sample. Mothers were happy, Educators were happy, Pampers was happy.

On Target created the idea, wrote the curriculum, developed the materials, created the distribution list, signed educators up, assembled and fulfilled the materials....and made quite a tidy profit. So On Target was happy, too.

Not unlike the way I discovered Procter & Gamble, I believed I had, once again, *stumbled* upon the next step in my career.

13

THE ART OF CLIENT ENTERTAINMENT

I COULD ACCURATELY attach a number of positive adjectives to working at Procter & Gamble during the ten years I was there: challenging, energizing, fast-paced, intellectually stimulating, just to mention a few.

But the adjective that comes to mind in describing work at On Target Media was one that I would never have attached to working at P&G: FUN.

As ex-P&G'ers at On Target, we became everything we weren't *allowed to be* at P&G. We were the guys who had made it in the corporate world and then cut off the neckties with switchblades and threw them into the river. We used to keep suits and ties in the closet at work for when we *had* to visit a client; otherwise, the dress code at On Target called for t-shirts, shorts and sandals. Footballs were routinely tossed across the office; nerf hoop games were ferocious. Our office was outfitted with Apple Computers (before Steve Jobs did his second stint at Apple) rather than PC's, and music blared out of our offices mid-day. We had the *Brainstorming Room*, outfitted with various toys, markers, crayons, and poster paper. I think the Silicon Valley start-up guru's may have come to Cincinnati in the early 90's to get office décor ideas from On Target before they started the Dot Com boom in the late 90's. We saw ourselves as the bad boy thirty-somethings — every product we created was *new to the world* — and we believed there wasn't a problem we couldn't crack.

I've commented with frequency that I've gotten a lot dumber in the last two decades — because when I was 32 years old, I knew EVERYTHING!! Or at least thought I did.

Arrogant as we were, the facts really were simple — the business was working well, we had developed a wildly innovative concept, and our business was growing like a weed. On Target already had a running start by the time I joined, and over the next several years, it experienced great success. On Target Media was named the 23rd fastest growing privately held company in America by *INC. Magazine* in its annual INC 500 rankings and was recognized as the Small Business of the Year by the Greater Cincinnati Chamber of Commerce. The business was on an incredible roll.

Above the receptionist's desk in our offices, the sign on the wall read "Welcome to the Land Where Dreams Are Created and Promises Are Kept." Armed with George's vision and Monk's creativity, Charlie would open the doors and we would all collectively close 'em — and then keep the clients happy as we diligently worked to deliver on those promises. And we had developed an incredible support team around us. It was a great group of people having a lot of fun. The business flourished… and so did we. I was very fortunate to have stumbled into this.

—⚬⚬⚬—

CLIENT ENTERTAINMENT WAS a concept not well embraced at P&G. If you had to entertain a customer or build a relationship with them, then it meant in the P&G culture that you had nothing of substance to sell them. And P&G ALWAYS sold on substance — product performance, superior end benefits, value to the retailer and the consumer. As such, client entertainment was frowned upon at P&G, and was something I never really learned how to do.

Fortunately, Charlie was a natural at it. Despite his decade plus at P&G, he overcame the behavioral conditioning, and he helped me to understand how building a relationship with a client was never a substitute for a product that delivered on its promise; rather, a good client relationship was an excellent *complement* to one.

I was awkward at first; I found the chit chat over lunch a challenge as I was much better at substantive topics. Charlie would get things going, usually with some sports-related conversation (if a man) or discussion about kids (if a woman). Maybe that was sexist, but it was hard to question its effectiveness. It worked.

I eventually learned how to find a way to turn the conversation toward the client's businesses challenges at the appropriate point. THAT was the value in client entertainment: you could get more insight to a client's business challenges at a dinner, over a drink, or on the golf course, moreso than ANY amount of time sitting in the office. It was just human nature. And that information was what we used to create business propositions and media property ideas to solve their problems. You can't solve the problem if you can't get them to talk to you.

And other times, it's just fun to get together with clients.

I recall one fall in 1995 when the Cincinnati Reds managed to get themselves into the National League Playoffs. Cincinnati was all abuzz since it was only 5 years after the Reds swept the Oakland Athletics and won their first world series in a decade and a half. Charlie looked at me and said "we've gotta use our tickets to get some of our P&G clients to the playoff game tomorrow night. *That* will certainly get them out of the office."

"Great idea. I'm on it. I'll set it up," I responded picking up the phone. We got two of our client Brand Managers to meet us for an early dinner and then head down to the game. The dinner lasted a little longer and had a few more beers than Charlie liked (Charlie didn't drink alcohol, but he recognized its beneficial value in opening discussion). By the time we made our way to the stadium, the Reds were two innings into the game and we were a bit more than two beers into the evening.

As we awkwardly climbed over an elderly couple to get to our seats, one of our clients, Bill Berry, noticed a beer vendor and called out, "we're gonna need 3 beers up here!"

With laser-like attention to the dollar, the beer vendor made his way quickly up the steps to our seats, pulling out a beer as he walked. As he reached for his bottle opener, he paused and cast a cautious eye at Bill. "I think I'm going to need to see some ID," the vendor said.

"No problem," replied the 35 year old, but quite young looking, Bill Berry. "But I want you to know, before you see this ID, that I'm the only person you're going to 'card' tonight who's had three kids AND a vasectomy!" I think the whole section cracked up when they heard that as the vendor forked over the beers.

We had so much fun that night that we invited Bill to join us again the following night for the second game of the series. Once again, we didn't manage to get there until the second inning. When we arrived and crawled over the elderly couple once again, the elderly woman looked at Bill and said, "Oh, I remember you. You're the one with the vasectomy!"

Without skipping a beat, Bill looked at her husband and said with a wink, "It's only hearsay. She doesn't know that *for sure*." Howls ensued. Even the woman giggled discreetly.

CHARLIE WAS A tremendous competitor, which is just one of the reasons he was a great sales person. Charlie played basketball in college in the Big 10. And as his basketball skills naturally faded over the years, he refocused his energy on golf. He became as good a golfer as he was a basketball player, winning his club championship multiple times and even competing on a national amateur level.

So when Charlie found a client who not only was a good golfer, but had also signed a multi-year, multi-million dollar deal with On Target, Charlie decided that it was time for some extra-special client entertainment. And he knew just the right place to do it.

Kiawah Island's Ocean Course was home to the 1991 Ryder Cup (and later, the 2012 PGA Championship), and Charlie knew that no real lover of the game of golf could resist an invitation to play the Ocean Course at Kiawah. The Ocean Course is consistently ranked in the Top 25 golf courses in the world, a 7,900 yard course designed by renowned golf course architect, Pete Dye. And if that wasn't enough, the Ocean Course is located on picturesque Kiawah Island, just outside of Charleston, SC.

Not surprisingly, when Charlie offered up a free trip to Kiawah to celebrate our new contract, our client (who shall remain nameless to protect the innocent) jumped at the opportunity. He brought his #2 lieutenant to round out the foursome, and we all headed to South Carolina.

The norm at the Ocean Course is to require golfers to use golf carts AND a forecaddie -- in both cases, to speed pace of play. The carts carried our clubs; the forecaddie advised us on how to play the golf course. We were pleased to have the forecaddie, because we certainly could use all the help we could get. The forecaddie would stand on the tee box, and tell us to bring our "175 yard club" – allowing us to select the club that we best felt would allow us to hit a 175 yard shot. I usually brought the "all I got club"; let's just say I'm more of a social golfer than a competitive one. As such, I was hardly the long ball hitter.

The course was absolutely beautiful and in pristine condition. We were fortunate that we had a calm and warm morning to play, with almost no wind, which is the real nemesis of any golfer playing on the oceanfront. The forecaddie not only showed us what to hit and where to hit it, he was kind enough to point out the various wildlife – fox, deer, osprey, herons – which helped us to understand why the Ocean Course was also a Certified Audubon Cooperative Sanctuary.

One bird we didn't expect to see was standing on the fourth tee box. As we finished putting the third green, we noticed the forecaddie speaking to an elderly gentleman. As we approached the pair, the forecaddie said, "Gentlemen, I'd like you to meet our course architect, Mr. Pete Dye."

This was a rare treat indeed, to which Charlie immediately quipped to the client, "See how much we'll bend over backwards to make sure our clients are happy? We brought in Pete Dye just to meet you." A little crass, but everyone chuckled, including Mr. Dye, who graciously autographed our scorecards.

I got a sparkle in my eye, as I realized the perfect opportunity of the moment.

But first, a little background. My wife Toni is from a small town in Northeastern Ohio, near Youngstown. Her uncle Vince is a retired golf pro. Vince is a prince of a gentleman, an excellent specimen of a human being, well into his 80's. I once played golf with Vince and was quite nervous, expecting to see him shake his head at my awful golf swing and mechanics. Not Vince. He'd just tell stories and help us relax during the game – including once how he had beat the famous golf course architect, Pete Dye, to win the 1944 Ohio State Amateur Golf Championship. We never really believed Vince, figuring that this was one of his tall golf tales – a tale we'd certainly allow a gracious, elderly man.

But now was the perfect opportunity to find out – for sure – if it was a tall tale after all....

"Mr. Dye, would you mind if I asked you a question?" asked the Mouse.

This raised a few eyebrows among the foursome.

"Certainly," Mr. Dye responded, unaware of what was about to come at him.

"If I'm correct, you hail from a small town in Ohio, don't you?"

"Yessir," as if he had to say 'sir' to me, which he most certainly didn't. "The town is called Urbana."

"I've heard of it. You see, my wife is from around those parts. She has an uncle who was the golf pro at a club called Fonderlac. His name is Vince…"

"…Leslie," Mr. Dye invoked, before I could even finish the name.

"So you know Vince?" I asked. This was a bad sign. I was instantly doubting if I really was going to nail Vince in his tall tail.

"Yes, Vince is a great guy and a great teaching pro. Probably one of the most patient pro's I've ever met." What a nice complement, especially coming from Pete Dye. It gave me pause, but I persisted.

"Well, sir, Uncle Vince claims that he played you in the Ohio Amateur in the 40's…" I continued, only to be interrupted again.

"…and until this day, I've never forgiven him for beating me to win the championship in 1944. You tell him I still haven't forgiven him," Mr. Dye said with a smile.

Then he noticed the look on my face and said, "I'll bet you didn't believe Vince when he told you that. You thought Vince was telling you an old man's tall tale?"

"Well, yes sir, I have to admit that we didn't quite believe the story," I sheepishly admitted.

"Well, your wife and you are fortunate to have an Uncle as nice and as honest as Vince. Not many like him. Please send him my best regards."

And with that he wished us a great round of golf. Which I played with a smile as I mentally rehearsed my apology to Uncle Vince.

14

IF AT FIRST YOU DO SUCCEED, THEN TRY, TRY AGAIN

ONE OF THE reasons television and radio became two of the most prolific forms of advertising is because they delivered a commercial message to a place where no one had been able to deliver before — inside a consumer's home. Think about it; prior to the invention of television and radio, advertising was static — on buildings, billboards, barns, newspapers, and magazines. Not only did television and radio bring advertising to life in ways no one had seen before — with moving pictures and sound — it did so right in your home. What better place to advertise a household cleaner or food product than while you were sitting in your own home, precisely where you'd use it.

Television and radio also allowed for better targeting of messages than previous forms of advertising. With TV, you could pick the show on which you wanted to advertise based on the demographics of who watched that show. This allowed companies like P&G who created products mostly used by women to reach that specific audience with advertising messages customized to their needs without wasting impressions on men. By contrast, with a billboard, you reached whoever happened to drive by.

As the US Food & Drug Administration began allowing more liberal use of advertising for prescription-based medications in the 1990's, pharmaceutical companies started to understand that they could begin to employ some of the tried and true consumer product-based forms of advertising to stimulate demand for their products. Of course, doctors still had to write a prescription for an ethical drug to be dispensed — so a prescription drug would never be purchased *exactly* like a consumer product. However, if a consumer better understood the benefits of a drug, asked for it by name, and a doctor determined that a patient needed that drug, then the chances of a better medical outcome were increased – everyone, including the doctor, therefore benefitted.

So a huge influx of pharmaceutical media found its way into the marketplace in the 1990's. Drugs, whose brand names previously were relegated to advertising on pens, notepads, and coffee mugs in doctors' offices, started filling the airwaves. The pharmaceutical marketing folks went crazy, and the television networks happily filled their orders of sixty second ad's with FDA-mandated and lengthy legal disclaimers discussing all the possible side effects. The most famous qualifier for Cialis and Viagra may sound familiar: "if you experience an erection lasting more than four hours, you should call your doctor". My brother commented once that he thought they should amend that to say, "if you experience an erection lasting more than four hours, you should call everyone you know!"

But I digress.....

While this influx of pharmaceutical advertising, despite all the qualifications, created the first billion dollar blockbuster drugs, the advertising was still suboptimized. Think about it, with a consumer product, the steps to a purchase were simple. First, you advertised the product on TV. Then the consumer went to the store and purchased it. All you needed was a TV, a consumer and a store to enact a sale.

However, with pharma advertising, there was an additional and *conditional* step: a doctor was required. That doctor not only had to initiate the purchase by writing a prescription that could be taken to a pharmacy, but, most importantly, the doctor had to believe you *actually needed* that medication.

So in reality, you needed a collection of things to come together to make a sale of a prescription medication: a sick patient, a doctor, a prescription pad, and (often) a pharmaceutical sample to try to ensure the patient had no adverse reactions from the drug. That way, the doctor could feel confident prescribing it.

Outside of a hospital, there was only one place in the world where all four of those things came together: the physician's examination room. Therefore, penetrating the physician exam room really became *the search for the Holy Grail* for pharmaceutical marketers. And we, at On Target Media's Health Solutions division, became King Arthur and the Knights Templar, determined to find the Holy Grail.

Pharmaceutical companies and their sales reps had spent decades trying to *invade* the physician's office – trying to find ways to get doctors to prescribe their medications more frequently than their competitors by keeping it top of mind to the physician.

They used many tools – ranging from the inexpensive nik-naks (pens, pads, key chains, bouncy things, you name it) to the informative (educational brochures, anatomical posters, and physical models), to the most expensive form, but also most likely to lead to a prescription – free pharmaceutical samples. Drug companies knew doctors often gave samples to patients who couldn't afford to buy the prescription or even to their friends, which drained the drug companies of revenue. However, doctors who wrote lots of 'scripts for a particular medicine – known as *loyal docs* – got the most samples. It was a chicken and egg game. You didn't know if the samples drove the 'script writing or if the 'script writing attracted the samples. But the data was quite trackable – every doctor was registered with the FDA and every prescription was tracked. So the correlation between prescriptions and samples was unmistakable.

The problems for pharma companies were really three fold: 1) how do I politely *invade* the patient/physician conversation with an advertising message? 2) how do I deliver samples and advertising cost effectively? and 3) how do I do this in a way that my competitor can't replicate?

On Target Media figured out how to solve all three of those problems with a new media product: the Patient Education Center.

The Patient Education Center was a locked wooden or molded plastic unit that was mounted on the wall in a physician exam room. It had three components: 1) a laminated flip poster of anatomical drawings, with an accompanying erasable marker; 2) brochures written to a sixth grade reading level explaining the most common diseases and treatments that physician's specialty encountered; and 3) a locked cabinet that held pharmaceutical samples. It was designed to enable a physician to educate his or her patients on specific conditions using multiple teaching tools, which was proven to improve patient health and outcomes.

Think about it - if a doctor told you that you had been diagnosed with irritable bowel syndrome, how would you react? For most people, after they hear the letters IBS, their eyes glaze over and they begin to tune out, wondering how their life will change, what they can't eat anymore, what medication they will have to take – for the rest of their lives! The doctor keeps talking, but what the patient hears is something akin to what the teacher sounded like in *A Charlie Brown Christmas* -- waaah, waaah, wa-wa-wa-wahhhhh. The patient appears to be listening, but actually hears very little. And partly because of that communication breakdown, the patient exhibits poor compliance and gets a bad outcome.

With the Patient Education Center, the doctor could use the anatomical flip chart to visually explain what part of the body was affected, hand the patient a brochure to further reinforce in plain English both the causes and the treatment, and then reach into cabinet to start the patient on the appropriate pharmaceutical treatment. Both the doctor and the patient got more out of the interaction through better communication. And this was becoming increasingly important as doctors were being asked by Managed Care providers, the ones who paid them, to demonstrate improvements in patient education and progress toward better patient outcomes.

While a great win for the doctor and patient, the Patient Education Center was even a greater win for the pharmaceutical company. For the first time, they were able to effectively penetrate the sanctum sanctorum – the examination room – since that was the place all the key elements came together – patient, doctor, sample and prescription pad. Prior to that, they were relegated to a different place, to the sample closet, where their competitors were as well.

Pharma companies were permitted to sponsor the Patient Education Center. In doing so, they would get branding on the wall unit and flip poster, advertising in the appropriate brochure, and their samples in the locked cabinet. Inclusion was sold on a category exclusive basis – meaning only one vasodilator, only one anti-depressant medication, only one statin, etc. And *only one* meant drug companies could keep their competitors locked in the sample closet while they got the exam room. Because of the pharma company sponsorship, the doctor received the units at no cost, including all the materials they needed and whatever service was required. Not a dime to the Doc.

The program was an instant success, eventually expanding through multiple physician specialties (e.g., Internal Medicine, Family Practice, Dermatologists, Gastroenterologists, etc.) and reaching ultimately over 70,000 exam rooms in the US. At one point, most of the top 10 ethical drugs in America were sponsors of the program, along with many over-the-counter (OTC) medications like Tylenol (for Internists) and Metamucil (for Gastroenterologists), and even consumer products like Crest (for Dentists) and Olay (for Dermatologists).

Charlie, Monk and I sold the living daylights out of this Program. Charlie could network his way into the executive suites of almost any company, Monk and I would make the compelling case for sponsorship, and we'd all do what it took to get the deal closed. We felt like a Superbowl-winning team. Each of us knew our individual roles and we understood how one complemented the other. It was a powerful and personally rewarding combination.

The PEC became On Target's largest program and cash generator and propelled On Target to become one of the 25 fastest growing companies in the United States according to *Inc. Magazine.* THAT is a hyper-growth company.

INTERESTINGLY, WHILE THE PEC solved many problems for physicians and drug companies, its success actually *created* a problem that had not been anticipated. As the physician/patient interaction improved, often resulting in a sampled patient, the need for more frequent replenishment of pharmaceutical samples emerged. Replenishment of printed materials to the doctor's office was fairly straightforward. We printed materials and kept them in inventory. The doctor's office called an 800 number, ordered more brochures, and we mailed them. Delivered in a few days. Pretty easy.

The challenge was keeping the pharmaceutical samples in stock. Since they are controlled substances, the US Food & Drug Administration has very specific protocols in place for handling and distribution. We understood those protocols in our planning and made a quick decision: we would simply use the Pharmaceutical companies' existing fulfillment processes for physician sample requests rather than recreate the wheel.

The primary means drug companies provided samples to physician offices was through in-person visits from their drug representatives. Samples were an important tactical sales tool for the drug rep's. Drug rep's were evaluated on their relationships with doctors – and how much value they provided to the doc. Thus, their goal was to see the doctor face to face as frequently as possible. And since delivery of a controlled substance required a personal signature from the doctor to document the chain of ownership, the more samples a doc used, the more face-time a rep got. So, at first, drug rep's loved the PEC, as it enabled more frequent interactions with doctors.

The problems that emerged were really for the doctors and for the pharmaceutical companies. First, the doc's didn't have time to see pharmaceutical rep's with such increased frequency. Managed Care was paying doctors less per patient visit; so doctors needed to see more patients in a given day, just to *maintain* their current level of income. Doc's liked rep's; but they liked feeding their families more. Drug rep's who weren't teaching them anything new soon became a distraction.

Second, delivering samples through a rep is expensive. Drug Companies estimated at the time that the fully loaded cost of a single sales call on a doctor was $150 — when you consider the sales rep's salary and benefits, training, automobile, insurance, etc. That's a fairly expensive delivery tool. You might think: why not just deliver the samples through FedEx or UPS? That would be an easy solution, but the FDA had a few thoughts on the matter. At the time, that would have been in violation of the FDA's regulations on controlled substances, because, with delivery services like FedEx, you couldn't always document the chain of ownership of the drug. And undocumented chains of ownership led to very steep FDA fines, and even possible legal prosecution.

So doctors needed an easier method of getting samples; pharmaceutical companies needed a less expensive method of delivery.

This was a solvable problem. It was called ProtoCall.

Utilizing pharmaceutical rep's to deliver samples was like using a Ferrari to drive the elementary school carpool. It was a way too elegant and expensive solution to solve what is essentially a pragmatic problem.

Protocol was a network of hundreds of service representatives across the United States whose sole purpose was to deliver pharmaceutical samples — initially to supply the PEC, and later on, it was expanded to include delivery of ANY pharmaceutical sample. They still had to get a doctor's signature and maintain compliance with FDA regulations, but it only took the doctor five seconds to sign the sheet — maybe less. Doctors can sign fast.

The pharmaceutical sales rep's were then freed up to spend time doing more value added activities — that justified the cost of $150 an hour. A Protocall sample delivery cost just $50 to the pharma company, a savings of two-thirds versus using a pharma rep. And even at $50 per call in revenue, ProtoCall could generate a tidy profit.

After we investigated the concept and ran the numbers, we realized we had a pretty compelling value proposition on our hands. There were a number of challenges in execution — particularly in hiring hundreds of people that you could trust to deliver controlled substances. But the biggest risks were in the liability of handling and documenting proper management of controlled substances. The first violation of FDA regulations in this area resulted in a fine up to $1 million. So we knew that to protect On Target legally, we'd have to incorporate ProtoCall as a separate company.

The other, less visible, risk was in starting up a new company and the distraction it would be to running On Target. We already had our hands full with a hyper-growth company. How could we manage a second one as it took off? And what about the capital required to start ProtoCall – which we estimated to be just shy of $1 million? Where would that come from?

We agreed we would use cash generated by On Target to fund ProtoCall rather than borrow it, or take on new investors. So that meant we would have to maintain sufficient focus on the On Target business to ensure we didn't kill the goose that was laying the golden eggs. This would prove to be one of our wisest decisions – but also one that had unintended consequences.

So we set up *separate* management, sales and operating staff for both companies. At a partner level, we agreed that I would oversee the existing On Target business and that one of our other partners, Worth James, then our CFO, would oversee ProtoCall. We also created separate operational staffing, splitting our top two operations people – one focused on ProtoCall, the other On Target.

The third, and most important decision, was in hiring separate Sales staff. The crowning move was luring an extremely high powered sales person, a twenty year veteran of IBM, someone who had made a career selling AS300 computers at senior levels of a company. We knew that ProtoCall would be a corporate-level sale, as outsourcing sample delivery might be a politically charged decision within a pharma company. So we believed somebody who can sell at the *C-suite level* with experience and confidence was going to be more important in this hire than pharmaceutical industry experience per se. The pharma industry could be learned.

We found that person in Denise Sobel. Denise was an attractive 6 foot tall brunette with piercing brown eyes that could look through you like you were glass. When she discussed a topic, you got the distinct impression that she knew exactly what she was talking about – and that you should listen carefully. She was serious, focused, aware of all going on around her. At the same time, she had an almost disarming charm about her – she could put you at ease while she elicited every piece of information she needed. And you wouldn't even know it. She had more gold than Fort Knox ; you could hear her bracelets clanging down the hall fifteen seconds before she arrived. Her perfume preceded her steps by a few seconds. She drove a jaguar that looked like dirt particles were scared to land on it.

It was almost as if she manipulated her environment, all in a grandly planned chess match, to achieve her desired end result.

And how true that would turn out to be.

To get Denise out of IBM, we had to promise her an ownership stake in the business. We tied it to achievement of business results, such that if she hit the kind of numbers we were talking about, we'd be happy to give her the stake.

She did. And we were.

ProtoCall grew on an even faster trajectory than On Target. Buoyed by the initial business of delivering samples for PEC, Denise did a very good job of targeting drug companies that had products late in their life cycles. Products that were still patent-protected, and therefore still very profitable for the Pharma company, and responded well to sampling. Yet, the doctors were very familiar with them, so they had no need to see rep's for educational purposes. Docs just wanted the samples. It permitted the Pharma companies to assign the rep's to new products that required more training.

Essentially, ProtoCall cracked the operational code so that doc's could get the samples they wanted and still let them focus on maximizing patient visits (and income). A win for everybody – including us.

WITH BOTH PEC and ProtoCall hitting on all cylinders, well, there's just no other way to say it -- life was good. The On Target partners were riding a wave that we never dreamed could happen. Not only was business good, but we did an excellent job of keeping our lives in balance with family and community matters. We all had young kids and we made sure each of us went to every school play, coached youth sports teams, served on community and church boards, took two-week vacations with our families – without interruptions – so we could disengage from work and come back from vacation truly refreshed. We were living the balanced lives we all wanted to live – heck, the lives that *anyone* would want to live. We considered ourselves very fortunate. We hoped it would never end.

15

JUST WHEN YOU THOUGHT IT WAS SAFE TO GO BACK IN THE WATER.....

WHILE BUSINESS MAGAZINES will chronicle the life of a successful start-up such that it looks like a vertical rocket-ride, every entrepreneur will tell you that it's more like a *rocking horse* than a *rocket ride*. It's *never* a straight journey upward. And anyone that tells you differently is either lying through their teeth, or their mind is doing that convenient thing where they remember only the good parts and somehow forget the "less than good parts". If the mind didn't work that way, women would probably never have more than one baby.

But even those few entrepreneurial experiences that actually seem like a vertical rocket ride – which I call *hypergrowth* -- present their own unique set of problems. Those problems almost always revolve around two things: good people and cheap capital. There's never enough of either. Never. Most people think capital problems just beset failing businesses. On the contrary, successful businesses experience tight working capital periods – whether it's trying to fund inventory expansion or addition of sales staff – or even just the tight times when every entrepreneur has a sleepless night worrying about having enough cash in the bank to make payroll that week. There are steps forward and steps backward in starting companies, and you just try to keep the general trajectory heading upward.

One thing experienced entrepreneurs and venture capitalists also know: every start up, and I do mean *every* one, hits a least one point where they bump up against a ceiling, where they plateau and have to evolve in some major way to take the business to the next level. Some fall for a while and regress before they can evolve and grow again. Some have an external event thrown at them.

It kinda reminds me of what my favorite philosopher, Jimmy Buffett, says in his song *I Will Play for Gumbo,*

It's a little like religion and a lot like sex,

You should never know when you're gonna get it next.

Most entrepreneurs can point to a period when their business hit that ceiling, that plateau, that barrier, when it got thrown for a loop. Usually, they can look at the numbers and pinpoint a year. Maybe they can even tell you the quarter when it happened.

I can tell you the exact day, the exact *moment,* when it happened to On Target Media. The moment we plateaued and, worse, things took a turn for the worse.

—⁓—

At On Target, we endeavored to become one of the world's great companies. A lofty goal. But we believed we actually could. To do so, we would create a lot of new methods of doing things; but we also tried to borrow what already worked by emulating the planning tools of the world's greatest corporations. George, the CEO and managing partner, was so into high quality, he also served as a national examiner for the Malcolm Baldridge Award – the award the US Department of Commerce gave to a select few US companies who demonstrated excellent quality. This award was created in response to the Japanese auto companies kicking Detroit's butt up and down the street in automotive quality in the 1980's, such that it likely forever changed the US's global dominance of the auto industry. Whatever the cause, and however defined, the US government believed getting better in quality is almost always a good thing. And they were right. So it enabled George to be up on the latest techniques, measures and operational processes for creating high quality output. We generally liked that and On Target benefited from it.

Each quarter, the partners would take a day or two off campus and *work an issue* that would help improve the quality of the business. In doing so, we'd also begin each meeting with a review of the previous quarter's financial performance. The CFO would provide us a financial overview. If things were good, he didn't believe we really needed much detail – and more often than not – that was the response he got from the partners, too. We didn't pay ourselves big dividends from the business; we largely reinvested the majority of the profit in the business to continue driving its growth, after paying taxes. At the business's peak revenues, we had nearly *one-third* of annual revenues held in cash in the bank. It was that conservative nature that allowed us to fund ProtoCall and to weather the inevitable downturn that always comes.

Early one May, we were at our quarterly offsite meeting, starting the day with a review of the first quarter financials. Worth James, On Target's CFO, was a tall, lanky fellow with forever tousled, blond hair and a broad white-toothed smile. He enjoyed a rather privileged upbringing in Louisville, Kentucky, and earned his undergraduate degree from Vanderbilt University and his MBA from the University of Pennsylvania's Wharton School of Business – ostensibly, without breaking a sweat. Through his family's real estate investments, he developed a good eye for cash control and structuring complex contracts. Both served On Target well.

Worth began the financial discussion with an unusual comment: "I'm happy to show y'all all the numbers if you want. But I don't think I can put it any more simply than this: based on the contracted revenue we have for this year already, we could all go play golf for the rest of the year and the business would still make several million dollars." That is a statement I'd never heard before. It sounded pretty darn good.

There was a lot of whooping and hollering and high-fiving all around the room. *Several million dollars* ain't chump change, especially to a bunch of guys who left corporate jobs with hopes of keeping their families fed and enjoying more of life.

I've been accused before of being hypercritical. Sometimes, even of being a pessimist. But as I heard the words come out of his mouth, I couldn't help but wonder if it sounded just too good to be true....

———

IT WAS. THE first blow came from a place we never would have expected – the Federal Government. Bill Clinton, President of the United States at the time, had enrolled his talented and experienced wife Hillary in an activity perhaps a little more high profile than those previously relegated to the First Lady, selecting the new presidential tea service. Bill had a vision for different delivery of health care in the United States and Hillary was leading the effort. At one point, discussion of capping the price

Pharmaceutical companies could charge for drugs entered the discussion. Needless to say, this spooked the pharmaceutical companies like little kids on Halloween. You'd have thought Jem and Scout had just seen Boo Radley in *To Kill A Mockingbird*.

The pharma companies – now a significant part of On Target's client base – moved fast to preserve their profits. They went on the offensive and the defensive. Offensively, they organized more K Street lobbyists in Washington than you could shake a stick at and stormed Capitol Hill. They called in markers from their congressmen and made sure that legislators understood that price controls were simply not the *American Way*.

But they smartly also recognized that Bill Clinton was a powerful and popular President, and that providing universal health care was a cornerstone of his presidential campaign platform. The man might just get what he wanted, despite the pharma companies' and lobbyists' best efforts. So they started looking for ways to protect their bottom lines. And among those ways was cutting marketing budgets.

It seemed every day we were getting calls from a different client: "Can we get out of our contract?"; "We're going to have to cancel that test"; "We're cutting back on samples". We heard it all, and none of it was good. We had a pipeline of new products and a dearth of clients with budget to spend on them.

When we calculated the impact, Worth was still right – we'd make several million dollars *that* year, because we had enforceable contracts and most – I repeat, *most* – of our clients honored them. But those contracts also had "out-clauses" after formal notice periods, and clients everywhere were exercising those out-clauses. By our best calculations, our revenue would drop by 50% or more from that year to the next. And for most companies, a 50% revenue drop in a single year is the harbinger of death.

NEEDLESS TO SAY, we scrambled. All hands on deck. Full panic mode. We didn't know how low things would go, but we could pretty much project when it would impact us. It was visible and we could see it coming like a freight train in broad daylight. We wrenched ourselves through late night *scenario sessions* trying to estimate their impact and explore proactive options we could take to manage the negative impact on our business.

Key was trying to figure out what the Federal Government would do and how that would impact Pharma company actions. Oh, is that all?? Predicting what politicians and bureaucrats will do should be easy! Was this a short term problem or a structural change in the way health care will work? If the government did place a cap on retail pharmaceutical pricing, would it stand legally, or be challenged in the courts? Worse, given the huge impact of health care on the US economy, would protracted litigation freeze the economy for years while we waited for a positive court ruling? Good luck forecasting the probability of any potential outcomes!

After weeks of debate, we concluded that we'd have to shed fixed costs in our business in line with our best guess at reductions in revenue. At the same time, we also made the tough decision NOT to lay off any of our people – even if it meant, as it did, that the business would operate at zero profit for a potentially protracted period of time. If this was indeed a temporary matter, then we would still have the human capabilities we needed to ramp up the growth curve to which we were accustomed.

We considered ourselves fortunate and good managers to come up with a plan that kept On Target cash flow neutral despite a 50% drop in revenue. We had built up cash reserves in the good times for a reason, and we could rely on those if needed. Our plan, fortunately, did not require us to use those cash reserves – at least, not yet. We'd just have to batten down the hatches and recognize no profit, pay no bonuses. Fortunately, most of us did not live lavish lifestyles, so this was manageable.

───

IRONICALLY, WHAT WAS bad for On Target was actually good for ProtoCall. Suddenly, a way to deliver pharmaceutical samples for one-third of the cost was of interest to pharma companies, who were in the midst of feverish cost cutting. And this led to an unexpected sales boom for ProtoCall. This sounds like good news, right?

Not exactly. The problem was that ProtoCall had not yet achieved a cashflow breakeven – meaning it was still requiring cash generated by the On Target business to operate. But On Target wasn't generating cash. The solution was obvious but risky. We made the call to keep funding ProtoCall growth out of On Target's reserve cash. And this turned out to be a fortuitous call for sure.

ProtoCall began to grow like we had not imagined, and achieved not only break-even, but also became nicely profitable at a time when On Target was struggling. For the ProtoCall employees, life was hectic, but good. On the flip side, for the On Target employees, life was hectic, but tenuous. Fortunately, we all managed to keep it together and made it work until the Clinton Health Initiative was ultimately withdrawn. It was only then that we all breathed a sigh of relief.

———⊗———

I CAN'T QUITE recall the first time I heard this quote, but it is probably apt for the way we had been feeling: "sometimes you're the butterfly, and sometimes you're the windshield". We felt like a butterfly there for a while, winging our way innocently through fields of flowers. And then a big Peterbilt semi-truck came along and we were a yellow splat on the windshield....

After the Clinton health plan was declared dead by Senate Majority Leader George Mitchell, we managed to sprout some wings again at On Target, albeit a bit more sobered.

Just a few weeks later, George, Monk and I were sitting in my office, plotting our next steps, when Worth came in.

"Y'all got a minute?" Worth intoned, in his bourbon-flavored Kentucky drawl.

"Sure, what else can you throw at us?" asked George with a wry smile. "We're still pretty wrung out."

"Well, I got a phone call you might want to hear about. The Chief Financial Officer of a rather large public company called to inquire as to whether ProtoCall might be available for sale."

That got our attention.

"No way," said George. There was no question in his mind.

"Did they make an offer?" Monk and I inquired, nearly in unison.

"They did," replied Worth, and proceeded to tell us of the all-cash offer that was made.

Now he *really* had our attention.

———⊗———

THE OFF-SITE PARTNERSHIP meeting began as it usually did, with an overview of the On Target quarterly financials. Not quite in the millions, but better than zero. The business was coming back, albeit a bit more slowly than we had hoped. We now added the ProtoCall quarterly financials and things were chugging along quite well there.

But we all knew why we were having this meeting. It wasn't to talk about the quarterly financials. It was to review the binding offer that the big public company had made for ProtoCall, now that they had gotten the chance to conduct their due diligence. In the parlance of mergers and acquisitions, due diligence roughly translates to a trip to the proctologist. They crawled through every facet of ProtoCall that they could – finances, operations, records, people interviews. You name it, they did it. They were, if nothing else, thorough. This was entirely understandable; after all, they were buying the company. But it didn't feel particularly good.

It had taken a lot of convincing of George to allow this to happen. George never liked to sell anything – if it had growth potential he wanted to own it until it reached its fullest potential. Which is not a bad point of view. Unfortunately, exactly when something has reached its true potential is often only visible *after* the fact. When you're looking in the rearview mirror. If you're still in the midst of it…well, whether it's reached full potential is a highly debatable matter.

And you better believe we debated it.

What clinched the decision to sell was Worth's analysis of how much money we'd have to invest in ProtoCall to automate sample tracking. We had watched as the administrative staff had grown, as they worked feverishly, tracking, documenting and filing all the seemingly infinite slips of paper that verified deliveries and matched inventories of pharmaceutical samples. When Worth detailed the expected millions of dollars we were going to have to invest to automate this process, primarily to comply with federal regulations, it really made the decision to sell a no-brainer.

Let's check our options: 1) mortgage our business (or homes) to borrow millions to invest in ProtoCall?; or 2) don't borrow anything and instead, receive millions to sell it? Hmmmm…..I'll take what's behind Door #2, Monty.

"So what's the buyer's plan for the ProtoCall people?" I asked. "Clearly, they need the Field Force, but what are they saying they're going to do with Management?"

"Well, I've already decided that I will not be going with the business to the new owner," replied Worth. Worth still commuted from Louisville to Cincinnati each week; if he wasn't moving to Cincinnati, he certainly wasn't moving to New Jersey or Connecticut or some other territory he would view as a Yankee Stronghold.

"So I've positioned Denise to take over the Presidency of ProtoCall," declared Worth.

"That's a great idea and nice thing to do, Worth," I responded. "How has the new owner reacted?"

"They're as taken with Denise and her capabilities as anyone. So they agreed."

"Then that should make her quite happy," Monk kicked in. "She's gonna become the President, and she's going to get a nice return from the sale of her stock in ProtoCall."

"Yeah," said George. "Her 'ROI' is pretty good when she didn't have to put a dime of 'I' in to get all that 'R'! I would think she'd be quite giddy."

"She is," laughed Worth. "And she'll be even giddier when I tell her the news of her promotion."

What we didn't anticipate was exactly how giddy she'd be.

⸺

As we all gathered around the table to sign the sale documents, Monk popped the cork on a bottle of Moet + Chandon White Star and started pouring classes of champagne for all the partners and Denise. With glasses filled, Monk raised his glass high and proposed a toast to Worth and Denise. Everyone clinked, everyone cheered Worth and Denise. Speeches were in order and we all looked in Worth's general direction.

"Well, I'm not much on words, but I can tell you this. Building ProtoCall has been an awfully fun ride. And I'm just proud as punch of Denise and the team for everything they've done to make this business a success. This is one of my most proud business moments in life," Worth blushed as he fought back a tear.

"Well, if Worth isn't much on words, then I am!" chuckled Denise as we all joined in the laughter. "I really do appreciate all Worth's done to build ProtoCall. It has been a labor of love for me, and I look forward to continuing it."

And then, in some very strange way, the mirth in both her eyes and voice disappeared. She continued, "But now that I've seen the sale documents, I have to tell you, I don't think I can agree to them under these terms."

If it were possible to actually see oxygen being sucked out of the room, it would have flowed out like water from an aquarium with a burst glass panel. I don't think people were really sure what they heard. We all looked at Denise with puzzled faces, with a collective look, as if we were muttering, "say what?"

George broke the silence, with the trademark equivocal tone of voice. "What exactly do you mean?" he inquired. I had heard that tone of voice from George before. It was what I'd best describe as *steely*.

Denise didn't bat an eye. "I mean, I appreciate that you all have given me a small equity stake in this company. But it's clear to me, and certainly clear to the buyers, that I made ProtoCall into what it is, and getting this puny amount of equity….well, it just doesn't seem, ah what's the right word? I know. It doesn't seem quite *equitable*."

Denise postured her best poker face and willingly stared down every single person in the room.

"So exactly what is it that you're saying, Denise?" George asked again, his steeliness turning a deeper blue.

"What I'm saying is that I'm not going to work for the new owners if you all don't double the amount of my proceeds from the sale. And if I don't go, the deal falls apart. Simple as that. After all, I'm the new President. Clearly, I'm *key* to you all getting what you want."

"And where do you propose the additional equity you want comes from?" George asked. A very cleverly phrased question, I might add. I learned right then and there the power of calmly asking questions when what you really want to do is come across the table and strangle someone.

"I don't really care where it comes from," said Denise as she looked around the room. And as her head slowly surveyed the room, her eyes landed on me, as if she had reached some epiphany. "Wait, I know what you can do. Take the additional shares from Michael. He's been running On Target the whole time. He hasn't done a single thing to make ProtoCall the success that it is. Not one single thing."

It was clear at this point that she really didn't *get* it.

She didn't *get* that it was the cash generated from On Target that funded ProtoCall. It was the cash that I as a partner could have put in my pocket but instead invested in ProtoCall.

She didn't *get* that the partners had actually made a plan to separate duties to ensure the cashflow necessary to fund ProtoCall still emanated from On Target. That's precisely *why* I had spent limited time on ProtoCall.

She didn't *get* that when On Target's revenues fell, we continued to fund ProtoCall out of the cash On Target had generated in previous years.

She didn't *get* that she was becoming President because *we insisted on it* as a term of the sale, for her benefit.

She didn't *get* that she was receiving ANY sale proceeds because we *wanted* her to, not because we *had* to.

And she certainly didn't *get* that playing this specific card, at this specific moment, and targeting me with that card was, in a word, *ill-advised*.

She didn't *get* a lot.

There was silence. Not a word. Not even from the Mouse.

"Denise, perhaps you might be willing to step out of the room for a moment and let the partners discuss your proposal," George intoned quite presidentially as the Managing Partner, breaking the silence. Denise obliged with a both satisfied and repugnant look on her face as she exited the conference room, champagne glass in hand. She liked the cards she had dealt herself. She liked the way she had played her hand. She was already beginning her celebration and counting the chips she had won in this round of poker.

IT WAS AT that exact moment that I learned three things about human nature that I will never forget. First, you never really know someone's true character until the stakes are really high — at least the stakes that individual *perceives* to be high -- and then, and *only* then, will you see their true character. Then you know who they really are, deep down, where it matters. And on that day, I saw who Denise Sobel was as a person, her true character -- fully, unabashedly, undeniably.

The second thing I learned that day was the *immeasurable depth of human greed*. I learned never to make assumptions about how people will behave when there's a significant money on the table. In Denise's case, though, it was not like the additional amount she wanted would be *life-changing*. Her net worth was already fairly significant. After all, she lived on a gated street in a neighborhood where the garbage men come to fetch the garbage cans out of your garage! You don't even have to push the cans to the street for pick up!

So this was not the case of someone recognizing the singular point in life in which they could grab the golden ring. This wasn't her one chance to win the lottery. This was simply a point where she grabbed for more because she thought she *could*, not because she *needed* to. She was dripping with unapologetic, unmitigated avarice. It was plain and simple greed.

The third thing I learned that day was when you find yourself in one of these rare moments, as painful as they may be and as vividly enraged as you might find yourself, the best thing to do is to sit quietly, look around the room, and gauge who your friends are. And watch carefully how they behave.

Since that day, I have not considered Denise among my friends. While the rest of the people in that room that day proved that they were indeed my friends - and for that, I am indeed grateful - they too fell prey to the allure of a very large payday and made a decision I would not have made. If someone like Denise will pull something like this on you when circumstances are good, imagine what they'd do to you when the chips are down.

That said, having even just a handful of genuinely true friends will always be worth more than a thousand Denise Sobels.

16

COOLER THAN THE FONZ

In the 1970's, there was a ratings-leading TV sit-com entitled *Happy Days*, that reminisced about how uncomplicated (and funny) times were in the 1950's. Ron Howard, the famous Hollywood director, played the main character: a red-haired, pimply teenager named Richie Cunningham, growing up in Milwaukee, Wisconsin. Each weekly episode explored the trials and tribulations of growing up in the 50's through Richie, his best friends Potsy Webber and Ralph Malph, his little sister Joanie and his parents Howard and Marian. Richie and his pals used to hang out at Arnold's Drive-In restaurant, where an even broader cast of characters would parade through creating antics, challenges and entertainment for everyone.

Perhaps the most enduring character from *Happy Days* was Arthur Fonzarelli, also known as "Fonzie" or "The Fonz", played by Henry Winkler. The Fonz was the embodiment of cool in the 50's. He was an Italian-American, leather jacket-clad auto mechanic who rode a Harley. As a former gang member, high school dropout and abandoned child, The Fonz had an edge that made him feared among the naïve teens who hung out at Arnold's. He also had a sense of mystery about him that included an ability to slap the side of the jukebox and magically have it play his favorite song. Women were powerless to the allure of The Fonz, and teens trembled with fear when summoned to his office – which doubled as the men's restroom at Arnold's.

Despite his rough edges, The Fonz possessed a great humanity. Fonzie had a clear moral code -- he treated others with respect and defended those who couldn't defend themselves. Pretty strong character traits, actually. When The Fonz intervened in a gang rumble that saved Richie, they became unlikely friends. While Richie learned all about the real world from his new ally, Fonzie learned what it was like to be part of a close-knit, All-American family from the naïve teenager.

The Fonz came to embody both a rebel and a soft-hearted soul that transcended television. This character was so real that in August 2008 the City of Milwaukee unveiled a statue, called *The Bronze Fonz*, designed with the Fonzie character giving his signature thumbs up sign.

Henry Winkler, who attended the dedication ceremony, was quoted as saying, "The Fonz was everything I *wasn't*. He was everything I *wanted to be*."

The Fonz embodied the character Americans love to lionize: the down and out son of misfortune rising above all odds to success. The guy who went from hoodlum to hero, from demon to deity. The guy we judged wrongly based on appearances who showed us there could be deep humanity beneath the leather jacket and rough appearance.

While the Fonz had many wonderful character traits, he lacked one particular trait that became the focus of a particular *Happy Days* episode. Despite knowing he was wrong The Fonz just couldn't seem to utter the words "I'm Sorry." He lacked the ability to acknowledge fallibility. He would begin to apologize, get two syllables into it and then swallow hard. "I'm sssss....I was wrr....", totally unable to finish and utter those simple few words.

It is perhaps this trait that made The Fonz most human to me. He suffers from the fate that befalls all too many of us. We're simply unable to utter the simplest of phrases – "I'm Sorry" – even when we know we're wrong. Even when we know that just allowing the words "I'm Sorry" to spill from our mouths will almost instantly fix a situation, eliciting the forgiveness that allows friends to remain as friends. We just can't admit it publicly, can't seem to bring ourselves to acknowledge our own imperfection.

We become The Fonz. Just not the part of the Fonz we wanted to become....

WEEKS PASSED AFTER the ProtoCall sale and we had once again returned our attention to feathering the Golden Goose, On Target Media. We were still facing a tough competitive environment and it was taking all our energies to get our Pharma clients to re-engage after the Clinton Health scare. It was taking longer than we hoped, and was tougher than we expected to get the business back on track.

I was standing in the men's room washing my hands when Worth dashed in. He had a concerned look on his face as his eyes darted around the room, searching impatiently. He walked toward each stall, tapped the door to make sure it was empty. Once he concluded we were completely alone, he looked at me as if he had just seen a ghost.

"Did you hear?"

"Did I hear what?" I replied. Worth was acting quite strangely.

"George just asked Charlie to resign. To sell his shares back to the partners. Charlie's leaving."

My eyes must have looked like saucers, my eyebrows arched in surprise. I was floored. I wasn't just speechless, I was *incapable* of speech. I heard words that simply didn't compute. How could we have On Target without Charlie? I had never contemplated that possibility. It didn't seem in the realm of the possible.

At that very moment while I struggled to breathe, much less fully comprehend what Worth had said, Charlie opened the door to the bathroom. He got about halfway in the door and stopped, seeing me standing at the sink with a stunned look on my face. He looked at Worth and saw equal surprise on Worth's face. He stared at both of us, contemplated the awkwardness of the moment, narrowed his eyes with the saddest, most hurt look I hope to never see again, and beat a hasty and wordless retreat.

I looked at Worth. Worth looked at me. We both looked at the back of the bathroom door. What had just happened?

A FEW MONTHS earlier, Charlie had gotten involved with a business outside of On Target Media. This was not uncommon as some of the partners at On Target had other business interests. And in fairness, the business that Charlie had become involved in bore no direct business conflict with On Target.

What concerned George were two things. First, On Target was at a critical stage trying to pull itself out of an economic tailspin. He was concerned about Charlie being distracted with *any* other business. Second, in addition to Charlie some of On Target's other employees and even some clients were involved with Charlie's other business. For George, this situation created a conflict of interest for Charlie that he felt was unacceptable. So George asked Charlie to extract himself from the other business on the grounds of this conflict of interest and the need for us all to focus on our collective future. At some level, George was acting in the team's best interest as the Managing Partner, and this was a very reasonable request. All the partners were aware of George's request of Charlie.

From Charlie's perspective, he wasn't doing anything many of the other On Target partners were doing. After all, Worth still had his real estate developments. Others had business interests outside of On Target. Why couldn't he?

In the end, unbeknownst to the other partners, Charlie was either unable or unwilling to extract himself from the new business interest. When evidence of that come to George's attention that morning, George elected to act swiftly and sever Charlie's relationship with On Target immediately. This was within George's rights as managing partner, even without consultation with the other partners. Despite the fact we probably would have preferred to have had a say. But when George saw new evidence, he acted swiftly.

Apparently while Worth and I were standing in the bathroom.

—— ∞ ——

By the time I got to Charlie's office, he had already left the building. I was still trying to understand what happened and was confused — since I assumed that Charlie had extracted himself based on George's request. Beyond my confusion, I felt horrible about the incident in the. All I knew is that when Charlie narrowed his eyes and stared at me, it was if he was boring lasers through my soul. I got the distinct impression that he was somehow blaming me for what was transpiring. And for the life of me, I couldn't figure out why.

I left a voice mail message for him at his home, asking him to return my call. When the second and third messages went unreturned over the next few days, I sat down and wrote Charlie a letter. I told him that I could tell by the look on his face in the bathroom that a misunderstanding was afoot, and that I'd like to have an opportunity to speak with him, to better understand the situation and how he felt.

But all attempts at contact went unreturned. And I felt awful. Charlie and I had been friends for nearly a decade and a half, back to my very first days at P&G. I had introduced him to his wife. He was my conduit to On Target. We had big wins together, we were a good team. There was a ton of common history here — too much history, in my view, to be tossed away over what was likely a misunderstanding. This was a wrong that had to righted.

I couldn't understand why he might believe this was my fault. Or at least at seemed by the look he gave Worth and me in the bathroom, that we were somehow to blame for what transpired.

It is said that the deepest need of the soul is to be understood. I felt terribly misunderstood, and by someone who I felt as close to as a brother. A brother who wouldn't speak to me. I suspect Charlie felt misunderstood also.

And if that loss wasn't bad enough, it got worse from there. Within weeks of Charlie's departure I started to feel a cold shoulder from some mutual friends of ours. While I felt it inappropriate and potentially hurtful to Charlie to discuss the matter publicly, it was clear that the story was getting out --some *version* of the story was getting out -- and some friends felt like they needed to choose between being friends with Charlie or with me. The only thing I can liken this situation to is a divorce, where friends believe they have to choose friendship between the splitting spouses. I don't know which I felt worse about – the friends I lost who chose Charlie or the friends Charlie lost who chose me. It was a lose-lose situation in my view, and one I felt powerless to fix.

It was a loss that, sadly, would stick with me for quite some time.

17

THE NEXT NEXT ADVENTURE

I CAN'T SAY exactly what it was. I can't put my finger on the exact moment I knew it or the specific event that caused it. I guess I'm not really sure.

Maybe it was the seven year itch. Maybe it was ego. Maybe it was that things at On Target didn't seem the same without Charlie.

Maybe it was arrogance and overconfidence. After all, I really hadn't had a business failure of any significance in 16 year career. So why not roll the dice again?

Maybe it was that the On Target business didn't rebound as quickly as we thought it would. Maybe I was a wee bit worried that we had lost our mojo as a team. Maybe I was scared. Maybe I was just giving up too early.

Maybe it was true what someone had once said of me: "every few years, Michael, you just have to reinvent yourself, don't you?" Maybe he was right. Maybe I felt some primal urge for reinvention of which even I was not conscious.

Maybe it was a lot of things; I don't know. I can't really put my finger on it.

All I knew was that every instinct inside me said it was time to leave On Target. That this thing I had loved so much had run its course. That it was just time for me to go. Like when you get that feeling when it's time to leave a party. No one's telling you it's time to leave; you just sense it. I was getting that feeling that it was time for the next adventure. The next chapter.

I WAS MEETING with my attorney Matthew Mazeroski. I am not a litigious guy; in fact, I've never sued anyone in my life. I've never been sued although I have been threatened by lawyers; does that count? I don't think so. Getting threatened by a lawyer seems like a rite of passage these days. I've never been divorced. I've never been a victim of malpractice, had a sudden neck ache after a traffic accident, or been arrested for DUI.

So it's not like I *need* to have regular interaction with an attorney.

But I meet with my lawyer fairly regularly so we can study. You could call us *students with a certain thirst for knowledge.* We like to explore the various combinations of hops and barley that exist in liquid form. Agrarians we are.

Matthew is devout catholic. He has not one, but two degrees from Notre Dame. He's actually met the Pope at The Vatican. Got a personal blessing from the Holy Father Himself. I am in awe.

Despite being a few years his elder, I am merely the student. He is the teacher. The subject matter is tasty.

I trust my attorney. And my good friend.

He listens to my ravings about work. About the kids. About life. His consumption rate is a little faster than mine because he talks less. Listens more. Teaches me a lot about listening, much of which I've sadly never adopted. To my own detriment.

"So why don't you just hang out your own shingle?" Matthew asks, cutting to the chase, challenging me in his own non-confrontational way to stop whining and start doing something. Testing to see if I'm serious about leaving On Target or just wallowing in self-pity. For which he has no patience, unless he's on the clock and billing hours. Then he's got all the patience in the world. A smart man. A good lawyer. But he's not billing hours at the moment.

"Hang out a shingle? I'm not a lawyer," replied the Mouse, not so artfully dodging the real question.

"Of course you aren't. You actually have meaningful accomplishments in your career. Lawyers just offer opinions. Create paperwork." Matthew is the king of philosophical self-deprecation. "What I'm talking about is *consulting.* Helping people start the business ventures of their dreams. Turn their dreaming into reality."

Matthew can certainly spin it, can't he?

"I thought *self-employed consultant* was just a euphemism for *unemployed and looking for a job.*"

"Often it is. But in your case, it wouldn't be. It would be for real." I wondered if the hops were getting to him. Or to me.

"Yeah, but I'm kinda missing one thing," I squeaked.

"And that would be?"

"A paying client base. Doesn't that help with that ol' *income thing?*" My squeaking continued.

"That's where your old lawyer pal and loyal devotee of the Fighting Irish might be able to help," said Matthew with arched eyebrows and a twinkle in his eye.

"And what might my favorite leprechaun have in mind?" I was intrigued.

"Hey, no short jokes," Matthew replied defensively.

"What short jokes? You're taller than me," I countered. "I was just saluting the Notre Dame reference. My bad. No offense intended."

"None taken. Get more beer. I'll fill you in on what I'm thinking."

I got more beer.

———

GREAT LAKES CHRISTMAS Ale. According to ratebeer.com, it has a "cinnamon and ginger spice flavor, and a rich copper color" that got it a 93 rating.

Whatever. Matthew liked it. So I bought another round. Personally, I'm just fine with Miller Lite. But I try to be, if anything, flexible. It doesn't always work. Anyway, with the second beer in front of us we now had each other's attention.

"OK, here's the thing," Matthew began, after a long pull on the bottle. "People come to our law firm all the time to help them start their businesses. We've been in business for over a century; hey, we were started by a former President of the United States! So that's one of the many things we do. As such, we see lots of business ideas come through our doors."

After another swallow, Matthew continued. "We're not consultants, we're not there to tell them whether it's a good idea or not. We're lawyers. So, of course, if they can pay we help them with the legal stuff. Sometimes, we even help them even if they can't pay. As we're beginning to see more and more start-up's these days, we see a lot more that can't pay - *yet*. In the past, there weren't that many. But with the dot com craze going on, we're seeing plenty. And we're wondering if we should start doing work for these start-up's and let them pay us with equity in their companies instead of cash."

"Could be risky," added the Mouse, "but equity is better than more pro-bono work than you want."

"You get it. I knew you were smart. As we see it, the risk in terms of attorney time is not that big. The returns, however, can be enormous. One of our clients, Up 4 Sale, just got bought by eBay for $75 million in stock. Three guys working over near 12ᵗʰ and Main Streets in Over the Rhine. In a loft space for which they were paying $2 a square foot. Couple card tables, couple laptops, couple cell phones. A few posters on the wall. Pizza boxes. Empty beer cans. A lotta coffee and a bunch of code. Good code apparently. Unique code. Ebay saw their code, and the online trading engine that code created. eBay decided that it was better than their own trading engine. And eBay is the *king* of trading. So these guys now have a lot of eBay stock and wear eBay employee badges. And oh yeah, they got eBay stock options on top of that. 25 years old. Gazillionaires working out of their $2 per square foot space in Over the Rhine."

"$75 million? Really?" the Mouse was amazed.

"That's all public information by the way," quickly offered Matthew. Always maintaining the proper legal propriety. Another thing I respected about him.

"So $75 million just for their code?" the Mouse squeaked again.

"For their code and equally important, for their brains. These guys are smart."

"I guess they can get multiple toppings on their pizza now. Maybe even buy some of this fancy Great Lakes Christmas Ale. After all, it's got 'a rich copper color and hints of cinnamon'. So I guess you and your law partners are wondering how many more Up 4 Sale's there are out there? So you're wondering how we find them? How do we bet on them? How can we predict if they will hit big too?"

"Bingo."

"And how are you going about answering those questions?"

"Well, we're not the only ones asking the questions. The local managers for Microsoft, Oracle, EMC, Compaq, Cincinnati Bell, Cisco…they're all asking the same questions. The guys from Deloitte, Ernst & Young, PWC are asking them too. The software development firms like Whittman-Hart. And the venture capital firms, too. Everybody's asking the same questions. So we've put together a small group that represent each of the firms and we're examining different start up's together as a team. Letting them pitch us. Trying to decide, using the various skill sets around the table, which ones have a chance of winning. Which ones we'd be willing to risk some of our time in exchange for equity."

"How's that working out?"

"Well, we've got various perspectives — legal, financial, technical, etc. But we're missing a critical skill set."

"And that would be?"

"The *been there, done that* perspective. We've got all these people who have worked for big firms all their careers, but no one who's actually *done* a start up. No one that's actually operating on the ground and knows what it takes to really take a business from a concept to reality. You know, the stuff you get only from having 'been there, done that'."

"And you think I have that skill set? You think I can fill in that missing part?"

"Absolutely. You actually went from *Fortune 500* to *Inc 500*. You've built start-up's. Twice, in fact. Sold one to a public competitor. That would qualify, I'd say."

"I think you've had too many Christmas Ales. Maybe too big a 'hint of cinnamon'? You're confusing me with Santa Claus."

"Santa isn't Jewish."

"As far as you know."

———

Two beers later, Matthew's idea was beginning to bloom. While it seemed pretty out there, I was warming to it. Or the beer was warming me to it. I couldn't tell which. As we discussed it further, he filled me in on two other parts that really made it come together for me.

First, Matthew genuinely believed that this would be not only good for the entrepreneurs and the service providers who helped them, but that it could also be good for the City of Cincinnati and the Over The Rhine neighborhood. OTR was a historically significant neighborhood in downtown Cincinnati that had fallen into decay and disrepair over time. OTR was about a 35 block area bordered by Central Parkway on the south and Liberty Street on the north. Before it was a street, Central Parkway itself was a canal off the Mill Creek in the 1800's and many of the Cincinnati workers had jobs in what is now downtown Cincinnati, south of Central Parkway. They lived just across the canal. Due to its largely German population the little canal was referred to, tongue in cheek, as the *Rhine*, a reference to the famous Rhine River in Germany. Therefore, the neighborhood where they lived was therefore dubbed Over the Rhine.

As the city grew, the canal was filled in and became Central Parkway, connecting it to downtown. For decades, people lived and worked in OTR. Yet, Cincinnati, like most US cities, experienced urban flight in the 60's and 70's, and OTR fell into disrepair and became largely lower income *Section 8* housing, supported by US government subsidies. Once containing over 100,000 residents, OTR had fewer than 7,000 in the late 1990's. While short on residents, it was not short on empty buildings.

"So here's the idea," Matthew continued. "We start a not-for-profit technology incubator in OTR. We use the group we've got to screen companies. For the best ideas, we give 'em the resources they need – legal and financial advice, software and hardware platforms on which to develop, internet access, and free office space. The more companies we have in OTR, the more economic development occurs – they all have to work, and possibly live, down here every day. They buy coffee, lunch, parking, and beers after work. They get the help they need to get their businesses off the ground through access to the best business support services for free. The City gets economic development. Once we get them to the point where they can secure venture funding, they move out of the incubator and into an OTR building. Wins all around."

I had to admit, this was an interesting idea and a compelling vision.

"So how are you thinking about funding this little incubator?" asked the Mouse.

"I don't think we're going to need a lot of actual cash, perhaps just for rent and utilities. I'm thinking we'll work primarily on in-kind donations -- get Cincinnati Bell to donate free internet access as their high speed lines run right down Main Street. We'll get Compaq to donate laptops and servers, EMC to donate storage, Microsoft and Oracle to donate software. Everyone will play somehow. They bring what they have already to the table; others can donate cash. If we don't get enough, we'll go hat in hand and we'll go to the biggest firms in Cincinnati. They all have a vested interest in doing something to help OTR. But they have a dearth of good ideas. Here's a *fundable* one for them."

This continued to be a very interesting idea.

"What do you need from me?"

"I need you to help me turn this beer-inspired idea into reality."

"That I DO have some experience with. And I'm happy to help. Actually, it sounds like a lot of fun and something that could work. Only one problem we haven't solved yet, and forgive me for being a bit on the selfish side with this question. But if I quit my job, and I devote all my time to this, how do I feed my family?"

"I neglected to mention that part, didn't I?"

"That is where this conversation started, wasn't it?"

"Well, given the work my firm does for start-ups that are already funded by venture firms, I'll help you get some paying gigs with them. They don't need the early help we're talking about providing in the incubator as they're already past that stage. But they still need the help you can provide and they have money to pay."

"Enough?"

"More than you make today."

Apparently, Leprechauns do lead to a pot of gold.

———

WE DUBBED THE incubator Main Street Ventures, as our offices sat at the corner of 12th and Main Streets. The firms we solicited for in-kind donations all stepped up as we had hoped. Matthew's law firm kicked in the first $25,000 cash contribution, followed by Deloitte and then Fifth Third Bank. Procter & Gamble had a keen interest in the concept. With the dot com boom exploding on the West Coast, P&G was losing Brand Manager couples rapidly. One spouse would join a start-up in San Francisco and the other spouse would get a bread-winner job at Clorox or Levi's to support the family. If Main Street Ventures could prove successful, P&G could keep at least one of those Brand Managers while their spouse scratched the start-up itch staying in Cincinnati. The P&G Fund ante'd up a three year, $50,000 annual commitment. We had operating cash. We were good to go.

Matthew became the Chairman of Main Street Ventures and I served as its founding President. Our three-person board included Matthew's good friend, Gary Harris, who was already an active investor in start-ups by night and a public servant by day -- Hamilton County's Clerk of Courts. His office was three blocks from 12th and Main. Perfect. Gary was a frequent student in our little hops-based study group.

We secured office spaces on around the 1200 block of Main Street, joining the Up 4 Sale, now eBay, guys. We believed the spaces could support up to 30 companies. In most circumstances, the buildings had retail space or a bar on the street level, and were empty on the second and third floors. The typical space was what one would think of as loft space – hardwood floors, exposed brick walls, tall windows. In major developed downtowns these spaces were redeveloped into condo's that sold for hundreds of thousands of dollars. In OTR, we leased our spaces on average for about $2 a square foot in four separate buildings. All situated around Kaldi's coffee house. For start-up's coffee was the elixir of the gods. As long as there was coffee close by, any space was workable.

Word of Main Street Ventures spread like wildfire around Cincinnati, aided significantly by the Cincinnati business press and the ebullient NASDAQ. Between the Dot Com phenomenon and good hearted Cincinnatians looking for something positive in OTR, help for MSV abounded.

A significant amount of help came from the local Herman Miller office furniture dealer. Herman Miller had taken a keen interest in San Francisco-based start-ups and designed a line of flexible office furniture that, according to their marketing materials, "thought outside the cubicle". A crafty turn of words at the time, I thought. Cincinnati's Herman Miller dealer offered to furnish our office free of charge, in exchange for being able to use it as a *showroom* for potential clients interested in their new lines. Of course, every resident company of MSV would be a potential customer when they secured funding. No brainer. For both MSV and Herman Miller.

Then the showroom concept caught on. Cincinnati Bell and Cisco wanted to demonstrate the power of wireless spaces. At that point in the late 1990's, the internet world was wired as there was no cost-effective mobile technology developed yet. In fact, of the wired internet world, most of it was still dial-up, as high speed DSL was developing and cable-delivered fiber optic internet access was just behind it.

But the 802.11 wireless standard was lurking right around the corner. And Cincinnati Bell and Cisco were eager to show the world what a wireless world might look like. We created a vision for what would become known as *The Wireless Community* and enveloped the entire 1200 block of Main Street in it — all four MSV buildings and Kaldi's. For free. Every MSV member company got plug-in wireless cards for their laptops, and soon you saw collaboration like never seen before. People carried their laptops building to building. They worked on the streets, in Kaldi's, or wherever their interests took them. The MSV Wireless Community made the wired world look so *20th century*.

Planet Feedback and Up 4 Sale became the first start-up's associated with MSV, with Planet Feedback being the first to actually reside in MSV-rented space. Others soon followed. Before long, we had 30 start-up's, employing about 300 people, generating about $60 million in angel and venture capital investments. When Planet Feedback (which is today owned by The Nielsen Company) got its first big round of venture capital funding, it held its funding party on Main Street at one of the group's favorite watering holes. Hundreds of people attended the party causing it to spill out onto Main Street. City council members, Chamber of Commerce officials, television stations, print media, you name it. All were there. The buzz was huge. And everyone wanted to be part of it.

Success has a thousand fathers; failure is a bastard child. *Fathers* abounded that night.

Cincinnati was on the map as an internet development hot spot, and Over the Rhine was on its way back. The Next Next Adventure was in full swing.

18

COMMON HISTORY

HAVE YOU EVER noticed that sometimes people feel a sense of affinity or relationship to others who have shared a common experience? I'm not talking about two people who have survived a plane crash together – there would be a really good basis for bonding if you had been through something that extreme. I'm thinking about something more commonplace than that, more benign. Something we all can relate to.

For example, think about two people who happened to spend a few years at the same place, at the same time – a high school, a neighborhood, a college, a summer camp, an employer, the military base, etc.

I've found there can be an unusually strong bond people feel for others, even decades later, who have that kind of shared history. I wonder why people often feel compelled to attend high school or college reunions decades after graduating? And why do they feel a particular kinship to those whose tenures overlapped – even if they'd lost track of each other? They might not have even been particularly good friends at the time; maybe just a social acquaintance. But for some reason, after decades have passed, people feel compelled to see others they knew for only a short time, many years previous, and rekindle some bond or relationship.

Maybe they just want to reminisce about the good old days. Maybe they get good vibes from remembering shared experiences. I can't say exactly.

But one thing is abundantly clear: it's a fairly unexplainable yet common experience. There seems to be an unmistakable bond, a relationship, if even solely on an emotional level, that exists — that holds people together. Psychologists must have some fancy term for it. But I'm not a psychologist.

So I made up my own term for it. I call it *Common History*. This is the term for this phenomenon. There! I just made it up.

Common History is powerful. Just look at the size of the college reunion business — and how much energy universities put into them — if you don't believe me.

I was not consciously aware of the phenomenon of *Common History* until the summer I graduated college and moved to Cincinnati. There were only a few people I knew in Cincinnati prior to my arrival, other than the people I met interviewing at P&G.

One of those few was a gentleman named Fred Diamond. Fred was fourth year at UVA (UVA speak for: a senior in college) when I was first year at UVA (UVA speak for: a freshman). It was not common for a *fourth year* to socialize with a *first year* at UVA, at least no more common than any other college.

Even moreso in fraternities. fourth year's didn't socialize with first year's in fraternities. Fourth Year's *hazed* first year's in Fraternities, which was technically a form of socialization. Just not a good form of socialization. By the time a first year at UVA was actually inducted into his fraternity, it was well into the second semester of the fourth year's final months of college. Not much time for bonding. Not much time for relationship building.

Despite this, during the little time in college I knew Fred I liked him -- even if for no other reason than he was too busy studying for the CPA Exam to waste his time hazing me. He was a nice guy whose basic history I had to memorize to get inducted into the fraternity, but someone I never actually *knew* very well. I got to know him a bit playing basketball. He was a taller guy that, as point guard on the fraternity basketball team, I fed the ball inside to score. When he rebounded on defense, he'd throw the ball to me on the outlet pass to start the fast break. But it would not be fair to say I knew Fred very well or that we were friends.

You wouldn't have known that when we met four years later for lunch in Cincinnati.

I had contacted Fred by phone. "Uh, Fred? This is Michael Elliott. Perhaps you remember me from Phi Ep at UVA?" asked the Mouse.

"Sure, I remember you," boomed Fred. "A Phi Ep Brother! What can I do for you?"

That was a nice welcome. "Well, I just moved to Cincinnati to work for Procter & Gamble."

"Really? Great! Is your office downtown? Mine is only a block away from P&G Headquarters. How about we meet for lunch this week?"

Wow. Another nice welcome. Who was this guy?

I walked into the Red Squirrel to meet Fred for lunch, about a block away from both our offices. I saw him sitting at a table when I walked in and he rose to greet me, hand extended. As I shook his hand, he gave me the *Phi Ep Grip*, the special handshake that brothers are supposed to secretly give one another. I don't think I had used the Grip since I was inducted into the fraternity one hazy night. Fred probably gave me the Grip then too. I can't really recall. After the Grip, Fred then gave me this big bear hug and said "Welcome, Brother."

At first, I wondered whether he was being sarcastic. Even my *genetic* brothers never called me "brother". But as I looked into his eyes, I could tell he was serious. To him, I *was* his brother. If we were in the same fraternity, even if we overlapped for only a semester, in his mind we were brothers.

Honestly, I never took the *brotherhood* part of fraternity life all that seriously. I enjoyed the social aspects of the fraternity. I enjoyed having ready teams on which to participate in intramural sports. It was nice to have a group of people ready to party virtually on call. But I never really went in for the traditions, the brotherhood, the rituals, the hazing….all that stuff. I understood that it was meaningful to people – I was just not one of those people.

Apparently, Fred was. It *was* meaningful to Fred. "Brother" meant something to him. And he treated me like a brother. I was invited to his house for holidays. He must have convinced his parents of this, too. They would always hug me when I saw them, like I was their long lost child who had simply wandered off for 20 years and had finally come home. I didn't really get it. But I had to admit, living in a strange city with no blood family around me, it sure felt good to be part of an *adopted family*. Though I couldn't really explain it, it felt good, so… I went with it.

I wouldn't say Fred and I became *best* friends in Cincinnati. Probably more like good friends and certainly more than acquaintances. We played in the same basketball league, we did some of the same kinds of volunteer work together, gathered for holidays together. Periodic lunches during the work week. We even attended each others' weddings. I remember walking down the aisle after being pronounced *husband and wife* and seeing Fred with his wife Amy. Fred was smiling broadly and proud to among the many Phi Ep brothers there. Amy was very pregnant and had an odd look on her face. It was shortly into the reception that I discovered that Amy was having serious contractions. Their first of their three children was born later that evening! It's pretty easy for to remember her birthday.

But I can't think of a single time we got together that Fred didn't greet me with the secret Grip and call me "Brother". Not once did he forget. Fred not only understood the power of common history, but he but was a strong practitioner of it.

<hr />

ABOUT 15 YEARS later, I enrolled Fred in helping me with our newly formed not-for-profit, Main Street Ventures. MSV was founded to help launch start-up companies in Cincinnati's historically relevant, but economically disadvantaged neighborhood Over the Rhine. Fred had left Arthur Andersen to become a very successful entrepreneur himself, having founded a firm that provided audit and consulting services for large Pension and Endowment Funds. This proved to be a lucrative business, extremely well niched, and Fred had quietly built quite a business that generated a significant income for his family.

Fred was a *gotta give back* kind of guy, one of the many reasons I admired him. And he had a soft spot both for Entrepreneurs and for the Over The Rhine section of his hometown Cincinnati. So he joined the Board of Main Street Ventures and helped us to make it a success.

One day, Fred and I made plans to meet at Kaldi's Coffee House on Main Street in OTR. Kaldi's was an eclectic spot, where all kinds of meetings happened. It was a confluence of many influences and many cultures in the city, as great coffee houses often are. Everything happened there from good coffee to good music to good food to the development of a legally binding term sheet to fund a start-up company. During the day at Kaldi's, you could find lawyers, bankers, businesspeople, homeless people, musicians, poets, politicians, and clergy. At night, the cross section of community was even wider! Kaldi's was truly a testament to coffee being the great equalizer – and harmonizer – of society.

I sat in Kaldi's noticing Fred come through the door. Oddly, he seemed to be favoring his left side a bit, more than his gangly, six foot four frame might normally. As he made his way over to the table it appeared he was even dragging his left foot a little.

"Brother," he said as he greeted me with his trademark secret grip, smile and hug. We were sharing our usual Kaldi's fare – the big pot of chamomile tea. We weren't into coffee. What a shame given Kaldi's offering. But we liked their tea.

"Are you OK, Fred? I noticed you favoring your left side a bit," inquired the Mouse.

"We need to talk, Brother."

"Whassup?"

"It's not good, but I'm going to get through it. I'm going to beat this thing as sure as I'm sitting in front of you," Fred said resolutely. And I knew then and there whatever it was, it wasn't good.

"What 'thing'?" I asked, with a quiver in my voice, fearing the answer.

"I've been diagnosed with an inoperable brain tumor. It seems to be causing some paralysis in my left arm and leg. I'm flying down to MD Anderson Hospital in Texas to see a specialist tomorrow to map out a treatment program. To figure out how to beat this thing."

How do you respond to a statement like that? What in the world can you say when your friend utters the syllables "in-op-er-a-ble brain tu-mor"? What can you say that *works* in that situation? What's appropriate? Lord, I didn't have the words. I didn't have the thoughts. I didn't have anything. I was floored.

But I recovered. I realized quickly that what Fred needed was not to see me break down and blubber all over him. He needed strength from anywhere he could get it. He needed me to tell him that the courage he was demonstrating, the optimism he was exuding, the belief he was espousing, was.... *warranted*. Was... *justified*. Was... *the way to be.* The way we *all* needed to be. For Fred.

"Well then, 'beat this thing' is exactly what we're gonna do," I responded echoing his resolve, mustering more strength in my voice than I really had, more brightness to my eyes than I really felt, more warmth in my tone than I really possessed. "How can I help? Do you want me to come with you to Texas?"

"I appreciate the offer, but not necessary. Amy's coming with me. She's my rock."

———

FRED EMBARKED UPON a fight like none I'd ever seen. He regularly travelled to Texas for treatments. Since the tumor was inoperable, he signed up for every experimental treatment therapy for which he could qualify. He flew to California, Colorado, wherever the therapy was offered. Pharmaceutical, Herbal, Transcendental, whatever. Fred went and we cheered him. A bunch of Fred's friends ordered t-shirts with a *Team Diamond* logo on the front and the phrase *FredWillWin* on the back. Fred wore them everywhere, determined to do just that - to win. And Fred did win.

For a while.

He'd make progress, build optimism, and then regress as the treatment inevitably failed. He'd find a new treatment, undergo it, brave his way through it, only to have it fail eventually as well. Though he would never give up the fight, I think he knew what was happening. I believe he participated in some of the latter treatments simply to help the doctors learn. He was so selfless that he allowed himself to become a human guinea pig, absent a true belief that there was really anything left that could cure his condition. He believed his participation in the study would help someone, even if it wasn't him. And that made the effort, the pain, the cost, in Fred's mind, *worthy*.

I had frequent visits with Fred during his extended illness. Since he was physically limited, he read a lot to keep his mind stimulated. He recommended a few books for me to read. And when he did, I went right out and bought the book to understand what he wanted to share with me. Most provided a particular perspective on life, one that my friend apparently wanted me to experience. Think about it. Someone facing the end of life as we know it must possess a unique perspective, difficult to attain, and likely elusive and rare. Certainly worth understanding before we faced it ourselves.

Despite the reality of the situation, Fred never outwardly gave up, never indicated he felt he was doing anything other than fighting. Anything other than "beating this thing." He didn't want to let *us* down by giving up.

The Saturday before Fred died, two friends and I went to his house for a visit. Fred was gnarled in pain, contorted and shaking. It's simply horrible what cancer does to the human body. It must be horrible to experience, because it's certainly horrible to witness.

It was impossible for him to even speak with us. He had no voice left. We went to his bedside to greet him. I watched him hold his hand out to shake hands with my friends, to nod appreciatively, and to try to frame a smile of thanks for them coming to see him, unable to form the words.

When I got to him, he held his hand out to shake mine, and then clandestinely adjusted his fingers to give me the secret Grip. The Phi Ep Grip. Soundlessly, he mouthed the word "Brother," with a smile in his weakened eyes. I was frozen. I held the Grip, and wrapped my hands around his, for an extended moment. Something passed between us in that moment, although I can't say exactly what. Maybe it was a bit of his spirit. I like to think so.

"Brother" was Fred's last word to me. This gesture remains my first, final and most fond memory of Fred.

The Power of Common History. When you have a relationship based on Common History, don't ever doubt its power. Don't question its logic. Don't ask how it works. Don't endeavor to explain it.

Rather, savor it. Practice it. Embrace it. It may lay fallow for years, for decades, but it can be rekindled in a moment's notice. That's how Common History works.

THE EXCITEMENT AROUND Main Street Ventures had been growing at a rapid pace, and not surprisingly occupying an increasing amount of my time. It was truly a labor of love. Every new MSV company presented a fresh start. And with all those new companies, it seemed that almost weekly we were seeing new restaurants, bars and renovations going on around 12th and Main Streets. I loved walking the streets of Over the Rhine bearing witness to its evolution from decay to renewal.

With all this work focused on my not-for-profit interests, I was reminded by the bills in my mailbox that I had a *for-profit* venture that needed to be developed also. I discovered that a business could really be operated with only a laptop, a cellphone and a nifty Herman Miller table and chair.

True to his word, Matthew had helped connect me to some consulting gigs and my new venture was born – Stablehand Advisors LLC. It was named Stablehand following an old adage in venture investing: *bet on the jockey, not on the horse*. That adage meant that a good business idea was certainly important (the "horse"), but it was the quality of the person running the business (the "jockey") that most determined the level of financial return an investor received. So my job was to help the start-up's president, or the jockey, win the race.

One of the earliest Stablehand assignments was with a company called Intellitecs International. Intellitecs was not a new software company and was not part of Main Street Ventures which was good because it meant it had money to pay consultants!

Intellitecs had created a new, breakthrough product in a business not quite as sexy as software – female urinary stress incontinence. This was a matter of which I knew nothing for obvious reasons. First, I was not female. Beyond that, female urinary stress incontinence wasn't exactly what you might call dinner party conversation. Unless, perhaps, you were at a Urology Convention.

But it is a very real problem. Apparently, many women over 40 that have given birth at least once struggle with a condition that causes them to emit varying amounts of urine involuntarily from simple body actions like sneezes, coughs, laughter, and exercise. Imagine having to hold yourself back from laughing or sneezing. Impossible! And no one should have to.

There were few good solutions to this problem on the market and those were uncomfortable and had serious drawbacks. Women could wear multiple maxipads and hope that would contain the issue. Or they could wear adult disposable diapers that were highly un-feminine and really made women feel old and *broken*. There weren't many other options.

Until now.

Intellitecs had developed a unique, feminine lace panty, coupled with a form fitting disposable pad that addressed the physical problem for women and catered to the emotional one -- still allowing them to maintain their dignity and femininity. In my experience, solving problems on both a physical and emotional level translated into great rewards – for both the consumer and the business.

Intellitecs called the product *Compose*, a fine brand name that elicited images of both femininity and confidence. Intellitecs was gearing up to begin national distribution of Compose when I was asked to bring both my experience in health care and consumer products to assist them.

Intellitecs' business plan called for raising sufficient capital to produce inventory for national distribution, fund an initial national advertising campaign to garner market share from humongous competitors Kimberly-Clarke and Johnson & Johnson, and then take the company public as it went cash flow positive. Intellitecs' primary angel investor funded much of the initial capital – many millions of dollars. It was decided to bring in a mezzanine capital firm to bridge the capital needs from Angel to the initial public offering of stock (IPO) and establish a bank line of credit, secured by the inventory primarily, to fund borrowings for working capital. In this manner, they could skip Venture funding altogether.

Intellitecs' sales staff had secured Wal-Mart and Walgreen's as its first two customers. Quite an accomplishment! And quite demanding customers, too. Now it had to create a supply chain capable of meeting Wal-Mart's stringent operational requirements. Minimally, Intellitecs had to be capable of accepting an electronically-generated order and ensure product could get to any Wal-Mart store in the lower 48 states within 9 days of order submission. The angel investor provided us with a seat on his company's JD Edwards Enterprise Resource Planning (ERP) software system. With only about half a million dollars investment, Intellitecs built a flexible supply chain that began with cut and sew operations to assemble panties in the Caribbean, pad manufacturing in Pennsylvania, packaging in St. Louis, and distribution throughout the lower 48 states.

In short, it more than met Wal-Mart's objectives. Kimberly-Clarke and Johnson & Johnson's global supply chain could meet Wal-Mart's standard in 7-8 days, just inside the 9 day requirement. Amazingly, through the magic of this new type of ERP software and great people-based planning, Intellitecs was able to execute this process start to finish in just 6 days.

It was clear that the world was changing in the late 90's. Previously, huge companies could erect high barriers to entry that created competitive advantages over start-up's in supply chain infrastructure. Now those barriers were coming down as software and the internet were *virtualizing* business in ways that had never been seen. And the impenetrable walls of big company scale were tumbling down.

It was fascinating to watch — and even more exciting to be a participant.

ONE DAY, I got a call from the Intelltics CEO, informing me that they had engaged an executive recruiter to help them find a Director of Marketing. Given my experience in consumer products, he wanted me to serve on the interview panels which were to take place over the next week. He was going to provide me with the resumes and the recruiters' assessments to prepare for the interviews. He had informed the recruiter that I would serve on the panel and gave him my background so the candidates could be as prepared as possible. I was more than happy to engage in this process. Choosing the right talent is one of the most leverageable moves a start-up company can make. It can also be the most devastating if executed improperly.

When I received the packet of resumes, I was stunned at the recruiting firm leading the search: Charlie MacAvoy & Associates. Yes, Charlie. My old friend from P&G. My former partner from On Target Media. My friend who was no longer speaking to me.

I had heard that Charlie had started an executive recruiting firm and remember thinking what a great match it was for Charlie's networking talent. He was a master at networking — and it made him an excellent recruiter.

Of course, now that it was apparent that Charlie and I would be interacting, I wondered how this interaction would transpire. I was hopeful the power of Common History would positively influence it

I have to admit that Charlie's re-entry into my world -- after three years had passed – caused me much more consternation than I had wanted, or expected.

After giving it days of thought, and probably way more thought than I wanted to allow, I decided that I had made more attempts than was necessary previously to reconcile the situation. I had made overtures that had gone unreturned – overtures I was sure had been received, even if not acknowledged. I was hurt by this and it weighed on me.

I decided that Charlie should now be well aware I was involved in this placement for MacAvoy & Associates as the CEO had told him I'd be on the interview panel and provided him with my background for the candidates. It's quite common for a recruiter to speak with panelists to get their feedback and input.

So I decided I'd just wait for Charlie to call me. He now had incentive, in the interests of his own business, to contact me and to engage with me. And I eagerly awaited that contact.

That strategy proved ill-fated. The call from Charlie never came. The interviews came and went. I gave the feedback to the CEO when he inquired and the CEO himself selected a candidate. He worked with Charlie to convince the candidate to join Intellitecs and she was hired.

But I never heard a word from Charlie. Maybe he thought talking to me now would appear disingenuous or self-serving -- seeming only to further his business interest rather than provide a genuine reconciliation. That it would appear he *had* to reconcile, not that he *wanted* to reconcile.

Or maybe he just never wanted to speak to me again. Maybe he felt that, as his friend, I should have gone to George and urged him to reconsider asking Charlie to resign. That it was my obligation as a friend to have rushed to Charlie's defense; that I should have stepped up for him and turned the situation around. Maybe he felt that the bonds of friendship should always supersede ANY circumstance. Maybe he felt that's what he would have done for me, so why shouldn't I have done it for him?

Perhaps I should have. Maybe I should not have watched it all happen, in a my stupor in the bathroom. May I should have stepped in. Maybe I was no better than Chip Sharp. Could that really be true? Had I abandoned Charlie like Chip abandoned me? I certainly hoped that wasn't the case. But how could I be sure if I couldn't speak with Charlie?

I rationalized that I wasn't driving the circumstances. Charlie was. The matter at On Target was between George and Charlie, not me. I found out when it was too late to do anything.

Or was it? Perhaps I'll never know.

Either way, the resulting effect on me was the same. I was just interminably bummed out.

———

DESPITE HOW HORRIBLE I felt about the situation with Charlie, I felt powerless to fix it. My only recourse, once again, was to rationalize the situation -- to put the situation in the past and move on. I had made those initial attempts to reach Charlie, to explain myself, to rectify the situation, and he wouldn't even take my call or respond to my letter. And then, with the Intellitecs opportunity to bring us back together, he wouldn't engage with me...once again. And I let him dodge it. I let him avoid me.

He wouldn't even give it a chance. And if he wouldn't even give it a chance to get cleared up, I rationalized that the problem was really his, not mine. I'd done all I could do. I guess it was simply not meant to be. The forces of the universe took over. So I felt my conscience was clear.

Or so I thought.

It was the fall of the year and the time of Jewish High Holidays. I was sitting in Synagogue on Yom Kippur, the holiest day of the year in Jewish tradition, the Day of Atonement. The day Jews seek forgiveness for the transgressions of the past. The Rabbi was speaking about how the Jewish faith teaches that sins between man and God can be forgiven on Yom Kippur — through penitence, prayer and charity. However, Jewish tradition also held that God cannot forgive the wrongs between people; only people can grant forgiveness to each other. One should be humble enough to ask for forgiveness from another, and the other should be merciful enough to grant it.

It's a good concept. A good concept for building a tolerant and cohesive community. If only it were practiced more.

The Rabbi went on to elaborate — which, if you know any Rabbis, *elaborating* is what they do a LOT of -- Jewish tradition held that a person who wrongs another is obligated to humble himself by making *three attempts* to garner forgiveness for that wrong. It was the process of humbling oneself to ask repeatedly for forgiveness that demonstrated the true act of contrition that warranted forgiveness.

If, after the three legitimate attempts, the wronged individual "hardens his heart" and refuses to forgive the offender, then the wronged individual now *bears* the sin for refusing to show mercy. The offender is officially forgiven and the *offendee* now becomes the *offender*. How's that for a twist?

This is a great way to encourage reconciliation through humility. Yet, I wondered how many people truly worked that hard. It required a great deal of perseverance and commitment to humble oneself to say *I'm sorry* three times. Especially, when you see how hard it was for The Fonz even to say it once. I don't think the Fonz was, at least in this way, different than most people. It seems everyone struggles with those two little words from time to time.

But that wasn't the end of the Rabbi's elaboration (as my wife says, "See, I Told You")! The Rabbi went on to extend the concept of "righting one's wrong" to *eliminating one's regrets*. He noted that regret can be as damaging to the human psyche as remorse and that if we really want to free ourselves we should extend the concept to include finding a way to fix situations that you *regret* — even if you felt you might not have been actually *wrong*.

And that's when it really hit home for me... like a ton of bricks. That's the moment when I found the word for the situation with Charlie. The whole situation was simply *regretful*. It wasn't about right or wrong, his fault or mine. I should attempt to fix it simply because I *regretted* the situation terribly. As much as I thought I had put things with Charlie behind me -- rationalized them away, convinced myself the situation didn't bother me -- it all came storming back in a new context, called *regret*.

Yet, was there really anything I could do about it at this point, after so much time had passed?

IN THE COURSE of human history when great triumphs are recorded, one tends to think about ending bloody wars, eradicating plagues or diseases, jailing evil dictators or toppling oppressive political regimes. We talk about the triumphs of great sporting events — like when the US Hockey team beat the USSR in the Winter Olympics or when Cassius Clay beat Sonny Liston in boxing -- or when ANYBODY beat one of Bobby Knight's Indiana basketball teams.

While those moments are all historical or at least memorable, I believe one of the great triumphs of humanity is a simple one: when an average human being – not a field general or super athlete, but an *average joe* -- decides to take that thoughtful intention of doing the right thing and actually puts it into action. I've heard it said that the road to hell is paved with good intentions and it's probably true. The world would be a far better place if we actually did half the things our conscience urged us to do.

And my conscience was screaming at me that day.

My conscience tugged at me, "you've really only tried *once* to fix it with Charlie. When the second opportunity came along, he could have taken the opportunity to step up and chose not to; but neither did you. You waited for him to come to you. You know you regret the whole circumstance. You know that as a result of this situation, others have experienced pain, intentionally or not. So if the Rabbi's right – if you're obligated to try three times to correct a wrong – you're only a third of the way there. Go make the second attempt. Don't wait. Do it now."

Instead of going down that paved road to hell, I chose to try again.

The next day I sat down and wrote Charlie a letter. I feared a phone call might go unreturned like the others and I might not even get the chance to tell him how I felt. If instead, I wrote him a letter, he might toss the letter without opening it…or he just might read it. It was worth a chance; so I took it.

In the letter to Charlie, I shared that I regretted what happened. I told him that I wished he had not endured pain and embarrassment. I told him that I appreciated the work he did for Intellitecs, and that, based on the quality of the great Marketing Director he had found, he was obviously great at this new business endeavor. As great as he was at On Target Media and P&G. And I asked him to give me a call. To give our friendship another chance.

I anxiously awaited a response. One day, one week, two weeks. Nothing. Despite my divinely-inspired efforts, I got zero response.

Maybe the Rabbis don't really know what they're talking about.

"So be it," I told myself, erecting my defensive walls, the self-preservation instinct kicking in. If that's the way Charlie wanted it, then I guess that's the way it would have to be. A friendship must be a two-way street.

My belief in the Power of Common History was diminished.

19

The New Economy And The Old James Brown

"Toto, I've a feeling we're not in Kansas anymore."

Those famous words spoken by Dorothy Gale to her little dog in the *Wizard of Oz* were no less descriptive of the world of internet start-up's in the late 1990's than the imaginary Land of Oz itself. It was an age of the *New Economy* and the catchphrase of the time was "The Internet Changes Everything."

For a while, at least, it seemed that the internet *did* change everything.

Take, for example, a business meeting. Business meetings were totally different in the latter part of the 90's than in the earlier years of the decade. First, take attire. In the late 90's, no ties. In fact, no suits either. Barely even shirt collars. Jeans, t shirts, Hawaiian shirts, shorts. Sweatshirts or sweaters in the winter. Whatever you're comfortable in. Shoes? Allen Edmunds and Cole Haan would have gone hungry. Sneakers. Wallaby's. Flip flops. The Casual Friday of the early 90's was *every* day in the late 90's. Actually it was more like Saturday-level casual.

Conference rooms? Hah! Forget 'em. Unnecessary expense. Leave them for the bankers and VC's (venture capitalists) -- the people scornfully referred to as *suits*. All you needed was a laptop that ran Microsoft PowerPoint software and an internet connection. Maybe a portable overhead projector if there were more than three people. Nothing printed; printed matter was way too *old economy*. The preferred venue for meetings became coffee houses, bars, parks, restaurants. It didn't matter. The more comfortable, the better. The less conventional, *even* better.

Business cards? Soooo *my dad*. If you wanted to exchange contact information, you simply pulled out your Palm Pilot and with the swipe of the stylus, you would *beam* your contact information to the other person. It would automatically create an entry for you in that person's address book. What could be easier? If you didn't carry a Palm Pilot and exchange information in this manner, it sent a not-so-subtle message that you really didn't get the new economy. It would have been like wearing a letter jacket to a 1960's protest sit-in.

It seemed that the more counter-culture you behaved, the more credibility you exuded. The more you eschewed the norms of the culture of the old economy, the more hip you were to the culture of the new economy.

Which created some challenges for me because I lived *between* the cultures. I was a product of the old economy and it was hard to shed that baggage. But I was also part of the start-up world and the new economy. As Matthew had so aptly put it, I had both *Fortune 500 cred* from my P&G days (my tie-wearing years) and *Inc 500 cred* from my On Target Media days. Sure, that was start-up cred, but it wasn't *internet* start-up cred. It was not new economy.

I didn't adapt quite as quickly as I might have hoped. I was still mired in some of the conventions of the past. Sure I could carry a Palm Pilot and beam with the best of them. And I loved the new norms for office attire for sure.

But there were some new economy notions that were just hard for me to accept.

Let me give you an example. I planned my first trip to Silicon Valley to visit with some of the largest and well-known Venture Capital firms. My purpose was to peak their interest in Main Street Ventures and some of our incubating companies. I flew to San Francisco, rented a car and headed down Highway 101 toward Silicon Valley. I had pre-arranged meetings all through the hallowed land – Menlo Park, Palo Alto, Mountain View, Santa Clara and of course, the famed Sand Lake Road. If you were a savvy investor in technology, these were Jerusalem, Mecca and Medina.

My conclusions from these visits: I was a dinosaur. The internet had changed everything, except perhaps *me*. Don't get me wrong - all our MSV companies were truly internet start-ups. They certainly employed internet- and software-based technologies. They were disruptive concepts that addressed expressed needs in the marketplace.

Apparently, what I didn't understand was how to *fund* these companies. I kept telling the Silicon Valley VC firms about how helpful MSV was in training these entrepreneurs to burn capital slowly, to extend their cash runway until the moment was right to maximize value for investors, to efficiently utilize their resources until they got breakthrough opportunities with customers. I explained how we helped them focus resources on gaining success with high profile reference accounts so that they would have the credibility that comes with success. I explained how we worked closely with personal reference groups of experienced and capable angel investors, who provided not only start-up capital, but also mentoring to the young firms.

I thought that would impress the VC's. I thought they'd be surprised to hear that our companies were getting such guidance in such an usual place as the Midwest.

I was politely told that was *all well and good*, but what really mattered was a single number – 100. One hundred? What the hell were they talking about? What was all this Zen mystery around the number 100?

It was simple. The Silicon Valley VC's wanted to meet start-up's that met two criteria: 1) they had at least 100 employees; and 2) they needed at least $100 million in investment to drive them to an IPO. No LESS than $100 million.

WHAT? 100 employees and $100 million? I was aghast. What did those two figures have to do with a winning business plan? I was informed by these new scions of capital that *everything has changed* – winning business plans were for business school papers. Silicon Valley was rewriting the rules for business. Deals were done on the back of napkins now and that once a company was funded, it was simply a race to take it public as soon as possible. That was The Goal.

Therein lay the problem. The business models we were espousing in our incubator were built on proven concepts:

1) breakthrough ideas that dramatically changed marketplaces through technology;

2) requiring limited funding to achieve them; and

3) could get to cash flow positive *before* going public

Didn't the Silicon Valley VC's *get* that these were tried and true concepts with decades of evidence indicating these were the rails on which to drive growth trains?

Apparently, these concepts were antiquated notions, decried as old economy concepts. Apparently, generating revenue and cash flow weren't really *necessary* in the internet revolution. Apparently, giant losses were OK as long as it was a commensurately *giant* idea. Apparently, accounting didn't matter.

I was politely told that I didn't get it. Everything had changed and I was going to need to change with it.

In some ways, they were right. The notion of businesses actually generating revenues and, dare I say, make money, *were* antiquated – at least within this weird bubble of time. Because the public markets were buying what these Silicon Valley VC's were selling. There were IPO's flying all over the place for companies whose websites generated more eyeballs than revenue – and in some cases actually generated *zero* revenue. The venture capital firms were making hereto unforeseen financial returns – literally billions in profits in a matter of months, not years. Who was I to tell them they were *wrong?* I had to consider whether I was, in fact, the one who was wrong.

What few realized at the time, including me, was while many of these IPO's later fizzled and the businesses themselves cratered after the DotCom bubble burst in 2000, the Venture Capital firms smartly sold much of their stakes in their portfolio companies during the company's IPO, generating huge and immediate returns for their investors. Huge returns, of course, was their *primary objective*. Creating businesses that were built to last was a Jim Collins idea that would come in later years for other businesses.

The VC's objective was the IPO itself. They often kept small stakes in the firms after cashing out at the IPO, which provided some further upside for their investors if the business did per chance find a lasting toehold. This was sometimes called the *lottery ticket*. Perhaps the business would keep on creating value; but if not, the VC didn't really care. Because they had already made their money through the IPO; the VC had already hit the *real* lottery. For the VC, the IPO was generally the *end* of their journey. The entrepreneur and his company were just the vehicle to get there.

That's when I learned that internet investing VC's never claimed to be great judges of business models; they just claimed to get outsized returns for their investors. *And that's what they were in business to do.*

The VC model wanted companies that needed $100 million because they didn't want to divide up their multi-billion funds into more than 20-30 or so investments. Otherwise, it would be hard for a few fund managers to guide their small set of portfolio companies to the IPO. It had nothing to do with developing a business to success. It had everything to do with getting "in" and getting "out" at the right time, buying low and selling high, leaving someone else holding the bag.

While these were clearly smart guys, I wasn't really sure they were the right type of investors for MSV businesses. And MSV businesses, in large part, didn't really fit their target start-up. However, I did want to get their feedback on what we were doing to hear what they had to say. I wanted their perspective even if it didn't come with their money. At least for now.

———

"So how did the West Coast trip go?" asked Matthew Mazeroski, my favorite attorney, as he brought over a pair of Guinness Draughts to the table. Not a Great Lakes Christmas Ale. Not a 93 rating. Tasty, nonetheless.

"Guinness? Brilliant!" I always liked those Guinness TV commercials.

"Was your trip equally 'brilliant'?" Matthew persisted.

"'Educational' is the better descriptor."

"How so?"

"I learned a lot about the New Economy."

"How's that?"

"Well, the New Economy works for the VC's and investment bankers who can make quick hits and huge returns on IPO's. But it's not always so good for the entrepreneur. Or the average investor."

"I dunno. It seems like it worked pretty good for the guys at Up 4 Sale." Matthew was quietly unconvinced. One of his hallmarks. And he was right. $75 million. For code written in $2 per square foot, pizza box-ridden office space.

"Yes, you are correct. It did work well for them. Perhaps because they didn't have VC investors in their business, and didn't have to go public to sell their company. Nor did they have to deal with hitting quarterly numbers and then face Wall Street analysts. They experienced a lightning strike. You can't count on that all the time."

"I see. So are you saying VC's are bad?" Matthew did enjoy a bit of intellectual banter. And perhaps seeing if I'd trap myself in my own logic. Which I was prone to doing.

"No. I wouldn't say VC's are bad. VC's serve a vital role in funding start-up's, perhaps even for a few of those in MSV. They can provide a significant amount of capital that just isn't available anywhere else in that quantity and on those terms. No one else is willing to take those kind of risks with their money. Plus, there's a lot to learn from VC's especially about investing in start-up's. That said, I'm just not sure the VC model is the only model we should encourage for MSV start-up's. I think of it as one arrow in the quiver of funding options. Albeit, an important and highly visible arrow that we should encourage when it's right."

"Makes sense to me. Sounds like the trip was worthwhile then. Learn anything else?"

"Yeah. I used each of the meetings to get feedback from the various VC's on a couple of the elevator pitches for MSV companies." An elevator pitch is the two minute description of a company's basic business idea. It's called an elevator pitch because you have to be able to summarize the basic idea and communicate it during the average time you'd spend with a VC during an elevator ride. If it's not easily understandable in the elevator, then you usually don't get invited into the office.

"Almost all of them responded positively to two new MSV companies in particular — VisualNet Communications and Digital Rx."

"Is that so?" replied Matthew with a broadening smile. Matthew was the primary investor in VisualNet Communications. "Sit tight, I'll go grab two more beers and we'll talk more."

———

FIRM HANDSHAKES. SMILES all around. "OK, you've got a deal," squeaked the Mouse.

Stablehand Advisors LLC had just signed a new agreement to serve as the CEO of VisualNet Communications to reconstruct and reposition its primary product ConnectMail. I would spend up to half of my time working on ConnectMail, leading its existing team of three. The objective was to reconceive ConnectMail, build its software engine, put together a new business plan, and obtain sufficient funding to get the business to cash flow positive. Oh, is that all?

What intrigued the VC's about ConnectMail was not what it *was* but what it *could be*. What ConnectMail was at the time was a kiosk that would sit in malls or college student centers. Think of it as a modern photo booth where you would send video email instead of having pictures taken. For a couple of bucks, anyone could stand in front of the kiosk and record a short video that could be emailed to friends. The VC feedback was that it was an interesting piece of technology being underutilized as a single use novelty experience rather than as a daily communication tool.

I had to admit it - they were right. Matthew raised sufficient capital to pay for my services along with VisualNet's three other employees for a year. During that time, we'd have to develop something interesting enough to generate further funding.

Such was the challenge of any start-up – do enough with this slug of money to engender enough confidence to garner you the next slug of money. Step by step. Like football, march down the field, gain enough yardage with each set of four downs to get a first down, and to earn you another set of four downs. As you march down the field, you get smarter, you build momentum, and eventually, you push the ball over the goal line and score the touchdown.

....And just hope you don't get sacked and have to punt.

———

I REALLY ENJOYED the walk to 1201 Main Street from the parking garage two and half blocks away. Blazing concrete hot, or icy, freeze-your-ears-off cold – it didn't matter. Walking the streets of Over the Rhine had purpose to me. I was honored to engage in it each day.

The brass key turned in the front door lock to 1201 and the radiated warmth enveloped me. The wide wooden staircase of the four story building wound around the corners of the atrium. MSV occupied the third story, so the exercise felt good through the two flights of stairs. The second brass key opened the MSV door, as I entered the single large room and saw the now familiar random plank wooden floors, exposed red brick walls, floor to ceiling windows, radiated heat, CAT-5 cable extending across the tin ceilings like spider webs because you couldn't run them through the plaster or brick walls. I could take it all in and find myself smiling once again.

The single closet adjoining the room housed the racks of servers, the computer stacks that ran MSV companies. The one small bathroom was always so cold without its own heat. The Herman Miller furniture sprawled all over the room in random patterns, creating the showroom Herman's minions desired. The collective Planet Feedback team spread over 90% of the space as they had grown like weeds, which we welcomed. They were MSV's new lead start-up. The last 10% of the space, closest to the Main Street windows, housed the small, three person ConnectMail team – plus me.

New Economy or not, I still relished the Monday morning sessions where we heard the stories of the weekend – a tradition I brought from my previous employers. We all huddled in the corner, hovering over whatever form of warm liquids we possessed – coffee, tea, hot chocolate – Monday Fuel.

Raymar Jersey was ConnectMail's sales leader. Raymar was a stylish dude, nary a hair out of place, bright eyed and bushy-tailed, and ready for the hunt. His wispy, dark hair, tussled, but perfectly placed, dared not touch his ears. His white teeth nearly met the vertical dimples that formed on his cheeks with his ever-present smile.

Raymar craved three things – the newest breath mints, a cool pen, and human contact. He was the proverbial Myers Briggs "E" – which meant he derived energy from being with people and loved to interact with them. He was also a master at making people feel good about themselves. Those reasons, among others, were why he was a successful sales person and particularly good at opening doors.

Raymar was dressed in a suit and tie that morning, uncommon duds on Main Street.

"What's up with the suit?" asked Jay Birch, ConnectMail's project manager and Raymar's former college roommate. They had traded in roommates for wives, a move that behooved them immeasurably. Jay was a unique mix of project manager and visual designer. He loved the creative pursuit and project managing gave him an effective role in the pursuit.

"Headed to California today to call on Logitech," responded Raymar.

"But why the suit?" echoed Cray Liggins, ConnectMail's resident techie and chief coder. Cray was tall and angular, and thought with the same linear focus. As a software architect, he lived in a black and white world – the code ran or it didn't. No in-between. No emotion. He thought in spreadsheets and liked things that fit neatly into boxes. If they didn't, it frustrated him ever so slightly, but always kept him a bit curious. "Who wears a suit anymore?"

"Funny you should ask," responded Raymar, and you just knew a story that was going to make us smile was to emerge.

"You see, about a month ago, I got a call from my brother. He was at Jos. A. Bank – at one of their numerous crazy sales. With this sale, you buy one suit at regular price, you get a second suit for free, and a third one for $99. Two suits was more than enough for him, so he wanted to know if I wanted to come and get the third one for $99. How do you turn down a Bank's suit for $99? You don't. So I hopped in the car and headed over. Found the perfect suit, got it fitted for alterations, and took delivery two weeks ago. I was fired up for this trip because I'd get to wear my new suit."

"But you've had the suit you're wearing today for years," said Jay, an observation only a former roommate could offer.

"I know," replied Raymar, with a sudden and somewhat sullen change in demeanor.

"So where's the new suit?" asked Cray.

"Well, I put it on this morning, all fired up for this call. You know, Logitech makes the webcams that consumers need to utilize ConnectMail's video software. A relationship with them would be huge for us – what if they want us to co-develop software? What if they will give us a deal we can offer our customers on discounted webcams? What if they like the idea so much they want to invest in us? Or maybe even acquire us one day? The opportunities are endless with them so this call is a *big* meeting."

"Yeah, go on," urged Jay, wondering where this was going.

"So, I put on the new suit. Even had a new shirt and tie. Buffed myself up, looked in the mirror, and gave myself the killer smile – the smile, you know, I'd give the Logitech guys....and hopefully, a Logitech girl. The killer smile works better on girls than guys."

"Right, *married man*," prodded Cray. "Like there's anything you'd actually do about that, being as whipped as you are."

"Regardless, this is a big day and I had to not only look on top of the world, I had to feel on top of the world."

"And what happened?" asked Jay, seeming to understand his buddy's budding concern.

"Well, all I could do was look in the mirror and look at myself and ask 'can you really *kill it* today in a $99 suit?'"

"What are you talking about?"

"How was I going to be on top of my game if I knew I was wearing a $99 suit? Who *kills it* in a $99 suit? I mean, really? It's a friggin' $99 suit!!"

We all looked at each other, wondering if this was a joke. When I was sure it was and was about to laugh, it occurred to me that Raymar was serious.

"Raymar, buddy," interjected Cray, with his Spock-like powers of logic, "you do realize that it's not *actually* a $99 suit. It's just the way they structured the promotion to get you to buy 3 suits for roughly $100 more than their regular price for one suit. They're just discounting a perfectly good suit to generate revenue while also moving inventory." I thought Cray explained it quite well.

"Yeah, in my left brain, I get that," responded Raymar. "But in my right brain, as I look in the mirror, I can't help but tell myself, 'you can't kill it in a $99 suit.' And there's no two ways around it, today, I have to *kill it* at Logitech."

"OK, so are you wearing the suit you can 'kill it' in today?" I asked, trying to spare Raymar the embarrassment of having to explain his logic, or lack thereof, to two of the more logical people on this earth. I also realized this negative talk was not what Raymar needed on the day of a big call. "Are you ready to 'kill it' on the left coast?"

"Absolutely," boasted Raymar, grabbing a broomstick like it was a microphone stand and breaking into his best James Brown imitation.

"I feel good, na na na na na nah,

Like I knew that I would, na na na na na nah,

I feeeeeel good; na na na na na nah,

Like I knew that I would yeah, na na na na na nah,

So Good, bahmp bahmp, So good, bahmp bahmp

I've got you! Bahmp bahmp bahmp bahmp! Hey!!"

And with that we broke into an air band, with bass, sax and drums, supporting Raymar. The Planet Feedback guys all looked over, shook their heads and smiled. It was not unusual to see unconventional office behavior on Main Street. Just one of the many reasons it was a great place to work.

"Well, speaking of James Brown, that's the perfect segue to something that happened this weekend," said Cray.

"Don't tell me," blurted Raymar in his best voice that sounded like Eddie Murphy when he did his James Brown impression on *Saturday Night Live*. "Don't tell me you got you a *hot tub!*"

"Well, not exactly," as we all laughed, incapable of resisting that JB imitation. "But I do have a James Brown story you will not believe. As you guys may remember, my sister is married to a tax attorney and lives in Augusta, Georgia – which coincidentally is James Brown's home town. He was born there and lives there when he's not on the road. So on Saturday afternoon, my brother-in-law gets a call at home."

"Tell me it wasn't James Brown," said Jay.

"Indeed it was......and the story goes like this...."

James: "I got a letter from the IRS. Says I owe them a lot of money. My friends all say that you are THE MAN in Augusta to make this go away. Think you can help me?"

Attorney: "I can certainly try, Mr. Brown. Let's get together first thing Monday in my office. You bring your tax records over and I'll clear my calendar for you."

James: "No can do. I'm headed out on tour tomorrow. I really need to see you today."

Attorney: "Well, uh, OK, Mr. Brown. I can make that work. The only problem is my office is getting painted this weekend, so it would be hard to meet there."

James: "How 'bout I come to your house?"

Attorney: "Well, sure I guess that would work. I live on Tripps Circle, right off Walton Way."

James: "I know right where that is. I'll be there in half an hour."

"Half an hour later, the doorbell rings, and it is none other than James Brown, in the flesh. And my brother-in-law welcomes him in," continues Cray, enjoying telling the story.

Attorney: "Come right in and sit down, Mr. Brown. Can I get you something to drink?"

James: 'Thank you, no. I can only stay a few minutes. So you think you can help me?"

Attorney: "I don't rightly know yet. I'll have to see the records first."

James: "I got 'em in a box right out in the car."

"And so they went outside, popped the trunk to the car and James Brown handed him a box that contained a copy of every LP Album he had ever recorded. Yes, when James Brown heard 'bring your records', that is exactly what he did!"

James: "What's wrong, you wanted my records right? What? You don't like my music????"

"C'mon!," exclaimed Jay. "You made that up! That can't be true."

"Here's the picture of my sister, her husband, James, and the full collection of his records. Yes, it really happened."

Sometimes, the truth is better than fiction. And the truth on Main Street was always better than fiction

20

THE DOT COM WORLD –
THE THEATRE OF THE ABSURD

It was Monday morning and First Watch in Kenwood was buzzing. Of course, all early morning business meetings on the east side of Cincinnati were going to happen in one of three restaurants. For the manufacturing community, it would have been the Sugar 'n Spice on Reading Road in Norwood. Not too far from the old GM plant. Good old blue collar neighborhood. Eggs, bacon, hash browns. Coffee. Juice. Simple. Get it done.

For the banking community, it was The Echo on Hyde Park Square. In one of the more upscale east side neighborhoods. Drop the kid off at school and head over to The Echo for breakfast. Same fare as Sugar 'n Spice. Same discussions. But different clientele. Some people would eat there just to be seen there. The thought process: "I must be someone in the banking community if I'm seen reading my Wall Street Journal and drinking my coffee at The Echo."

For the New Economy players, it was First Watch. You could get eggs there, but they'd be in a frittata. You could get pancakes, but they'd be an apple, walnut, banana and whole wheat pancake. Better yet, maybe a yogurt smoothie and a bran muffin instead. The New Economy; The New Menu.

No matter what you ate, or where you ate it, your objective was the same: *business*. Or as they would say in my Southern home town: *bidness*.

This particular Monday morning, I was meeting Ron Conklin and Bud Kennedy from Whittman-Hart for breakfast at their request. Whittman-Hart sold outsourced software development services. I had met Bud Kennedy on Main Street and liked him as soon as I met him. Bud was 5'-10" and stocky, with the strut and stature of a former football player. The notes of gray hair at his temples gave him an air of experience that was uncommon in the New Economy. Like me, Bud was on the *older* side of the New Economy, which meant we were in our late 30's and rounding 40. Bud had been through a few start-up's himself, some successful and some not so successful, similar to most who had worked in start-up's Bud had the *been there, done that* experience a lot of his compatriots at Whittman-Hart lacked. Including Ron Conklin, his boss.

Bud was Vice President of Business Development; Ron was the new General Manager of the Cincinnati office. Ron had just turned 30 and was a Sales superstar. Ron had taken Whittman-Hart's basic model of selling outsourced software programming resources to mega-corporations to a new height in Cincinnati. His red curly hair, freckles and John Lennon/John Denver rounded spectacles gave him a certain boyish charm, an affability that formed the platform for the selling machine that he had become.

After a kind exchange of pleasantries and a little moaning about the performance of the Cincinnati Bengals that weekend, I officially called the meeting to order. "So what is it I can do for you guys?"

"Maybe it's more like what we can do for you," Bud offered with a bit of a Midwestern hint in his accent.

"Whittman-Hart has already extremely gracious in helping Main Street Ventures and we really appreciate it," I responded, endeavoring to thank those that helped our little not-for-profit enterprise. Whittman-Hart had donated money and time as Bud served on our Board of Directors.

"And we're happy to help MSV. It's a great organization serving a great purpose. But this morning, we're here to talk about ConnectMail," interjected Ron with a certain deliberateness that I caught.

"What's on your mind?" asked the Mouse.

"We understand that you've secured a small round of funding and are going to be redeveloping the ConnectMail software from kiosk-based to web-based delivery. We've expanded our capabilities at Whittman-Hart and have a lot of talent that could be applied to your project. Especially in the areas of web interface design and the codecs necessary for the compression algorithms required for video." It was clear

Ron and Bud had done their homework – and had their proverbial ear to the street. I liked that.

"Well, Ron, you've now delved into a depth of software expertise that exceeds my knowledge base, which doesn't usually take very long. We'll have to bring my team in to understand that capability. But even before we get to a software development capability discussion, I mean, are we even in the same ballpark from a price standpoint? You guys write code for Procter & Gamble and GE data centers. Those guys have budgets that a start-up like ours couldn't touch. And while we have raised some money, we didn't raise the kind of money that could afford Whittman-Hart prices." I wanted to see how easily deterred they were…or misinformed.

Apparently, not very. They were on a mission.

"We understand that the pricing structure for writing code for start-up's is going to be different than for P&G and GE," said Bud, with a clarity indicating he knew quite well what I was saying. "We are quite aware that we have a reputation for being priced in a league that wouldn't be possible for start-up's. Which creates a bit of a PR problem for us."

"We think we need to develop our business in different markets," Ron jumped in quickly. "A little diversification, if you will. And doing web development for start-up's is the kind of diversification we need – one in which we clearly have capability, but have not really pursued. It's time for us to jump in. It's time for us to pursue this business and we're starting right here, right now. We look at our capabilities and the type of programming you'll need to make ConnectMail work and we think there's a fit."

"Let's assume that, from a technical perspective, there is a fit. Because honestly, I'm not smart enough to assess that. But for sake of argument, let's assume so. I have enough money to hire a few guys to write code for ConnectMail, but I don't have the capital required to pay for a cadre of Whittman-Hart developers nor am I in a position to start offering equity in ConnectMail in exchange for work. So how do you think an arrangement with us might work?" I figured I'd toss out the challenge *point blank* and see what they're willing to do. What did I have to lose?

"Well we know that we've got to prove ourselves in this market. We also know you've got to prove the ConnectMail concept works to raise your next round of capital. So here's how we could help each other. What do you think of this idea: ConnectMail hires us to develop a working model of video email to your specification that you can use to prove that the technology works. Something that you could show to potential investors and customers. We charge you *nothing* for this work now. You pay us back when you use the model to secure your next round of funding for the business. That way you get a working model within your current financial constraints; and we get a reference account that shows our capabilities in web development for start-up's. It shows that we can do more than the big corporate work we're known for."

Well, as Popeye used to say, *blow me down*. I had to admit this sounded pretty good. Maybe too good. I had to poke at it a bit.

"So what happens if we can't successfully secure another round of funding?" asked the Mouse.

"That's our risk. If you don't have the money, clearly, you can't pay us. We lose out," said Ron. "But we don't think that will happen. You've got a good track record personally and we know we can develop the technology. So I think it's a manageable risk that I'm willing to take."

They didn't know that the ConnectMail development team had already been out taking stock of the market and getting estimates to develop this model. We just hadn't talked to Whittman-Hart yet. At least we thought they didn't know. And so far, it was looking like it would cost $250,000 or more to get a model developed. Gulp.

Until, perhaps, now....

"Hmmmm. Very intriguing, gentlemen. And I thank you for your interest. We're quite flattered that you'd want to do such a program with ConnectMail. Tell you what, why don't we set up a meeting for my team to come talk with the Whittman-Hart team you'd assemble for this project and we'll make an assessment of technical capability and personal compatibility. You can also get the information you need from us to scope the project and tell us what we'll, at least eventually, owe you for this work. How does that sound?"

"Sounds like a plan," beamed Ron, very proud of himself. Could he sell or what?

I enjoyed the rest of my healthy banana apple walnut whole wheat pancake. Slathered in syrup.

———

"So what's the catch?" asked Matthew Mazeroski a few days later as he watched the waitress place two Harpoon Winter Warmers on the table.

"Is this really a cold beer called 'Winter Warmer'?" I asked. "That seems rather contradictory."

"Yes, it's a problem for English professors, but not for me. Try it. You'll like it. If you don't, then feel free to get a Miller Light."

"How very kind of you. For the record, I happen to like Miller Light. I was raised on Miller beer; Miller High Life, in fact. It's the 'Champagne of Bottled Beer.'"

"Please don't confuse my interest in beer variety with snootiness. I am above no beer."

That is one of the many things I like about Matthew. He is very democratic, especially for a Republican.

"So, I repeat," said Matthew, "what's the catch in this Whittman-Hart deal? Sounds too good to be true."

"Yes, it did to me, also. I've turned over a bunch of rocks and I'm struggling to find the catch. After looking at the detailed proposal and terms, it's pretty straightforward: they do the work. We pay them out of the proceeds of our next capital raise – if and when we do it. They have no claim to any patents developed nor an equity stake in the business. They're essentially an unsecured creditor."

"And do you believe the story of what's in it for them?" inquired Matthew, sniffing around all the angles, as any good lawyer would.

"You know Whittman-Hart as well as I. You can see the whole transformation they're putting themselves through – from software specialist for the Fortune 500 to cool developers to the dot com world. You see the office space they're taking and the non-software staff they're adding – project managers, graphic artists, copywriters, you name it. They're building a veritable advertising agency within a software development firm. Every time I see someone from Cincinnati's ad agency world, it seems they've joined Whittman-Hart. I think they're gearing up for their own IPO. This all feels very 'silicon valley' to me."

"Yes, I've noticed that. If they're doing in other cities what they're doing in Cincinnati, then something big is going on with them. OK, if you don't think we'll get lost in the shuffle and delay our timing then let's do it."

"On the contrary, I think it will accelerate our timing to market. They have people with the skill sets we need now and critical mass that I'd have to hire for. We'll get done in three months there what it would take us up to a year to do on our own. Plus we assume no risk and give up no equity. If we hire employees, we burn the cash we've already raised. This deal is like a free cash raise."

"What's the total amount we'll owe Whittman-Hart for the work when we're done?"

"Two hundred fifty thousand dollars."

"That's a chunk of change."

"It's also remarkably close to the other bids we were getting from other firms. This is a tight community I suspect. So I'd say it's a *market price*. It's about equal to about two and half developers fully loaded with taxes and benefits for a full year if I hired them myself. Instead, we get so much more talent than we could assemble on our own and we get the output in three months instead of twelve. It should save us cash burn of nine months of the rest of our overhead, too."

"Makes sense. OK, I'm on board. Sign the deal."

The Winter Warmer went down better than I expected. It's not a Miller, though.

———

DEVELOPMENT OF THE ConnectMail software and the working model went very well. By adding a small webcam to a desktop or laptop computer, you could go on line and access the ConnectMail website. Using a mouse you could simply point and click to record up to a 60 second video message. The software would automatically compress the video, upload it to a database over the internet that resided on the ConnectMail server, and send a notification to the email recipient(s).

The recipient would get a normal email message through their existing email system with the body of message indicating they had received a video email with an invitation to simply click on the link provided. The click would instruct the ConnectMail server to begin streaming the video. The video would play uninterrupted for up to 60 seconds using a turtle-slow dial-up connection. We even tried it on the MSV wireless network and the video streamed without interruption. Amazing. No waiting for files to upload, no cryptic software messages to figure out. Nothing complex. Just some easy points and clicks, and just sit back and watch it all happen.

"So what do you think?" beamed Ron Conklin after the demonstration of the system, knowing precisely what the answer would be. Ron was quite proud of what his team had done and rightly so.

"It's everything we hoped it would be. Pretty cool, I think," replied the Mouse. Of course, this was not the first time I had seen it. This was our business; you didn't just go away for three months and hope the outsources created what you wanted. I had been watching the progress daily! But I wanted to give Ron his *moment*.

"Delivered as promised, on time, too, Ron. I really appreciate the work you and your team have done for ConnectMail. People are gonna love this" I gushed.

"Thanks. We appreciate the opportunity to show what we can do. How's your business plan coming?" asked Ron. A curious question coming from him, but I guess it would be fair for him to start wondering when he might get paid. After all, he didn't get paid until we raised our next round of capital.

"We finished the business plan last week. I've been previewing it conceptually with five or six venture capital firms. You know you have to *date around* a bit to build relationships with these firms before investors decide to write you a check. They want to see how you progress over a period of time. I've built up the promise of ConnectMail in these meetings. But no words can hold a candle to actually seeing it work. I think this demonstration will be pretty visually impactful."

"That's very good to hear. But is 'visually impactful' the best you can do? I think it will *blow them away*," boasted Ron, who did nothing in a sedate fashion.

As the two of us shook hands and walked away from the crowd, I asked Ron quietly, "So how are the discussions going on Wall Street regarding Whittman-Hart's initial public offering of stock?" I knew Ron would want to talk about how rich he was going to become. It had been mentioned in the *Wall Street Journal* that week.

"The investment bankers are pricing the IPO this week. It will start trading next week. Bob Bernard is going to be a billionaire." Bob Bernard was Ron's boss, the primary shareholder and CEO of Whittman-Hart. I wanted to ask Ron what his share of the proceeds was going to be, but I thought that to be a bit gauche. Besides, the programmers would be scouring the web for details and then cackling about it – as they always do – so we'd find out later.

Ron continued, "Speaking of Bob Bernard, he's coming to Cincinnati as soon as he rings the opening bell at the Stock Exchange. He's asked me to prepare a review of the most exciting projects we're working on. We intend to show him ConnectMail as our prize project."

"That's great. I'm glad you think that much of the technology," I demurred.

"Well, I'd like you and your team to be present when we demonstrate it for Bob," Ron requested.

"Sure. If that will help you with Bob. Just tell us when and where."

"Thanks. By the way, did you hear that coincident with the IPO, we're rebranding Whittman-Hart?"

"No. I hadn't. Rebranded as what?"

"MarchFirst."

"What?"

"Seriously. Our company name will be MarchFirst – one word. You know, as in to *march forward*, to *lead*. And of course, it coincides with the IPO date – March 1, 2001. Is that cool or what?"

Ron clearly thought so. And I was not going to burst his bubble.

"*Very* cool," I replied with a smile, much to Ron's pleasure. It had to be the most ridiculous thing I'd seen yet in this crazy dot com world so far....and *that* was saying something. Little did I know that I hadn't seen *anything* yet....

———

"CONNECTMAIL HAS GOT to be the coolest thing I've ever seen," exclaimed Bob Bernard, CEO of the newest publicly held company in the United States, MarchFirst. "This is 2001 and this is definitely 21st century technology! I can't wait to tweak the guys in our San Francisco office on the cool development going on here in Cincinnati. They think they're the center of the software universe! Let's hear it for the Midwest!!" Bob was from Chicago and took great pride in one-upping the left coast.

All of Bob's minions gathered in the large conference room echoed his glee with Ron leading the pack. It was good to see Ron share the credit with Bud Kennedy and the development team, something Sales guys don't always do. Maybe Ron was maturing a bit as a general manger.

Bob turned his eyes on me. "Michael, so what's your business plan for ConnectMail look like?"

Everyone got quiet. I was not anticipating this question but as a start-up CEO, you've always got to be ready to sell the vision! I figured he wanted more than the elevator pitch though. He'd already seen the best pitch I could give – the software in action.

"We've divided the market into two segments – consumer and enterprise. We envision the consumer version integrating seamlessly with web-based, carrier class email systems like Openwave's, that's offered by most telephone companies and internet service providers. The enterprise version will have to integrate with the Lotus Notes and Microsoft Exchange email systems," I offered, hoping to establish that we'd done our homework. "It can't look markedly different than the email client the user is already comfortable with and these companies spent years defining."

"Makes sense. What's the revenue model?" Bob asked. Finally, SOMEONE in the New Economy asked a meaningful question about generating revenue! What a comfort. I was starting to like this guy, despite the whole goofy MarchFirst thing.

"Well we've still got some proving out of this theory to do which will be part of our next stage of development of the company. But preliminarily we're thinking we will sell ConnectMail as an add-on to your basic internet service in the consumer model. In the same way HBO is an add-on to your cable television package, you can have ConnectMail for an extra few dollars added to your monthly bill. We'll revenue-share those dollars with the internet service provider. Since they have the infrastructure already set up they do the billing, collections, etc., and send us a check each month for our share.

It's less clear on the enterprise side since corporations will have to buy webcams for employees to enable the program. We're thinking of a site-license model where the corporation basically pay a one-time upfront fee. We want to avoid on-going billing which could be cumbersome and create a lot of staff costs. If we establish both models successfully, we will get two types of revenue streams – a steady, ongoing one, and one with big, hopefully regular, hits."

"Lessee. Hmm," Bob thought carefully. "When you think of the number of people with an email box, even if you could net a dollar a month for the service, that adds up to an awful lot of dollars pretty fast - just on the consumer side of the model."

"Yessir. It does. We've begun to design consumer research on this that would initially validate the ConnectMail concept and positioning. The second step would then allow consumers to try the system MarchFirst has built. Participants in the study will send and receive ConnectMail messages and then rate their experience so we can understand how well it lives up to the promise. The third step would help us nail down the price point that maximizes revenue for the experience. We'll need to find the right balance between price and penetration of the product into the marketplace that maximizes profitability. It's a tried and true consumer testing model we've experienced dozens of times at P&G."

"I like it. I haven't seen consumer products thinking applied like this in software yet, but it certainly makes sense. How much money do you think you'll have to raise to get ConnectMail to cash flow positive? And how many rounds of funding do you anticipate?" Another set of good questions! I was really starting to like this guy. He seemed to have solid Midwest sensibilities. I also wondered if he was trying to figure out when he might get paid for the work they'd done.

"Actually, based on Ron's team's estimates we're thinking it'll take $2 million or so to fully develop the software to integrate on both the consumer and enterprise sides. Plus, we think we'll need another $2 million or so in operating capital. This really isn't a capital-intensive endeavor because the telephone, cable companies, and corporations host the system and pay for the infrastructure to run it. The user base then scales really fast especially given that you've only got a handful of carrier-class email systems and email providers, like Hotmail. It's a fairly concentrated market. One installation and you can hit tens of millions of potential users."

"So $4 million is what you've got to raise?"

"Give or take. Plus the $250k I'll need to pay you guys for the working model you developed. I've been having a number of conversations with funding sources now and explained the business model with our projections. There's a lot of interest. I believe seeing this model work will be the icing on the cake to push us over the top and get us to some term sheets." (Term sheets were the preliminary steps to getting financing.)

"Well, you'll need no other funding sources," said Bob, with a flash of fury on his face.

"Come again?" I was not quite sure what he meant or the sudden change of tone. He became *very focused*. His eyes bore down on me in a way I had not experienced before. It was almost as if he were willing himself telepathically into my brain. Then, in contrast to the look in his eye, his voice softened.

"I like this idea, Michael. I like it a lot. The business model makes sense; the software is differentiated. With some of the proceeds from the MarchFirst IPO, I have started my own investment fund. I'll use that to fund your $4 million. I *want* to fund this deal -- as long as you let MarchFirst do the development of the software. In fact, we'll do more than that. We'll do the branding, we'll do the testing, we'll do the user interface and operability work, we'll do it all. We'll fund your travel costs. We'll be your bank. Just say yes to letting us be your investor and partner on this."

Wow! I was blown away. I wasn't sure what to say. "What about the $250k we owe you already?" That was about all I could come up with.

"We'll roll that into the deal. Call it a $4.25 million funding. Hell, tell you what. Start-up's always have unanticipated costs. Let's just round it up to $5 million, with the $250k rolled in too. Bud, email Michael a term sheet this afternoon. I want this closed by the end of the week. We have no time to waste on an idea like this."

Apparently, Bob Bernard did want to MarchFirst.

—◦◦◦◦—

"HE SAW IT for the first time in the meeting, asked you a few questions and offered to fund it with $5 million — *on the spot?*" Matthew was equally shocked as I reported the day's events.

We both went silent for a moment and let the words *$5 million* linger in the air a moment while the waitress placed the two Kentucky Bourbon Barrel Ales on the table, served in glasses that look like brandy snifters.

"Is this beer served in its own special glass?" I asked the waitress, as I could immediately detect a sweet hint of bourbon aroma emanating from the beer. Plus, I wanted to shift the conversation while the waitress was present.

"Yes," she said. "The Distributor brings us these special glasses just for this beer."

"This is really unique," I said. "I've never tasted anything like this before."

"Concocted by a mad scientist in Lexington, Kentucky. Very wealthy guy. Loves to mess around with fermentation techniques and horse breeding." She seemed to know a lot about this.

"I'm glad he doesn't confuse the two," quipped Matthew. And that was the waitresses' cue to let us get back to our conversation as she laughed heartily and moved to the next table.

"So he rolled in the $250k we owe him into this funding, too?" asked Matthew.

"Yup, essentially, he's going to personally take a stake in ConnectMail to pay MarchFirst to do the work — past and future."

"What's the term sheet look like? How much of the company does he want to own in exchange for a $5 million investment?" Now we were getting down to brass tacks.

"That's the weirdest part of the whole day," I responded. "As if it could get any weirder. The term sheet came by email. I scoured it. Standard terms. Nothing unusual. What you'd expect. What amazed me was not what was in the term sheet, but what *wasn't* in it. No Board of Directors positions, no requirements to review progress or hit stage gates to get tranches of cash. No convertible debt or associated interest payments. The only thing it stipulated was a liquidation preference, which is really fairly standard in new rounds of funding."

A liquidation preference is essentially a way to ensure that in any type of *liquidity event* — any form of funding that would allow investors to cash out or take a cash return on their investment — Bob Bernard would get the first dollars to come out of the company.

"OK, but how much equity does he want for his $5 million? How much of ConnectMail does he expect to own?" repeated Matthew.

"Again. That *wasn't* in the term sheet. There was no offer. There was a *blank* in the document where the percentage ownership he expected to take would normally be specified. He was allowing us to fill in the amount. I guess he wants us to provide the opening salvo in this negotiation. He is going to let us set the valuation of the company." My eyes were as wide as saucers.

"You're kidding me." Matthew's eyes were now wider.

"Yeah, so I called Bud Kennedy and asked what the story was on that. Figured I'd fish around and see if this was some kind of trap. Kennedy reaffirmed Bob doesn't want to be on boards and he doesn't want management responsibility for his investments."

"That sounds like *code* for he's not expecting a big stake," ruminated Matthew.

"That's how I read it. What do you think we should offer in terms of equity? What do you think would be fair?"

"That would be the proverbial five million dollar question, wouldn't it?" said Matthew with the smile of the Cheshire cat.

So we concocted a plan...over another tasty Kentucky Bourbon Barrel Ale.

MATTHEW MAZEROSKI SAT at his desk in his law offices the next day, responding to emails in the few minutes he had before his next client meeting. He noticed a new email come in from Michael Elliot with a subject line "Fasten Your Seatbelt".

Matthew opened the email and whistled. He blinked his eyes and shook his head, as if to shake himself from something that he must have been reading wrong. He read it over again. And again. And then wished he had a cigar.

All the email said was:

$5 million, 8% equity, $40 million valuation. For a business with no revenues, no customers, and fewer employees than you have fingers on your right hand. Let's get this bad boy papered before they change their minds, Mr. Lawyer!

And, by the way, he gave me this.

Michael

Attached was a photo of something that looked to Matthew like the old metal charge card his mother used to use at the department store before plastic MasterCard and Visa credit cards were given to every man, woman and child on the earth. As Matthew studied the picture carefully, he realized that it was a photo of Bob Bernard's business card. Only it wasn't paper; it was metal. Yes, metal! And printed on it was Bob's name, phone number and email address.

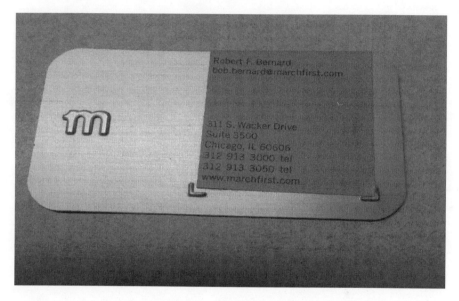

THE DOT COM era was most certainly the Theatre of the Absurd.

21

BLOWING THE BUBBLE

PERHAPS ONE OF the most quintessential signs of excess from the DotCom era was something called the Funding Party - a concept imported from the West Coast that even made its way to Cincinnati. The idea was a simple one: *Some VC's just gave you millions of dollars. Throw a party.* In *Animal House* parlance, that would roughly translate to: *Toga, Toga, Toga....*

Funding Parties on the West Coast became rather lavish events because of course, the fundings themselves were lavish. It was the opportunity for everyone to celebrate that the precious start-up, that was just a twinkle in an entrepreneur's eye, had become *real* enough to get funded. In San Francisco, funding parties became *de rigeur*, appearing with regularity in the society pages of the newspaper. And when that happens wide collections of people attend to be part of the celebration even if they had no idea what the start-up actually did.

Main Street in Cincinnati had its most lavish party when one of MSV's earliest start-up's, Planet Feedback, generated a "Series A Round," measured in the *tens* of millions of dollars, funded by a collection of venture capital firms in both Cincinnati and Silicon Valley. There were a lot reasons to celebrate - for Planet Feedback, for Main Street Ventures, for the City of Cincinnati, and for everyone who was dreaming of becoming an entrepreneur.

For Planet Feedback, the reasons to celebrate were quite obvious – someone just gave them a boatload of money!! The team at Planet Feedback put in a huge amount of work to even get funded, so it was only fair for them to take a little time to celebrate. For MSV, Planet Feedback's funding was the largest realization of the vision – that we could start technology companies in Over The Rhine that could not only garner tens of millions in investment, but could also garner the attention of both local and Silicon Valley venture capital firms. It proved that we didn't have to be on the West Coast or in Boston or New York to get attention in the New Economy. For the City of Cincinnati, well, ANY good news out of Over The Rhine was welcome news for sure.

While the Planet Feedback folks expected to fill one of our Main Street drinking establishments with perhaps 100 people, word spread fast, and before they knew it, over 350 people were spilling into the streets in celebration. Of course, the Main Street technology community attended, and the extended Cincinnati technology community attended – the stalwarts of the New Economy. The unexpected part was the attendance from the Old Economy - the television stations, the city council members, the chamber of commerce members and even a few aspiring politicians. We even hosted a new crowd. Evidently, a whole bunch of wanna-be entrepreneurs found themselves wondering if they should dump their Old Economy jobs and just give this New Economy thing a whirl.

The party was incredible. An incredibly bubbly spirit filled the space with an incredible collection of celebrating Cincinnatians. It likely generated two or three months' income for the host bar on that one night alone and created huge buzz for Planet Feedback. It was a shining example of how the New Economy could rapidly change fortunes.

Believe me, I wasn't one to pooh-pooh the Planet Feedback celebration. I was smack in the middle of it having as good a time as anyone. Maybe even better. It felt good to feel some wins for our budding community and for the Planet Feedback guys I knew so well who toiled next to our ConnectMail team day in and day out. It felt good to attract more faces to Main Street and too demonstrate the possibilities our little not-for-profit held out as promise for OTR and our fair city.

At the same time, I just didn't feel right throwing a funding party after we secured the $5 million investment from Bob Bernard for ConnectMail. Sure, having such a party was often justified by the *buzz* it created – it could cost more than the party to *buy* that kind of publicity. But ConnectMail was not *live* yet – we weren't ready for that kind of publicity.

It just felt a little premature to me for ConnectMail. Maybe we should party when we're making money for your investors, not just *attracting* it. Maybe I was still a little too Old Economy, a little too *Old School*, to go spend money that way. So when ConnectMail signed the funding deal with Bob Bernard, we did not have a funding party. Instead, we just got to work. Yup, call me what I am -- *Old School*.

A HUGE FLURRY of work began. We subscribed to the notion that you begin a huge project with the end in mind. So we spent an inordinate amount of time upfront flying around the country trying to understand what our customers (email purveyors) and our end users (either consumers or business people) want from our service.

Early meetings with customers such as Microsoft and IBM/Lotus Notes were very encouraging. They liked the idea of being able to take their current text only email systems to the next level of video. At the same time, they were non-committal as they could have filled *every* day with some company dangling some new idea and appearing as if they were just trying to get acquired. They wanted to encourage us but not *too much*.

The carrier-class email purveyors also warmed to ConnectMail. Since it cost them nothing to encourage us (and they could ultimately benefit from our success) they cheered us on too and we thrived on it. They helped us determine specifications and performance requirements for the system and brainstormed software interface methodologies and *skins* for the software – that is, how the system appeared to the user, i.e., the User Interface.

All of this was very helpful to us in our design phase. As we came to understand, if you don't know where you're going, you'll probably end up somewhere else.

Meanwhile, the MarchFirst and ConnectMail teams were busy as bees. MarchFirst brought in experts of all types – in computer usability, video compression, market research, branding and visual identity – a dizzying array of talent that was totally energizing. I kept asking Ron if his team was tracking the cost of all this. He indicated so although I suspected he had no idea what it all really cost. He kept telling me, "Don't worry, Michael. We'll do whatever it takes to get this working and operating in the marketplace."

And I believed him. So I just kept sending every bill I got to MarchFirst, other than the costs of the salaries of our four ConnectMail employees. Travel, t-shirts, testing – even costs that didn't begin with "t" – MarchFirst paid for it.

While the energy and feedback from potential customers was quite positive, I continued to be quite nervous because I couldn't see a concrete path to "yes". No matter who we talked with in our discussions with these huge customers, I had trouble defining exactly how and when the customer would actually buy it. The degree of inequity between a big corporation and a small startup is essentially the size of the Persian Gulf. When I tried to delicately pin a potential big customer down as to what we'd have to do to get to "yes", things got a little shaky, and this worried me.

I pushed and pushed, trying to understand why we were always encouraged by potential customers but no one would pull the trigger and actually buy it! Finally, I was able to pin down the concern. These big companies had trouble believing that whatever we developed in Cincinnati would be robust enough to work on systems the size of theirs, created in Silicon Valley. Aha! That's what I needed to find out! Whether the concern was valid or not was irrelevant – any lingering concern a customer has is a barrier to getting to "yes" and it must be addressed.

I also realized that to get the customer to "yes", I was going to have to create some incentive for them to move faster and to take even a modicum of risk. The problem was they were so big and we were so small. I was going to have to find a way to prove ConnectMail could operate effectively on a *carrier class* system (millions of users). At the same time, we had to incite consumer demand for the product. Finally, we had to create a competitive environment among the customers, so they would feel worried that they might lose out to someone else if they didn't move fast enough. While the team busily toiled on getting ConnectMail designed and built, I needed to solve these problems.

THE ANSWER CAME to me at a kids' soccer game one day.

I had run into Tommy O'Leary, an old P&G friend at the soccer game. Tommy's younger son and my middle son were the same age and their teams were playing each other in soccer. I had not seen Tommy in quite some time.

Tommy and I worked together in the Beauty Care Division at P&G. Tommy started in Sales and moved into Brand Management. We worked together very well and built business together when he was in Sales. We knew how to win together, which is not always so common with the fierce internal competition at P&G. By the time we had both become Marketing Directors, he and I were overseeing all of P&G's Hair Care brands in the US. We had a terrific working relationship.

Over time though, Tommy became frustrated with the somewhat plodding P&G ways. His patience for P&G's methodical analysis thinned over time. So he decided to take a job with another Cincinnati-based consumer products business at the time, Chiquita Foods, a company he believed made decisions faster and more decisively than P&G. Tommy moved to Geneva, Switzerland to become the General Manager of Chiquita's European business. I had not seen Tommy since he left for Europe a few years back.

"So this means you and Clarice are back in town?" I asked Tommy with a big smile.

"That would be so," he said with his thick Bostonian accent.

"So what are you doing with Chiquita now?"

"Decided to quit the banana business. I spent more time fighting with governments and human rights groups than selling bananas."

"Say what?" I had no idea what that was all about.

"Believe me, you don't want to know. But I could tell you stories that would curl your hair."

"OK, so what now?" It seemed best to move on.

"I came back here to work for Cincinnati Bell."

Cincinnati Bell was one of the smaller telecom systems that was created when the US government broke up AT&T decades ago. While some of the Bell Systems covered whole regions of the country, Cincinnati Bell mostly just covered Cincinnati. It was an incredible cash cow but needed to expand beyond wired land lines to grow its business. It had a rich history of creating different businesses and spinning them off, including its outsourced call centers and billing services, Convergys. In the late 90's, Cincinnati Bell had decided to take advantage of the internet boom and was investing in fiber optic networks around the US – even outside of its primary regional locale.

"So what are you doing for Cincinnati Bell?" I asked, genuinely curious as to what both he and they were up to.

"President of Zoomtown.com."

I was aware of Zoomtown, which was the brand name for Cincinnati Bell's high speed network. Because of Cincinnati Bell's vision and ability to invest in advanced networks, it had made Cincinnati one of the most *wired* cities in America. As West Coast companies were building internet-based applications that required broadband or high speed networks, the problem they often faced was how to test the new software in a real-world environment. Most cities still had primarily dial-up connections, and while they were upgrading to broadband lines, there were very few places in the world that had as large a residential population wired with broadband as Cincinnati. So Zoomtown became a testing site for data-heavy software like thrived on broadband, like video applications, and was seeking new software companies to demonstrate the power of its advanced broadband network.

What? ConnectMail was perfect for Zoomtown. How had I missed this?

"O'Leary, you and I need to talk."

IT DIDN'T TAKE Tommy very long to *get* the ConnectMail story. Even though ConnectMail was designed to work on dial-up connections, it worked even faster on broadband. Tommy was looking for video-based applications that could generate revenue and demonstrate the value of broadband's high speed capabilities. It also helped that O'Leary and I spoke the same *language* -- that ConnectMail had utilized all the P&G-type testing methods to prove out the model – concept and use testing, conjoint analyses, pricing models, etc.

And if that wasn't enough good news, the email software platform that Zoomtown use was provided by a company called Openwave, the largest provider of email software in the world at the time. If we could prove ConnectMail could work on Zoomtown's Openwave system, it could expand readily to a number of email providers globally who also used the Openwave email software.

So installing ConnectMail on Zoomtown was the perfect next step for us:

a) it provided an in-market test of consumer interest and willingness to pay for ConnectMail as a service;

b) it demonstrated the ability for the ConnectMail software to integrate seamlessly into a major carrier-class email system; and

c) it created some competition among the potential email system customers that didn't exist because Openwave's was the largest – and they didn't want Openwave beating them again.

I tapped my fingers together like Montgomery Burns on the Simpsons. *Eggggselent.* This was shaping up perfectly.

ZOOMTOWN HELD UP its end of the deal. They became ConnectMail's first major licensee and O'Leary made the necessary resources available to us for our targeted September 1, 2001 Zoomtown launch. The requisite Sun Microsystems servers were acquired in Zoomtown's data center and software installation and testing had begun. Raymar's relationship with Logitech had been developed (thank God he didn't wear the $99 suit) so consumers could acquire a Logitech webcam and microphone as part of the sign-up process with Zoomtown. MarchFirst and I had worked diligently with Zoomtown's advertising agency to get the introductory advertising and promotions set to build awareness of ConnectMail all over Cincinnati. It was all going according to plan.

Until I got the call. The call I will never forget.

It was late August, about 10 days before launch, when I saw O'Leary's name light up on my cell phone.

"Yo, Tommy! Whassup?"

"Uh, I got a problem, Michael. I gotta conflict we gotta deal with." This didn't sound good.

"OK, gimme the scoop. I'm sure we can figure something out."

"Yeah, well, we've already figured it out. I'm just calling to inform you of the revised plan."

This did not sound good either.

"What revised plan, Tommy?"

"OK, here's the thing. I gotta delay the ConnectMail launch by two months to November 1. I've got another product that has to launch September 1 and I can't launch both simultaneously. Too much risk to the system. Cincinnati Bells' CEO has prioritized the other project. My hands are tied."

"Sorry to hear that." What else was I going to say? It was clear they had made a decision and Tommy wasn't in the driver's seat.

"Hey, but here's what I'm going to do to make it up to you. We're going to make ConnectMail Cincinnati Bell's primary holiday promotion. Given it will kick off on Novermber 1, it will be marketed not just on Zoomtown, but across Cincinnati Bell's wired lines, too. It will get the full attention of the entire corporation. Plus, just think of how many Grandma's and Grandpa's are going to want to be able to see their grandkids faces every week while they're snowbirding in Florida. ConnectMail will allow 'em to do it. It's going to be even bigger than we imagined with the original plan."

OK, this didn't sound so bad. I hated to waste the two months, but this plan was a good one, especially for a back-up. It was clear Tommy wasn't leaving me in the lurch.

"Got it, Tommy. I'll get with your team and we'll get the new plan detailed out. I appreciate your commitment to the program, Tom. I really do. Thanks."

"Great. See ya', Michael. I'll be in touch."

This didn't sound so bad. Change of plans, maybe. A bit of a delay, maybe. But it also seemed like we'd get a more impactful launch with the new plan. In fact, it also sounded like I was going to actually get to spend Labor Day weekend 2001 with my family. Fire up the grill.

22

MICHAEL BANY WAY

MICHAEL BANY'S LOVE of music began at an early age. Growing up in the working class Cincinnati suburb of Finneytown, he learned to play the guitar from his older brother and Beatles' songs were among his favorites. Michael also possessed a sense of humor. During Christmas one year, he slipped a Beatles figurine into the family's nativity scene adorning the fireplace.

Michael was going to need that sense of humor — and love of music — to cope with some of the challenges of growing up. His parents divorced when he was very young. Shortly thereafter, his father disappeared and his mother died. Along with his two younger siblings, Mark and Mary, Michael was placed in foster care while his older two brothers, John and David, went out on their own. John and David supported themselves by playing music and this inspired Michael to be like his older brothers.

In a world that made no sense to him, Michael took solace in two things: music and relationships. And it was through music that he built and sustained relationships that were important to him. He played Beatles music in bands with his foster brothers as early as age 11. As he grew older and finished high school, Michael played both guitar and piano and became a welcome addition to many local Cincinnati bands, the most successful of which was named *Wheels*. Combining local harmonies with a funky Little Feat groove, Wheels became one of Cincinnati's successful local bands in the 70's and early 80's. Michael had written and recorded a hit song *Amaretta* which really put *Wheels* on the map. They even signed a major label deal and produced an album. But it never resulted in a national contract, and *Wheels* eventually broke up.

The relationships that Michael created through music — what he called his "musical family" — made him a favorite to sit in with a variety of bands, including the *Blue Birds* and the *Goshorn Brothers* who played frequently in downtown Cincinnati.

"There's never been a better team player in all of music," commented *Wheels* drummer Mickey Foellger of Bany in a 1996 *Cincinnati Enquirer* interview. "The way he played, the way he sang, he always thought about the group. He was the kind of guy you always want in a band."

On a late December evening in 1995, not long after his 41st birthday, Michael had just finished playing bass with The Goshorn's at the Cincinnati club Tommy's On Main. As he was walking home, Michael Bany was robbed and killed. His assailant stole the only possession Michael had on him at the time, the $60 he made that night. However, Michael's assailant stole much more from the world.

He stole the life of a man who created harmony in so many ways.

On May 21, 2009, City of Cincinnati Ordinance Number 141-2009 renamed Jail Alley, the short narrow street that ran the single block between Main and Sycamore Streets, in the heart of Cincinnati's Over-the-Rhine entertainment district, Michael Bany Way.

"Michael was the kind of musician whose positive spirit and talent turn players and singers into a community," wrote Larry Nager of the *Cincinnati Equirer*. Michael possessed a gift: he brought people together who might not otherwise come together naturally.t

— ∞ —

I WOULD OFTEN be at a cocktail party, safely ensconced in the quiet, tree-lined suburbs in which I lived in Cincinnati, and someone would invariably ask me *the* question: "do you really feel safe walking the streets of Over The Rhine every day?"

"Absolutely," I would respond. "Without question."

That was part of the front I needed to put up. I was an ambassador for urban renewal. I was President of a not-for-profit organization that believed that the unbridled economic opportunities of the digital age and the optimism of entrepreneurship could change what decades had eroded in the inner city. My job was to be an evangelist. Just getting people to come down to OTR was part of the whole plan. The more people who came down there, even for a cup of coffee at Kaldi's, the more economic opportunity would be created and prosperity would, of course, follow.

You gotta have unbridled optimism to change the world.

However, the truth was that I had more than my share of uneasy moments walking the streets of OTR. Though generally benign, the signs of deeper dangers lurked. You could see the crack cocaine vials in the gutter in the morning. The broken glass bottles in brown paper bags. The cigarette butts. The crushed tallboy cans of malt liquor. All remnants of the activities that had transpired the night before and had mostly disappeared from the streets during daybreak. Only these remnants left behind.

During the day there were plenty of panhandlers and drunks sleeping restlessly in doorways and alleys. Sometime in the late morning they'd get up and wander the streets a bit looking for something to eat, nearly always harmless. I'd always say a friendly "hi" when we met eyes. I was convinced that engaging anyone with a smile and a kind word almost always worked to de-stress a possibly dangerous encounter. Unbridled optimism.

And what I discovered walking the streets of OTR with frequency was that a drunk doesn't intend to do anyone harm (other than perhaps to himself and even that is unintentional). I discovered that he homeless often have some very entertaining stories they'd share with me. More than anything, the homeless living on the streets just didn't want to be as *invisible* as the world generally treats them – when people walk by them, pretending not to notice them. They craved human interaction just like anyone else. And were mostly deprived of it.

As with most things, familiarity breeds some level of comfort, and it was walking those streets and having those conversations that eroded whatever fear I had initially. That made the years I spent in OTR as familiar as the big glass and marble office buildings that comprised my work environment previously.

Realistically, however, I knew that it was never wise to fully drop my guard or I might do so at my own peril. All it would take was one bad event. Everyone remained painfully aware that things could go awry and it could happen quickly. All of us, including the homeless of OTR, kept an eye out for potential danger. A survival instinct as old as humanity.

I'LL NEVER FORGET the day as long as I live.

It was Friday, September 14, 2001. Three days after 9/11. Two weeks after the postponement of our original "go live" date on Zoomtown's network.

Everyone was already edgy, with frayed nerves and a sense of dread and uncertainty following the atrocities of 9/11. The world as America knew it had changed. No one had ever attacked the US mainland in times of modern warfare. And worse, the ones who dared attack us used *anything but* modern warfare to do it – crashing our own civilian planes… full of American passengers… into crowded buildings, killing thousands of people and a tremendous number of safety workers trying to rescue them. Unthinkable!! I remember being glued to the TV the morning of 9/11 with the visual of the first of the World Trade Center towers pouring dense, black smoke. And if that wasn't bad enough, another huge airliner smashes into the second tower while I watched. I sat there wide-eyed, incredulous. I wondered how the towers could have tolerated the impact and tremendous heat from the fireball and ensuing inferno. How were those buildings still standing?

Asking the right question never felt so wrong.

We had trouble working that day at 1201 Main Street. Trouble concentrating. And it only got worse when we heard about the plane that crashed into the Pentagon and the one that crashed in the field in Pennsylvania at the hand of the brave and selfless passengers to save others. What was happening? What was the world coming to? Was it over? Was there more to come? How? What was considered *out of bounds* in civilized society anymore?

People had a strong need to reach out to one another. To mourn for the loss of the families involved even if you didn't personally know anyone in the tragedy. Just to phone someone close to you to remind them that you love them; to hold your children just an extra moment or two when they left for school; to count your blessings, and pray they would continue. Pray this wasn't a total change in the world order.

Some people walked around in a daze. Some people acted out in anger. Some people just inexplicably cried off and on, quietly at their desk or in the shower. But no one really knew how to deal with what was happening. Very few had experienced anything like this before.

I stumbled through the week until Friday after lunch when I was finally able to kick it back into gear and focus on something else, *anything* else. Work seemed a fitting salve. The normalcy of work was welcomed and somewhat therapeutic. I got on a roll, wrapped my mind around the rescheduled ConnectMail launch at Zoomtown, and before I blinkd it was already 6:30pm and starting to get dark. I packed up my briefcase, locked the office and headed to my car to drive home.

The most direct path from my office, at the corner of 12th and Main Streets, to the garage where I parked on Sycamore Street was through Jail Alley, which was the street that would later be known as Michael Bany Way. Alternatively, I could walk a block south to Central Parkway, then a block east to Sycamore, and then it was a half block back to the parking garage.

But Jail Alley was direct, short and simple. It was a hundred yards instead of two and half blocks. The only problem was that Jail Alley was a very narrow, cobblestone way with tall buildings on either side, which only accentuated the narrowness of the passage. This was surely not the safest way to get to the garage. But I managed that each day through a quickened pace, squirting through the narrow passage like a tail-back in football traverses the small gap opened up by his offensive linemen. It opens quickly, you get through it untouched and you're fine.

Tonight, however, would be different.

As I took the quick left into Jail Alley committing myself to the shortcut, I saw three hooded figures turning into the alley from the opposite direction. I instinctively stiffened while almost imperceptibly the hooded figures did the same. They were laughing when they entered Jail Alley. I was whistling when I entered. Yet, silence engulfed us as we approached each other. Everyone took a sudden interest in the cobblestones, eyes down, pace quickened, words elusive.

Though not logical, something embedded deep in my consciousness called out to me: I was somehow programmed to *fear* the presence of three African American men approaching me alone in a dark, narrow alley. I had no reason to fear these particular men. I had never been hurt before by them, or any other African Americans for that matter. And these guys had done nothing that was remotely intimidating; they only stopped talking. They had given me no reason to fear them. Their posture betrayed no evil inclination or plot.

So what was driving this primal fear?

The three men, walking side by side, suddenly began to line up, one after the other. I wondered what they were doing — what, in my increasingly paranoid psyche, were they *plotting* ?-- only to realize that the alley was so narrow, we couldn't fit four people astride.

As we came within feet of each other, I made eye contact with the man at the head of the line and murmured, "how's it going?" in a low, modulated voice, greeting potential confrontation with a kind smile as was my practice in Over The Rhine.

"Alright," I heard back, in an equally low, equally wary voice. Nothing more. Our shoulders nearly touched as we passed. I realized that I was holding my breath for some reason. I was so taut that if we had touched, I probably would have emitted a musical cord.

We passed and I found myself deeply exhaling. Why was I so uptight? Why did I feel threatened? What was it in my subconscious that elicited this fear? How did it emerge only now, and not before? What was it all about?

And then I heard the voice.

"HEY!" one of the men behind me shouted in my direction.

I froze. Stopped walking. But did not turn around. Could not turn around. Couldn't move.

What did I think would happen? Would they be standing behind me with a gun or a knife? Were they just going to rob me? Were they going to kill me? I thought to myself *I should just run now. Take off. Run as fast as I can. Flee for my life. Leave my briefcase. It would only slow me down. Make them chase me if they wanted to harm me. They were going to have to work to hurt me.*

But for some reason I didn't run. For some reason, and to this day, I'll never understand why, I just turned around, faced them and responded simply, calmly and evenly.

"Yeah?"

All three of the men faced me, standing only about 10 feet away. They were side by side now. We looked each other in the eyes. I was expecting to see malice in those eyes. Intent to do harm.

What I saw and heard and felt from these men wasn't anything like malice at all. It was *pain.*

"What do you think about what happened this week?" one of the men asked me. We both knew the topic was 9/11.

"Bad stuff. *Really* bad stuff," I replied, not sure what else to say other than what I felt.

"Yeah. Never seen anything like this before," the second man said, shaking his head.

"Me neither. Kinda concerns me about what the future holds," I engaged, reaching out, a little less stiff, a little softness creeping into my voice.

"Me too. Do you think we're going to war?" the third man asked, with more than a hint of trepidation in his voice, the humanity of his concern clearly present. He was worried. His fear was almost palpable.

"I sure hope not. I saw the Viet Nam war happen, at least on TV. It wasn't good and that's just what they were allowed to show us on TV."

A conversation was emerging here. An exchange of feelings, shared concerns. One that could have been in my living room rather than a dark alley. And probably should have.

"Man, I don't want to go to war. But you know what?" the first man said, as much to his friends as to me. "If they call on me to go, I'm gonna go. I swear I am. I'm gonna fight. I'm gonna defend us. They can't do this to us." He said this resolutely, almost as if he had just decided, as if he was convincing himself as much as any of the rest of us.

"Well, I hope it doesn't come to that. I really do. But I want you know that I really admire and appreciate your willingness to fight for our freedom. Your willingness to defend *me and my family*. You're a better man than I," I said to him quietly as we connected, completely seeing one another for who we really were...and embarrassed, perhaps ashamed, of our initial fears.

"Yeah. Thanks for saying that. Take care, man."

And with that, the three men turned around and walked through Jail Alley to Main Street.

I realized at that moment that I hadn't been talking to men. I was talking to teenagers. Maybe 16 or 17 years old. They stiffened as much as I did when they turned into the alley and saw me. To them I was an older white guy, probably someone that held some undeserved and unearned authority, but authority nonetheless. Authority that could, and probably has, been used against them. They were scared boys, conditioned never to show fear, wondering if their country was going to call them to go to war and possibly end their lives early in the name of our country's security. Probably wondering if it was worth giving up their lives for a country of old white guys like me.

It was at that moment that I realized that no matter where on earth we're from, no matter the color of our skin, no matter the size of our bank accounts, no matter the religion observed or lack thereof, Abraham Maslow had it figured out when he put forward his theory. Safety and security are at the root of ALL human concerns. Safety and security are at the base of the human hierarchy of needs.

When personal safety and security are threatened, we all wallow in the same fears. We all react the same way. We all hum the same tune. We are all part of the same community.

And it brings us all together.

Perhaps Jail Alley actually turned into Michael Bany Way a few years earlier than 2009. Perhaps that very night.

23

THE BUBBLE IS BLOWN

MARK TWAIN WAS famously quoted as saying, "When the end of the world comes, I want to be in Cincinnati because it's always twenty years behind the times."

The NASDAQ Composite Index, the standard-bearer and benchmark measure of technology stock investing at the time, peaked on March 10, 2000, with an intra-day high of 5,132.52. It is widely accepted that this was the day the collapse of the stock market's DotCom bubble began, making its fall through 2000 and much of 2001. By July 2001, a mere sixteen months later, it had fallen to 1,387 en route to its nadir of 1,160, nearly 80% off its high. The bubble had certainly burst.

Perhaps in New York. Perhaps in Silicon Valley. But not in Cincinnati. I suspect Mark Twain was right, because all of us at Main Street Ventures proceeded as if *none of this* was affecting the Cincinnati tech start-up community. We believed we were immune to the excesses, because after all, we hadn't yet *experienced* any excesses. We would plow right through it. It would not derail our purpose.

Or so we thought.

The global signs were overwhelming. Especially for telecom-related stocks. Even the titan of internet-driven stocks, Cisco Systems - which produced the equipment that connected what was known as the backbone of the internet - dropped from $82 per share at its high to $11 in September 2001. JDS Uniphase - which developed wave division multiplexing equipment - dropped from $1,059 to $40 a share. Even our own Cincinnati Bell, which had changed its name to Broadwing as it started building global fiber optic networks, had dropped from $41 to $14 a share, and was still in the midst of a dive toward an all-time low of $1.80. A drop of more than 95%.

It was impossible for the global market declines not to affect us in Cincinnati, despite Mr. Twain's musings. And it most certainly did.

We started noticing it in various ways - some subtle, some not so subtle. On the subtle side, we saw a lot fewer venture capital investors around Main Street. They seemed to have just disappeared. They were largely occupied figuring out how to generate liquidity within their portfolios in an attempt to save their funds. VC's certainly weren't looking for new ways to commit what precious little capital they possessed. They were propping up any portfolio company that still held some chance of a sale or IPO. Those hopes were dwindling fast as start-up's dropped like flies as they ran out of cash and couldn't attract further financing.

Among the not-so-subtle signs, nearly all of the potential customers we were talking to about licensing ConnectMail software were experiencing massive layoffs. It seemed every contact we had at every potential customer and their bosses were getting laid off, effectively extinguishing any momentum we were building in that company for licensing ConnectMail. And those that remained employed were not looking for new applications. They were just trying to pare back, hunker down, protect their jobs and survive the massive and unprecedented downturn they were experiencing.

Ron Conklin at MarchFirst was among those crying the blues. He lamented that their new project work "fell off a cliff," and many of the projects they had just signed got cancelled "out of the blue." He was spending more time dismantling the staffing they had so feverishly built in the six months since their IPO, desperately trying to save cash. He assured me that they would continue to fund and staff ConnectMail, although I had my doubts. They were hemorrhaging cash; how could they help me when they were fully occupied trying to save themselves? Fortunately, we had already built the ConnectMail software and utilized much of the funding we were provided by Bob Bernard's investment. Nonetheless, I appreciated Ron's commitment to us.

We literally had no customers on which to call. Nobody interested in new products. No one wanting to even talk to us. Or talk to *anybody*. The lights were on in telecommunications companies, but no one was home.

So we had focused all our energies on Cincinnati Bell and our upcoming launch with Zoomtown. I had wondered how long it would be before Zoomtown and Cincinnati Bell would feel the effects of the global meltdown in telecom. It was unclear just how immune they were to the massive amount of infrastructure overbuild that had occurred. By the end of 2001, it was estimated that only 3% of the fiber optic network capacity that had been installed globally was in use. Only 3%. I wondered how many telecom companies could survive at that paltry utilization rate? How exposed was Cincinnati Bell, our *only* customer?

It wasn't long before I got my answer. It came in the form of a call from Tommy O'Leary explaining to me that Cincinnati Bell was going through the same downsizing that every other telco was experiencing. And the impact on ConnectMail was that we would still launch, but through a "soft" rather than "hard" launch. In layman's speak, that meant that Cincinnati Bell would still offer ConnectMail as a service, but all the holiday marketing that Cincinnati Bell was planning would be scrapped as a cost savings measure. Essentially, ConnectMail would still be made available, but no one would know about it unless they deliberately looked for it.

It's hard to look for something you don't know is there.

Simply put, the ConnectMail launch was *doomed* without any marketing efforts to build public awareness. Tommy was as sullen as I had ever seen him; I knew he felt as if he was letting us down. That he was personally letting *me* down. But I suspected that his call to me was simply one of many similar calls he was making that day. He was in the midst of a corporate meltdown, doing all he could to keep it together and standing by people and relationships the best he could in the incredible fury of a storm.

This was bad. *Very bad.* Unrecoverable, I feared.

———

THE WAITRESS PLACED the two Palmetto Porters on the table, as Matthew Mazeroski and I took stock of the situation. At least we had a 95-rated beer, a "blend of Munich, Crystal, Pale Ale, Black Patent, and Chocolate Malts." I have no idea what a chocolate malt is but I am certainly indebted to the guys at Palmetto Brewing Company who most certainly do. Matthew flashed the waitress his ever gracious smile with gratitude for her service hoping in some way it might delay the continuation of our grim conversation.

"How bad is it?" Matthew asked after a hearty gulp of the Porter.

"I wish I had better news," I responded eagerly taking my own gulp, hiding from reality. "It's like hellooo, hellooo," I said with my hands cupped around my mouth, making the reverberating sound of speaking in an empty room. "No Zoomtown launch. No prospective customers. The industry is caving in on itself. Total meltdown."

"Well that sounds pleasant," replied Matthew, trying to strike a happy chord with a little sarcasm and gallows humor. "How's MarchFirst holding up?"

"Dead men walking," I coughed out. "If it weren't for the miles of brand new, empty cubicles in their offices, you'd hear the same echo. Nearly everyone on our account has been let go. I can't see how they are going to survive."

"Incredible. What, they went public just last March! How could they run out of cash that fast?"

"If you spend money as fast as they have with limited revenue coming in, the fixed costs will bury you."

"Wow. What about Main Street Ventures? How bad is it for us?"

"Well, because of our low operating costs, MSV itself will be fine for a while. We've got enough operating cash for another 15 or 16 months. A number of the incubating companies are hanging in there too because we preached to them to keep their cash burn low. But with no investors on the horizon, and limited customers, they see the writing on the wall."

And now for the *next* question. The question he really wanted to ask. Or maybe not.

"And how about ConnectMail?"

"We've still got about $250,000 in the bank. However, we're burning about $50,000 a month," I counted, giving him the cold, hard facts. "So that gives us five months of operating dollars which means we run off a cliff sometime around early next April. When we run out of cash we're done, because I doubt we can raise more capital in this environment."

"What do you suggest?"

"Well, I have no reason to believe that the overbuild in telecom is going to correct in the next few months. In fact, I'd say it will take years to come back and that will likely cause some very high profile telecom bankruptcies. Our business model and software are built on selling to telecom companies. Without healthy telco's, we're dead."

"What about the Microsoft and Lotus Notes versions?"

"Largely completed, but all our testing was done on the telecom version. It's possible something could happen with the enterprise software side and corporations could consider buying. But remember, their stock prices are falling with the market, warranted or not, and they're cutting costs like there's no tomorrow. Corporate IT spending is in a downward tailspin. ConnectMail is a luxury for them, not a necessity."

"So how do you think we should handle this? It's possible I might be able to raise some more capital."

"Matthew, that would be awesome. But, honestly, I can't look investors in the eyes and tell them that I think I can get them a return on their investment of new money into ConnectMail at this point. I can't say with confidence that I can get a return for even our current investors. Neither you nor I want to be in that position – even if the investor has confidence in us. People around here have long memories."

"Yes, they do. So what can we do?"

"Here's what I'm thinking. We have to extend the runway so we don't crash in April. Flat out, we have to start reducing our cash burn as soon as possible. If we keep cash in the company, it may give us the flexibility to wait out the telecom downturn. When things start to turn back up we can pick up where we left off. As long as we keep cash in the bank, we keep our software. We stay alive. We live to fight another day."

"But how can you keep the team together AND reduce the cash burn."

"We can't. Simple as that. We shouldn't sugar-coat it. We should be proactive. So here's what I suggest. I tell the three ConnectMail employees tomorrow that we're going to do three things. First, I'm renewing health insurance for everyone through December of next year, more than a year from now. Second, everyone stays on salary over the holidays and through end of January. Third, *Job One* starting tomorrow is for me to help to get Raymar, Cray and Jay new jobs ASAP. I've already started putting in a few calls."

"I like the way you're taking care of the guys. They'll appreciate it. It's the right thing to do and I support it. But what about you?"

"I'll stay on salary-free, man the ship, try to license the software to anyone who'll see me, and get some cashflow going. When I began doing start-up's, I knew a time like this would come eventually. So I have the equivalent of six months' of my family expenses stashed away for such an occasion."

"You'll stay on without pay?"

"Yeah, but I can't do it indefinitely. Like I said, I can bankroll six months. After that, with a wife and three kids, I'm going to need to find a money-paying gig."

"Wow. I really appreciate that. We'll work out some kind of pay in equity instead of cash for the risk you're taking."

"Sure. I appreciate it. I just hope there's something I can do to get our investors' money back and make that equity worth something. For everyone."

———— ∞ ————

THE GUYS TOOK the news like champs. Truth be told, they saw the writing on the wall too. They knew what was coming; they just weren't sure how they would be treated. We were, after all, a start-up.

We developed networking plans for the guys to find them new jobs while we still had payroll for them. As a salesperson almost always in demand, Raymar hit paydirt first. He was able to find a good job with a more established software firm before Christmas. For the other guys, it was tougher and we went through the holidays with good leads, but nothing substantive. I'm sure it was an uncertain holiday for them. It was for everyone.

During the first week in January, I had lunch with one of my buddies from my P&G days. While we were catching up, he was telling me how he was expanding his consumer promotions business to include more web-based development for his client-base. Telecom may have been off, but consumer products was a steady business and his clients' businesses were holding up well.

"Do you happen to need a great web developer and a project manager?"

"Absolutely. I've got a new contract and I have needs for both." Ah, the Old Economy strikes again.

"I think I may have a solution to your problem."

By mid-January, Cray and Jay were firmly ensconced in their new jobs and I could breathe a sigh of relief. Having them taken care of was a huge load off my mind. They promised to work at night on whatever development work ConnectMail needed or whenever they had spare time. They were incredibly loyal and I was eternally grateful. I still had a few precious resources at MarchFirst working on the business, but not much work really to do. It seemed ConnectMail was going to have a long, excruciating wait until the market emerged from the DotCom hangover.

And that forecast was accurate. Things just got worse with each day. Bankruptcy filings, layoffs, restructurings, mergers of weakened players with other weakened players (the worst kind of mergers). It became clear to me that this would not end in my six month timeframe and that I would need to find other ways to generate income. This telecom *malaise* would take years, not months. And I didn't have years to wait. Because we kept cash in the bank, ConnectMail might be able to wait, but I couldn't.

Then it happened. The final shoe dropped.

There was no market for ConnectMail, and now, no resources to help anyway. I was now officially alone. MarchFirst declared Chapter 11 bankruptcy on March 1, 2002, exactly one year to the day after they IPO'd. A sad end to an improbable journey.

The legal dissolution of MarchFirst and the resulting sale of its assets took over 3 years to complete. Matthew and I watched it carefully in part out of morbid curiosity, but also to see how much cash was recovered for debt holders from the fire sale of MarchFirst's assets. We also had an admitted interest in a particular asset – MarchFirst's 8% interest in ConnectMail. With its liquidation preference, MarchFirst was senior on ConnectMail's capitalization chart. That meant that if anything positive ever happened with ConnectMail, whoever owned MarchFirst's stake would have first dibs on any proceeds. MarchFirst's interest in ConnectMail languished for many years in bankruptcy court untouched. During the final days of the liquidation process, with almost all other assets gone, a buyer petitioned the court and successfully procured MarchFirst's $5 million investment in ConnectMail - for a mere $1,500.

That buyer was Matthew Mazeroski.

———

THERE WASN'T A lot to do each day when I got to 1201 Main Street. The ranks of start-ups had thinned somewhat, so I spent much of the time encouraging those that were left, brainstorming the last desperate moves most companies have to consider when their very existence is on the line.

I was also contemplating my own career moves. A couple of opportunities to start new companies had surfaced, some quite interesting. When I told a number of ConnectMail investors that things were looking grim for ConnectMail given the murky outlook for telecom in general, they were appreciative of my candor. I guess they understood the risks of early stage investing and felt we communicated with them with frequency and transparency.

A few investors even asked if there might be other business opportunities in which they could support me. That was an incredibly gracious response given that

I had just told them that they were likely going to lose the money they had already invested. I was very fortunate indeed.

As I contemplated the future one morning, I noticed an email flash on my computer. Emails were a lot less frequent these days and with very little to do, emails did not sit in my box very long unnoticed.

The email was from my friend Ron Marinelli. Ron's friendship went back twenty years to my earliest days at P&G. Ron had been Brand Manager on Head & Shoulders when I joined P&G and had welcomed me to the Beauty Care Division's softball team. Ron later became my boss and we had worked well together. Ron was a die-hard P&G'er and I expected he'd retire from P&G. He was also a die-hard Cincinnati Reds fan. Ron coordinated our Cincinnati Reds season ticket group for the previous 15 years. Eight of us split four seats for the season which meant we each got the seats for ten Reds home games. A trip to the ballpark for the family once every three weeks is good for the soul, even if it required enduring some ugly Reds seasons.

The ticket group had largely stayed the same for many years although we tended to lose someone each year given the mobile nature of the P&G employee base. I wondered who was dropping from the group this year so I perused the names in the "To" section of the email.

And there I saw it. Something I had not in my possession: the email address of my old friend and ex-partner Charlie MacAvoy. I did not have the email address for a simple reason. Email had only come into existence in the six years since that awful day in the bathroom at On Target, the last time I saw Charlie.

I sat there and stared at the email address for what seemed like three hours.

Six years without speaking. Wow….that's a long time. Probably too much time. After that long, does it really matter? Well, it only mattered to me for one reason: the way my stomach felt when I saw his name. I still felt *the regret*. And the thought of the word "regret" made me realize that I had really not fulfilled the Rabbi's suggestion from a few years back. I had not made the third attempt to fix the situation. I had tried calling and writing twice, to no avail.

Now I had a new tool — email! Maybe this might work…maybe it was worth a try.

As I started to type out a message, I pondered what to say *this* time. Saying that I believed I was misunderstood certainly hadn't worked….and suggesting that he misunderstood the situation hadn't worked either. Trying to rationalize the situation, justify it, rectify it….no, none of that felt right.

So I swallowed my pride and tried the simplest approach – just saying *I'm sorry*. If that didn't work, I just didn't know what would. And I would have given it three efforts. How much more could I be expected to do?

So I got to typing. I said I was sorry for the whole situation, that I was sorry for any hurt it may have caused him, and that I was sorry for any role I had in it. I couldn't say it any plainer – I was *just sorry*. Then I took the final risk and asked him if he wanted to get together, perhaps to have lunch, and talk about it.

I typed out the message, reread it about a half dozen times, edited it a dozen times, reread it again, overthought it some more, edited it again, drew a breath, and hit *send*.

When I sent the message I knew my odds of getting a response were pretty low. After all, if he hadn't responded to the ones I sent before, what in the world would make him respond now? Six years is a long time. He's probably managed just fine without me as a friend. I've heard it said that time heals all wounds, but I hadn't seen much evidence of it. So I set my expectations low....yet I stared at the inbox, willing it to respond. Imploring it to flash with a response.

I Waited. Nothing happened. I waited a little longer. Nothing happened. The in-box was silent.

The phone, however, rang. "What time can you meet me for lunch today?" asked the voice on the other end. I recognized that voice instantly.

"Just name the time and the place, and I'll be there."

Finally.

As I drove to the restaurant to meet Charlie, my mind was a whirlwind. On one hand, I wanted to talk about what happened. I *needed* to talk about what happened. But that was not Charlie's style. Charlie's optimistic outlook in life was buoyed by the fact that he didn't dwell on the negative. He moved past it quickly and I suspected that he might want to do that today, too.

He might also want to simply tell me off. Maybe he wanted to meet to *unload* on me. Tell me what he thought of me. Maybe it had been festering like an open sore for six years. Maybe he was ready to move past this, heal the sore, by putting me in my place. That would not be fun. That was certainly not what I wanted, but what I quite possibly faced.

As I pulled into the parking lot, I concluded that I simply had no way of knowing what was going to happen, so I would just have to take what's coming and improvise. I also made a very important decision – that *I would let Charlie determine the outcome of this conversation*. It had taken me six years to get him to even speak to me. I sure as hell wasn't going to drive him away now just to satisfy my own ego needs.

When I got to the restaurant, he was waiting outside. As I approached the door, he rose to meet me. Firm handshake. Friendly smile. Awkward moment.

"It's good to see you, Charlie."

"And you, too, Michael."

After we were seated at the booth, we exchanged pleasantries. We talked about the wives, the kids, who was in which grade, what sports were being played. It was very friendly, in a detached sort of way. The air was still thick.

After we finished placing our lunch orders and had exhausted all the pleasantries, I took a deep breath, and cast a glance at Charlie.

"So do you want to talk about it or do you want to just put it behind us and move on?" I asked, tentatively. I hoped I hadn't ruined it by asking too soon.

Charlie looked down. A bit of pain on his face as his eyebrows furrowed. And in a moment I'll never forget, he looked up slowly, stared at me for what seemed like an eternity with a little glassiness in his eyes and a bit of hesitation in his heart.

"If it's all the same to you, Michael, I'd just like to move on. Just try to go back to the way it was... *before*. Like it never happened."

I wasn't sure how to respond to this. This was really hard for me. The manner in which I worked through my emotions was to talk them out not bury them. Yet this was apparently not the way Charlie wanted to work resolve the matter. The way I sought to get resolution was simply not his way.

Over the six years I had come to believe that this situation would *never* be reconciled. And in the narrow chance that it did get reconciled, I didn't expect it to happen without so much as even a small discussion.

I realized at that very moment that the end I desired justified the means. If I wanted to eliminate my regret – and finally, here was the opportunity, right in front of me for the taking -- I was going to have to play by Charlie's rules.

And so I did. We didn't discuss it. We didn't dwell on it. Just like he wanted. Like it never happened.

Even until this day, I don't really know if I did anything wrong. I don't know if I was at fault. I don't know what he was thinking. I don't know for sure why two friends spent six years without uttering a word.

And while there's a lot I don't know about the situation, there are two things I know for sure. First, I believe with all my heart that expressing two simple words *mattered:* "I'm sorry". That those two words were, at least in part, the difference-maker, the ice-melter. That we couldn't move on until those words were spoken.

And I'm awfully glad I did.

The second thing I know for sure was that it felt a hell of a lot better to eliminate that regret than to live with it. No matter *what was required.*

I felt cooler than The Fonz.

—⚬—

THE GREAT RADIO personality Paul Harvey coined the phrase, "…and now, for the rest of the story.'" His use of the phrase began after World War II as a segment within his weekly radio show. Later, *The Rest of the Story* became its own show in 1976, running nearly until Paul Harvey's death in 2009. *The Rest of the Story* was constructed as a fact-based recounting of some amazing thing in history that hinged on a particular and usually small event – which created some unexpected twist of fate. Had that small occurrence not happened, then the much larger and more impactful event would also have not happened. Paul Harvey always ended the astounding story with his signature dramatic pause and famous ending, "…and now you know the rest of the story."

Just rekindling my friendship with Charlie certainly would have been sufficient reward for gathering courage to say those two difficult words, "I'm sorry." My full intent was simply to get my friend back, and alleviate the regret.

But there's a "rest of the story".

After the reconciliation Charlie and I saw each other every couple of weeks. We had a few more lunches, a few emails and phone calls here and there. It wasn't quite like when we worked together, but I didn't expect it to be since we no longer saw each other every day as a matter of course working for the same company as we had twice before.

And neither of us wanted to force it. Didn't want it to feel *faux.* Plus, we had families and kids now. We were up to our ears and time was precious. We had to *grow* to become friends again. So we made it a point to get together. To become friends all over again. And that's what counted. We were rebuilding a great friendship. Allowing the friendship to take its own natural course.

Charlie and I met for lunch in May, a little over a month into the baseball season, to trade tickets for an upcoming game while he was travelling. I was sharing with him the disheartening ConnectMail experience as it was withering.

"So what are you going to do?" he asked as he loaded a big bite of hamburger in his mouth.

"ConnectMail has enough cash to last out the downturn as long as we don't spend it frivolously."

"No, I mean what are *you* going to do? You aren't ready to retire are you?"

"Hardly! I only in my early 40's. But I have to admit I'm getting antsy. Sitting there with little to do every day isn't conducive to the way I'm wired. I've got a few other start-up ideas brewing."

"I have something you may want to consider."

"OK, what? I'm at a point where I'm certainly open to new ideas."

"I 'm conducting an Exeuctive search to find the next General Manager at The Valvoline Company down in Lexington, KY. You know, the motor oil company. There's been a management change there. The current President of Valvoline just became a Group Operating Officer for the parent company, Ashland, and the General Manager got promoted to President of Valvoline. So they've got a hole to fill, they want to go outside to fill it, and I think you'd be a perfect fit."

"Me? Back in consumer products? Back in a large public company? Are you kidding? I think I've played that game out."

"Really? Are you sure?"

"Well, it's just not something I ever considered doing again. I guess given what I've done for the last decade, I kinda defined myself as a serial entrepreneur."

"Well, I'll tell you this: if you and I were ever to do a start-up together again, we'd want one of these two Ashland guys I was talking about as our partner. Maybe both."

"That's a pretty strong endorsement, Charlie. You like these guys that much? You really think I should look at this?"

"It's an eighty mile drive down I-75 to Lexington. Go have a look. Go talk to them. See what you think. Candidly, it doesn't appear your calendar's all that full at the moment. What do you have to lose?"

While initially resistant to the idea, I had to admit that I had nothing to lose by opening my mind to this possibility. And once again, I stumbled upon what would become another great opportunity. Stumbled upon.

Within two weeks, I had accepted the job of Senior Vice President and General Manager at The Valvoline Company, a division of Ashland Inc.

Which would never had happened if I had not tried multiple times, not swallowed my pride, not found a way to reconcile that regret. Not uttered those words "I'm sorry."

And now you know the rest of the story.

24

THE INDOMITABLE
DUKE DOMINIC

IF YOU'VE MANAGED to make it this far through this little collection of tales, you've come to realize that I've had a few jobs in my time. Is that an understatement? Probably so. To get those jobs I've had to do my share of interviewing. As such, I've learned a few things about interviewers. Here's one: Some employers interview job candidates to understand their capabilities and experiences. Some interview purely to see how well the candidate "fits" (also known as: "Do I like you?"). However, very few interview for both.

The President of Valvoline certainly interviewed me for capability. He was a career consumer products guy and he wanted to know how I analyzed business, how I developed strategy, how I turned strategy into execution, how I supervised advertising agencies to create breakthrough advertising, how I developed relationships with customers, how well I had mastered finance, and how I developed people. All the right questions to evaluate whether I could do the job. I welcomed the scrutiny and certainly had enough fodder for what I felt were appropriate responses. I would have interviewed him the same way if the shoe were on the other foot.

The balance of the interview panel, comprised mostly of those who would be my peers on the company's executive team, interviewed me for fit. Most were long tenured Valvoline employees and I was to be the highest ranking officer ever to be hired from outside the company, one that largely promoted from within and comfortable with the *familiar*. For some on the interview panel, my outsider status didn't sit well. Especially since the individual to previously hold the dubious position of the "highest ranking person to be hired from the outside" was now sitting in the President's chair. That immediately qualified me as a suspicious character.

Fair enough. Forewarned is forearmed. At least I had some insight into the territory I was entering.

As I was lunching with the leader of the Valvoline Instant Oil Change business - one of my would-be peers - he asked me who was next on my interview schedule.

"A gentleman named Duke Dominic," replied the Mouse.

"That would be *'Mr. Dominic'* to you," I was admonished. At first I bristled a bit at the belittling tone accompanying the comment. But as I thought more I realized it was actually a gift – advising me to show the proper respect for Mr. Dominic. A piece of advice to which I would listen.

Duke Dominic started with The Valvoline Company after enlisting in the US Navy in the 1960's. He grew up in the hardscrabble world of the Pittsburgh steel mills. There wasn't a piece of work that was too challenging for him and there wasn't a fight from which he would back down. At 5'9" and 160 lbs, with a sharp wit and a willingness to speak his mind, you can be sure that as a young man Duke Dominic's mouth wrote a few checks his body couldn't cash.

Duke Dominic was the classic *company man* of the time. While holding the title of Senior Vice President of Operations when I met Duke, he had spent his entire career with Valvoline, rotating through a succession of jobs through which he learned the business from many angles – sales, marketing, and supply chain (the wise leaders of Valvoline knew better than to attempt to train him in Accounting or Human Resources). The in-depth knowledge he garnered, achieved over four decades with Valvoline, gave him both depth and breadth of understanding as to what makes Valvoline tick. It also gave him decades of relationships inside and outside Valvoline that made him a highly valued employee.

Duke Dominic also became a source of very good guidance to a certain senior manager who would come to Valvoline from outside the company.

At my very first meeting with Duke Dominic, I realized that this was one unique character - unlike anyone I had met before. His passion for the Valvoline business was unparalleled. His blue eyes sparkled beneath his broad forehead and thinning hair when he spoke of the Valvoline Brand and what it meant -- to him and to legions of consumers and customers. He tested me to see if I was worthy of carrying the mantle of furthering the brand he had come to love and treat as one of his children. To many people, Duke Dominic wasn't just an employee of Valvoline, he *was* Valvoline. The only face of the company they would ever know, or *need to know*. He promoted dozens of employees; he was the provider of bonuses for hundreds more. Many felt they owed him their careers and were deeply loyal to him.

Over the years, Valvoline employees would come to appreciate – or, shall I say, *tolerate* - Duke's mercurial style. Over time, they would come to realize that Duke's bark was worse than his bite. They'd learn to put up with his rants and come to quietly giggle at his signature phrases, usually as they quietly slinked away after a famous "Duke Ass-Chewing." He was known for having a low tolerance for poor performance.

As Duke's office was next to mine, I would often hear voluminous *Duke-isms* floating out of his office. "Are you kidding me? If what you're telling me is true, what do I need you guys for? A dog with a note could do as good a job as you guys!!" I always loved the "dog with a note" Duke-ism that would be invoked whenever someone would transfer a problem to him instead of think it through and solve it themselves.

Another famous Duke-ism: "What? If I ever heard you speak to a customer that way, I would rip your lips off!" The visual of the lipless employee with a Valvoline "V" on his shirt always amused me.

And the most common Duke-ism, when you'd stick your head in his office and inquire as to how he was doing that day, he'd reply, "I'm busier than a one-armed paper hanger with the crabs!" Now you know why Valvoline Management never considered Duke to be a good candidate for a role in Human Resources.

Duke was crude and bawdy but loveable. I sensed early in the interview that Duke's opinion of me was going to be important, not only in getting me the Valvoline job, but also in succeeding in that job if it were to be offered. Apparently it was.

—⋘—

EARLY ONE MONDAY morning, Duke strode into my office and plopped down on one of the chairs opposite my desk. Like a rooster in the barnyard, he commanded attention whenever he desired. After all, in his view, it was *his* barnyard.

"How the hell are you?" he crowed. "Three weeks on the job. Are you keeping your head above water? Or am I going to have to dive in, drag your ass off the bottom of the pool and give you mouth to mouth?"

When Duke was in the room, you knew Duke was in the room.

I shook off the visual of him giving me mouth to mouth resuscitation, knowing that Duke always fired for effect.

"Yeah, I'm drinking from the fire hose for sure," I responded shaking my head. Duke liked colorful metaphors so I offered them whenever I could quickly conjure one. He also liked to be the guy to *show you the ropes*, to allow you to benefit from his experience (which I greatly appreciated). So I quickly calculated that he didn't pop in my office to have latte, share feelings and sing kumbaya.

"So, Duke, you got any guidance for me?" I asked, noting that giving me guidance was the full intention of the visit. I tossed him a softball, so to speak.

"Well, have you noticed the biggest line item in your marketing budget yet?" prompted Duke. He was asking about the highest expenditure of Valvoline marketing dollars.

"You mean television advertising?" responded the Mouse.

"OK, the second biggest line item in the marketing budget?" corrected Duke, with a little frustration. The facts were getting in the way of his point.

"You mean trade spending?" responded the Mouse again. Trade spending was the money Valvoline spent with retailers to run periodic sales.

"Dammit. OK, the *third* biggest line item," Duke said with even more frustration. Now you know why Duke wasn't a good candidate for Accounting either. "Oh screw it. Have you noticed how much money Valvoline spends on racing?" Now we were getting to the crux of his question.

"Yeah," I responded. "I have noticed it. Anything in the budget with that many zero's garners my attention. But I haven't had time to learn much about racing yet."

"Well, that's what I'm here for. I oversee Valvoline's racing program — I've done it since Christ was a Corporal — and when you're ready, I'll teach you what you need to know," Duke proudly offered. I was still trying to determine exactly when Christ was a Corporal and at what point he was promoted to General. As the uninitiated, I came to realize that was yet another famous Duke-ism.

But I digress.

Duke not only oversaw Valvoline's racing program, he built it. Over decades. He had relationships all over NASCAR, Open Wheel racing, and NHRA (drag racing), sponsoring more drivers than you'd ever heard. Not only did he build Valvoline's racing program nearly from scratch, he also formed the NASCAR cup team (the highest level of NASCAR racing) for which Valvoline was both a primary sponsor and co-owner. At the time, Valvoline was the only major sponsor in the sport that was also a team owner. If you looked on the NASCAR website under the #10 Valvoline Chevrolet at the time, you saw Duke's picture as the "designated team owner". The title was even on Duke's NASCAR credential that he wore proudly at races.

It was not hard to tell that Duke absolutely loved it.

"Well, given what we spend," I continued, "I will need to have a very clear and deep understanding of the business, and I'd welcome anything you could do to help me, Duke." Another softball. The words he wanted to hear.

"The best way to learn racing is to go to races. So I'm going to need not only time from you, I'm going to need *weekend time*, because that's when the races are. I'll put together a schedule, you and I will go together. As sure as I'm standing here, if you stick with me you'll meet everyone you need to know - and learn everything you need to learn - about racing," crowed Duke.

"And when you go with me, baby, you go in style," he winked as he wandered out the door.

And I did not doubt a single word.

25

THE CAR RUN GOOD ALL DAY

It was a clear and warm Saturday morning in late August. I was to meet Duke Dominic at the Lexington, KY, airport at 10:00am, "ready to ship out". Navy jargon rolled off Duke's tongue like he was still wearing his dress whites and saluting the flag over the yardarm. "Ready to ship out" meant wearing a uniform – only this was not a US Navy uniform. It was the Valvoline Uniform his assistant left for me the day before – the raceday uniform of an owner and sponsor. It included a khaki-colored, Valvoline logo-embroidered dress shirt, Valvoline fitted ball cap with the "V" logo on the front and personalized to include "Elliott" embroidered on the back. Dark long pants and comfortable black shoes (no shorts or open-toed shoes allowed in the pits by NASCAR regulation).

When Duke said "meet at the airport", he didn't mean the main terminal. He meant Tac Air, the fixed base operator (FBO) where private aircraft departed. Duke had arranged use of one of Ashland's corporate jets to transport us to Tri-Cities Regional Airport in Johnson City, Tennessee. This was the closest airport to Bristol Motor Speedway as my first NASCAR race was to be the famed Bristol Night Race. The *Night Race,* as it was known, was sold out and had done so for each of the previous ten years.

As we boarded the Cessna Citation V jet aircraft, Duke tipped his hat to the Ashland pilots, familiar faces due to his frequent race travel. They knew that when they transported Duke, they didn't just have to fly the aircraft and then wait around.

They knew they were going to get to see the race, too. Better than endlessly waiting at the FBO at Teterborough in New Jersey, sipping coffee like most corporate pilots.

As we landed at TRI after the short 45 minute flight, we taxied past an expansive collection of private aircraft that transported the NASCAR entourage every week. This was TRI's busiest weekend of the year, and there were aircraft parked everywhere there was room. This included the expensive private jets the drivers and team owners flew to the larger twin engine prop planes used to transport pit crews and marketing support staff.

In some cases, it was easy to pick out who owned which planes. Jack Roush was a famous NASCAR team owner known for wearing his trademark panama hat. Roush's jets had a silhouette of the "Cat in the Hat" himself in profile painted on the tail. Understated! More modestly, Rick Hendrick, perhaps the most successful of NASCAR team owners, simply had the Hendrick Motorsports logo painted on his planes.

For most jets, you might have to do a little detective work to figure out to whom it belonged. For example, Cup Champion Rusty Wallace's plane was simply painted white. Yet, the clues to the ownership were there if you looked carefully. The jet's tail number began with an N, by FAA requirement, but ended with "RW". It was a fun puzzle to put together.

Subtle or not, the expansive collection of aircraft was another indicator that NASCAR was not just a bunch of rednecks driving cars in a circle on Sunday as so many of the uninitiated presume. This was a $3 billion, well-financed professional sport. At the time, it was the fastest growing spectator sport in America, second only in television audience to the National Football League (NFL). Televised NASCAR *practices* drew larger television audiences than regular season National Basketball Association games (NBA). This was *real* money in a very real business.

We stepped off the plane and were greeted by ground support staff who whisked us to the other end of the small airport to the waiting helicopter taxi. Bristol Motor Speedway was sold out of every one of its 165,000 seats for the race that night which made the traffic around the track horrendous. Any company that owned a helicopter within 200 miles of a NASCAR racetrack provided shuttle services on raceday. It was by far the best way to get in and out of the track and Duke availed himself with frequency to the service.

As the helicopter lifted, I had that vertical sensation usually reserved for elevators. Except in this elevator, you could see the ground below you and full expanse of the airport. We headed west, flying at a few thousand feet, above the fields and barns and farmhouses dressing the landscape below. The helicopter lifted to clear the furrowed brow of east Tennessee mountains. Moments later, the massive track leapt into view, nestled between two mountains.

Imagine the largest football stadium you've ever seen — perhaps the Rose Bowl in Pasadena, California. Now imagine a stadium that seats 60% more fans and encircled a half mile high banked concrete track with an asphalt paved area larger than a football field in the center. You've now visulized Bristol Motor Speedway.

The traffic to get into the track was backed up for miles, having begun nine hours before the race was to begin. Cars were parked along to the roadside for more than a few miles from the track. The track was surrounded by pods of campgrounds with RVs of all sorts collected in small communities of NASCAR fans. Most had taken their vacation this week and had been here since at least Thursday — some as early as Monday. They flew their flags of glory. Whether it was Jeff Gordon's #24 or the #3 of the late Dale Earnhardt, they planted their flag to mark their outpost and display their driver pride. They would recount racing stories around the campfire at night accompanied by good friends and a cooler or two of cold beer — and come back year after year to tell those same stories again. These were the NASCAR traditions of committed fans.

I had always been inspired by the committed NASCAR fan who camped at the track for the entire weekend. Once I decided to wander through the campground to meet these folks. It was a great opportunity to meet enthusiasts, not just for NASCAR, but also for the Valvoline brand. And let me tell you, when you do this, you meet some of the nicest, friendliest people in the world.

You also meet some characters.

Once, I came across two guys sitting in folding beach chairs with a cooler of beer placed between them and a sign perched on the cooler. These guys could have been mistaken for the brothers of Larry the Cable Guy. Dressed the same. Sounded the same. Laughed the same. I liked them instantly.

It was 9:30am and they were already a few beers into the day. A barley breakfast. The sign perched on the cooler between them read:

WANTED: WOMEN INTERESTED IN…

Full Contact Sex

Three-Ways

Lesbian Action

...and assorted other descriptions of reasonably explicit sexual activity followed, capping off a list of about 10 items. The best part of the sign was the line at the bottom of the poster, written in the same capital letters as the line at the top:

NO WIERDO'S!!!!

This, I couldn't resist. I had to stop and talk to these guys.

"Hey, guys, how's it going?" asked the Mouse.

"Right as rain. Gonna be a beautiful day and we're gonna see a Cup race. What could be better?"

"Not much, I guess."

"Hey, you want a beer?" Nice of them to offer me a beer, I thought. Even at 9:30am.

"Thanks, but I'm good right now. Just finished breakfast."

"So did we!" they laughed. OK, got it. Told me just what I needed to know.

"So I'm curious. Do you mind if I ask you how your sign's workin' out?"

"You mean, are we catchin' any fish with this bait?" One smiled as he rubbed his hands across his copious belly. He looked about eight months pregnant.

"Yeah. I like the direct approach you're using with the sign. I mean, why bother with small talk? Just wanted to see how it was workin' out for you."

"We've been doing this for years, ya' see. It don't catch much fish in the mornin'. But we like to sit out here before the race with the sign so women see it when they're walkin' to the track. 'Cause they *remember* it later when they're walkin' back. See, the fishin' gets a lot better when they wander back after they've had about ten hours of beer drinking in 'em."

And the other guy chimed in, "Yeah, that's when it *really* gets interesting!"

I guess beer goggles work for women as well as men. You gotta respect the fact that they've put a lot of thought and practice into this.

———

As the helicopter landed in the cordoned off, makeshift helipad at a corner of the track's parking lot, onlookers gathered to perhaps catch a glimpse of celebrity. They seemed disappointed to see *me* disembark, discounting me for what I was – just a privileged sponsor who had not really earned his way into racing, hadn't *made his bones*. Hadn't fought traffic, hadn't sat through the intense heat, hadn't saved up for months for the ticket, hadn't *earned* it. I had hoped the Valvoline logo I wore might give me a bit of legitimacy, or at least a pardon. Hoped.

Duke and I were met by Valvoline's Racing Marketing Manager, Mitchell Hardy, who greeted us with a smile and offered us a lift in his golf cart, the main means of transport once you get on the track grounds. If you're ever driving on the interstate highway, and you see a motor coach towing a pick-up truck with a golf cart nestled in its bed, you should immediately know that unique trio of vehicles likely belongs to a NASCAR driver. The motor home is where they live when they're at the race track (which is 38 weekends a year), the pick-up truck is how they get around in the city where the track is located, and the golf cart is how they get around the grounds of the track. Only NASCAR drivers seem to have that specific combination of vehicles at any given time.

It became instantly clear that Duke had given Mitchell Hardy instructions that he was to babysit me that day – or to borrow the euphemism that Mitchell offered, "I'm here to show you the ropes." Like many things at Valvoline, even though Mitchell was in my organization, reported up through me and his marketing budget was under my control, Duke clearly called the shots! And Mitchell clearly understood the marching orders he had received from Duke. Much to my benefit.

Knowing that I would initially want to understand racing from a marketing perspective, Mitchell immediately carted me to the NASCAR Fan Walk. This is where the sophisticated marketing trailers were set up to allow NASCAR sponsors to interact with fans and to ply their wares – and the fans tended to walk away with all kinds of sponsor swag. These were the freebies fans loved and showed to their friends at home as souvenirs of their race weekend. At the Fan Walk the ubiquitous and never subtle NASCAR clothing was sold, which was a sponsor's dream.

Think about it. If a company sponsors major league baseball, the NBA or the NFL, do the players wear the sponsor's logo on their uniforms? Perhaps if you're Nike or UnderArmour and you actually supply the uniform. But have you ever seen the Budweiser bowtie on an NFL football helmet? Nope. Yet, in NASCAR, the sponsor logo is not only on the driver's uniform, it's on the driver's racecar, the semi truck that transports the race cars (the *hauler*) and every piece of merchandise that is sold supporting that driver – tee shirts, sweatshirts, jackets, coozies, golf balls, you name it. The Valvoline brand was everywhere!! And people wore the shirt with our logo on it with pride.

Once on a business trip to Atlanta, I was arriving in baggage claim and saw a man wearing an old jacket with the Valvoline logo broadly displayed on his chest. The jacket looked to be at least a decade old, if not more. So I stopped and complimented him on his jacket, which elicited a broad smile.

"Where'd you get that cool jacket?" I asked. He had no idea that I was employed by Valvoline.

"I got this jacket at the Atlanta NASCAR race in 1995. And look," as he unzipped the jacket to show me the lining, "I got Mark Martin to sign it for me." Mark Martin drove the #6 Valvoline Ford for Roush Racing for much of the 90's, always contending for the championship. Mark has probably finished second in the cup championship standings more than anyone in history and has been a fixture in the sport driving well into his 50's. This man was so proud of the decade-old Valvoline jacket he was still wearing.

"Do you actually use Valvoline oil?" I asked, baiting the hook, conducting my little one-person test to determine if loyal racing fans were also loyal Valvoline consumers.

"I sure do. I've never put anything other than Valvoline Maxlife 5w40 in my Ford 150!" he beamed with pride. "Wouldn't trust my baby to anything else!"

Music to my ears.

"Wow, that jacket is really cool," I complimented him. "And a great piece of racing history." As I handed him my business card, I revealed my allegiances. "Tell you what. I work for Valvoline and we really appreciate your support and loyalty. If you'll email me your home address, I'll send you a brand new Valvoline jacket for free."

I thought this would bring a smile to his face, but he stepped back, cautious.

"Is something wrong?" I asked, suddenly not so sure I had done the right thing.

"Well, you don't expect me to send you THIS jacket in exchange for a new one do you? I'm not giving this up for anything."

"Of course not," I smiled with relief. "I want you to wear that jacket for the rest of your life. I'm just going to send you a brand new one so you don't wear this one out."

"Well in that case, you're on, Mister! And thanks!"

"No. Thank *you* for being so loyal to Valvoline."

Fans love freebees. Fans love stories they can tell their friends about how they were treated special and fans will commit to your brand if you can show them the right love and respect. Having that guy tell his story over and over again about how he got his new jacket is better than any television commercial we could air. You can't buy that kind of authenticity.

I bet that guy will ask to be buried in that Mark Martin-autographed Valvoline jacket.

AFTER A DETAILED walk-through of the Valvoline marketing experience on the FAN walk, Mitchell took Duke and me over to the tunnel. The tunnel was the way you got to the pits - under the stands and underneath the track. Mitchell had already secured my Pit Credentials for that day. To get into the pits, you had to have one of three passes. A *cold pass* was a one-day pass that got you in until shortly before the race began, at which time the crowd in the pits thinned considerably for safety reasons. A *hot pass* was also a one-day pass, but you were permitted to stay in the pits throughout the race. This is the pass Mitchell had for me. The third type of pass was a permanent *hard card* that most members of race teams, Mitchell and Duke included, possessed – a season-long hot pass. All passes had to be displayed prominently at all times or NASCAR officials would promptly boot you out of the pits and possibly the race.

We were getting into the pits just in time for Happy Hour. In NASCAR parlance, Happy Hour doesn't have anything to do with drinking. Rather, it was all about driving. Happy Hour was the term used for practice prior to a race. It is a specified interval of time where teams could log some laps and get their car tuned perfectly for the race. NASCAR mandated highly specified requirements that all cars must meet; at the same time, they also provided flexibility for teams to adjust a number of areas in the cars. The collection of individual adjustments teams made to the car was called the car's *set-up* and it was highly confidential.

Not only will teams adjust set-up's from track to track, teams will typically use different set-up's at the same track for qualifying and for racing. There is a wide set of variables in set-up that could include everything from having fluids with different characteristics in the engine to adjustments that account for the differences in aerodynamics for when you have a single car on the track versus forty-three cars. Qualifying at Bristol had been the day before so today Valvoline's crew was testing in Happy Hour practice the set-up changes made from *qualifying trim* to *race trim*.

As we got to the #10 Valvoline hauler, the crew was scurrying all about preparing for Happy Hour. Mitchell procured two headsets for Duke and me that would allow us to hear the team communications during practice. We climbed the ladder to post on the top of the hauler, along with the team General Manager and the Crew Chief, to watch Happy Hour. An unobstructed view of the track was available from the top of the hauler. Team communications consisted primarily of the feedback the driver was giving the crew chief about how the car was handling in practice. After a few laps, they'd bring the car into the garage, make some adjustments, and send it back out, hopeful the handling was improved. This triangulation process continued until they got the right *balance* on the car, the one they believed would maximize both speed and handling at the start of the race. Of course, the balance would change as the race proceeded, as track conditions and temperature changed, as tires were changed, as the car itself evolved during the race, and on and on. Many of the adjustments during a race are fundamentally directed to keep the right *balance between* speed and handling. One was no good without the other.

Now I understood why the standard line delivered by a NASCAR driver after winning a race was, "The car run good all day." That was the trick — to keep the car running good. Maybe not the best grammatical articulation, but then again, fine command of the English language rarely wins races.

After Happy Hour, we gathered in the hauler's office, to understand the decisions the Crew Chief, the Car Chief and the Driver were making as to the final race set-up. After completion of final adjustments, the car would proceed to NASCAR's pre-race inspection, the method in which NASCAR tries to police compliance with the rules on car set-up. A great Crew Chief will understand these rules, especially the more vague or *gray areas* within the rules, and push the car set-up such that it stays within the rules, but creates as much competitive advantage as possible. Or if he chooses to bend the rules, he better figure out how to hide it well. NASCAR's objective is to make sure no one strays from the rules. If the Crew Chief gets caught breaking the rules, he gets fined, suspended, and/or docked championship points — in short, he's in the doghouse. It's a cat and mouse game between the teams and the NASCAR officials. And half of the fun.

———

"Now THIS IS where the real fun begins," Duke stated as we headed toward the small cramped building where they held the Drivers' Meeting. The Drivers' Meeting was held about two hours prior to the race start. It's a mandatory meeting for all drivers and crew chiefs where any rules specific to this race are announced or clarified. It's also where NASCAR will make sure everyone understands what they expect to happen, or in the case where fireworks between teams may have flown in previous weeks, what they expect NOT to happen.

The Drivers' Meeting is the single location at the track where everyone involved in the show gathers, face to face. A pre-show cast party of sorts. As we all funneled through the narrow doorway into the meeting, Duke noticed four-time cup champion Jeff Gordon next to him in line.

Duke put his arm around Jeff and said, "Man, I have heard some nasty rumors about you – and honestly, I just couldn't believe them."

"What are you talking about, Duke?" Jeff said earnestly, surprised to hear about anything negative to his finely buffed image.

"Well, I heard that you were going to abandon your traditional car number and change it to the #12," baited Duke.

Gordon, unsuspecting of Duke and taking the bait hook, line and sinker, responded "Why on earth would I abandon the #24? It's been my number since I've been in cup racing!"

"Well, you idiot, you're giving half of everything else you own to Brooke in this stupid divorce!" scolded Duke. "I thought I taught you better than that!"

Not many people would dare to rib Jeff Gordon about the way his very personal divorce matter was being exposed in the media. Jeff, realizing he had walked into Duke's trap, just closed his eyes, gathered himself and looked at me. At me!

"Hey, I don't know who you are, but you're wearing a 'V' and are foolishly willing to be seen publicly with this crazed man. I just want you to know there are very few people in the garage who could have said that to me and gotten away with it. And Duke is one of them. And probably only because he was one of the first people to sponsor me when no one expected me to become anything in this sport."

Then he looked back at Duke, "But Duke, you better watch out. Because if I see you tooling around in your golf cart at the track, I'm going to put you in the wall!!"

Duke hugged him and bellowed, "That's my boy!!"

I was glad to see Gordon took it well. I'm not sure I would have. But that was the Duke magic at work. As we got through the hallway into the Drivers' Meeting, it was as if Duke was at the head of a receiving line. He greeted many of the car owners he's known for so many years – Rick Hendrick, Jack Roush, Rodger Penske, Ray Evernham, Richard Petty, Chip Ganassi, having sponsored all of them at one time or another. Duke knew their kids, their wives, and in some cases even their girlfriends.

Duke's relationship with Rick Hendrick was strong enough that when tragedy struck the Hendrick organization, Duke found a way to lend the support they needed. On a foggy morning before the October 2004 Martinsville race, a Hendrick Motorsports airplane crashed into a mountainside, killing 12, including Randy Dorton, who headed Hendrick's engine building organization and Ricky Hendrick, team owner Rick's son. As a sign of friendship and support, Duke commissioned a six foot tall oil painting of Ricky, which he presented to the Hendrick family. It hangs today in the Hendrick Motorsports Board Room.

There weren't many drivers in the room that Duke didn't greet. Dale Jarrett, Ken Schrader, Rusty Wallace, Mark Martin, Joe Nemecheck, Bill Elliott, Michael Waltrip. Even some of the *younger* drivers like Dale Earnhardt, Jr., Tony Stewart, Matt Kenseth, Jimmy Johnson. They knew who Duke was, and Duke knew who they were too. Duke greeted them all and wished them all good luck in the race.

Duke was in his element. And I was happy to be trailing along in his wake.

———

As DRIVER INTRODUCTIONS began, I could feel the excitement amongst the 165,000 fans starting to build, nearly three times the fans that attend an average NFL game. At this point, most people were in their seats as *the show* was beginning. Each driver walked across the stage after being introduced, shook hands with a few dignitaries, and then jumped into the back of a Chevy Pickup to ride around the track and wave to fans. You could hear fans in sections alternately cheering and booing as their beloved or hated driver went by. Drivers didn't really care whether they were applauded or boo'd; they just didn't want to be ignored.

Duke and I parked ourselves along side the #10 Valvoline Chevy, lined up in qualifying order after clearing inspection. We waited for the driver of the #10 car, a young, up and coming driver, Scott Riggs, to finish his fan trip on the pickup. We all stood at attention, with Scott's wife Jai and their two darling toddlers, during what has to be one of the most thrilling displays of patriotism -- the national anthem at a NASCAR race.

At Bristol, it began with Lee Greenwood singing his famous song *Proud to Be an American*, accompanied with video on the four-sided JumboTron screen high above the track, patriotically displaying images of the United States' military strength and the freedom which it seeks to guarantee. During the rendition, two US Army paratroopers had jumped from airplanes and were parachuting their way right into the track, streaming red white and blue smoke toward their perfect landings. Fans occupying about one-third of the stadium held up placards that when connected, portrayed a picture of a waving American flag. It was all just an awesome display leading up to the national anthem, which just sent chills up my spine. Indeed it was a day to be proud to be an American.

At the exact moment the national anthem ended, we all covered our ears for the US Air Force flyover as the fighter jets screamed by and the crowd burst into cheers.

Duke looked at us and said "now watch this."

As if on cue, as the jets finished their pass, the 50,000 fans holding the US Flag placards flipped them over to form a giant Valvoline Logo at the south end of the track. The crowd cheered wildly.

Duke just smiled, looked at us, and said, "Who's your daddy, huh?"

———

As we were flying back to Lexington after the race, I looked at Duke, who still had a smile on his face after the day.

"You really seem to like being at the track," I offered, teeing him up. "You seem to just suck in the whole atmosphere with a joyful smile."

"Yeah," Duke replied, "When I'm at the track, I'm happier than a puppy that just discovered his peeder."

The people in Human Resources needed not fear for their jobs.

26

It's In The Bloodlines

IT WAS CLEAR from the very first moment I walked into Valvoline's headquarters that racing was a vital part of what defined this brand – and its employees. I have been to quite a few corporate headquarters in my time. But never, ever, have I seen one whose waiting area was adorned with race cars and jammed with dozens of trophies.

Yes, during the first decade of this century, in the reception area of Valvoline's headquarters, you'd find two race cars. The first was the Galmer chassis driven by Al Unser, Jr. to win the 1992 Indianapolis 500. 1,550 pounds and 111" long, Unser won the Indy 500 by the narrowest margin on record -- .043 seconds – over Scott Goodyear. Valvoline was Unser's primary sponsor.

The second was the #10 Valvoline Chevy, driven at the time by Scott Riggs, with a Gen 4 NASCAR body, which weighed roughly 3,600 pounds and was powered by a 358 cubic inch standard block engine. That was about as close as the car got to being a stock car. It was anything but *stock* when you looked inside it.

Trophies jammed the shelves around the vehicles – from races of all forms and types. There were only a few chairs because, after all, while you were waiting, how could you not resist getting up and having a closer look at the cars and trophies?

It took me a while to *get* why racing was so sacrosanct at Valvoline and had become a literal part of the Valvoline brand equity. Over the years, many brands put their logos on a race car by sponsoring racing. Detergents, Hardware Stores, Beer, Restaurants, Candy Bars, Soft Drinks, Cigarettes, Movies…you name it.

But Valvoline wasn't just *on* the car, Valvoline was *in* the car. In the engine, that is. Valvoline was the thin line of protection when that 358 cubic inch engine was turning over at nearly 10,000 RPM and putting out over 800 horsepower. Valvoline was the difference between an engine that won the race and an engine that seized up and put you out of the race early. Valvoline scientists worked on race engines day in and day out, figuring out how to help them generate more horsepower without jeopardizing their ability to finish the race.

To most sponsors, racing was a way to advertise their brand in a manner that built brand loyalty. But to Valvoline, racing was a *rolling demonstration of the product's promise*. If Valvoline could protect these racing engines imagine how it could protect yours.

And for that reason, and many others, racing was an integral element of Valvoline's corporate culture. And so was winning. In addition to Al Unser, Jr. winning at the Indy 500, over the years Valvoline had sponsored Cup champions like AJ Foyt, Cale Yarborough, Darrell Waltrip, and Jeff Gordon. There was a winning legacy spanning decades. It was forever part of the brand.

But sadly, since Valvoline had started co-owning a NASCAR cup team in the late 1990's, the team couldn't break into the Top 20 - despite Duke's immense love and caring. While owning a team was a significant source of pride for Valvoline, the performance of its namesake team was not. Fortunately, Valvoline still sponsored other teams who performed well, and that helped. But when your brand's prominently displayed on the car and you are used to seeing it win, when the winning stops, you feel it. And it doesn't feel good.

This was weighing on my mind and the mind of Valvoline's President when Duke and I jetted off to Richmond, Virginia, for the spring race there. The #10 Valvoline Chevy qualified well, but ran into trouble with too aggressive wheel camber in the set up (i.e, how much the wheel bends out or in at the top to aid in steering). While aggressive camber helped the car carry more speed deeper into Richmond's turns, the heat that built up from constant braking on the short track ended up melting the bead on the tire. When the tire let go, the car veered sharply to the right and into the wall. We would get the car back on the track, but effectively had lost our shot at winning that race.

Duke wanted to stay with the team to investigate the matter further. That was his role as a member of the team's Board and as the designated car owner. I used it as an opportunity to get off the pit box and see the race from different perspectives.

GOING TO A football or basketball game has its excitement. It's both a visual and audible experience. You see the players competing, you see replays on the scoreboard, you hear the crowd, the marching band. It's an exciting thing to watch.

But the experience at a NASCAR race goes a couple of steps further. You're thrust more deeply into the excitement in ways that just doesn't happen in other sports or get communicated through television. In NASCAR, fans get electronic scanners and headphones that allow them to hear the team communications between any of the forty-three drivers and their crew chiefs. You know that in football, the quarterback and offensive coordinator are communicating. In baseball, the third base coach and batter are communicating. But, for competitive reasons, the fan doesn't get to hear what being said.

In NASCAR, all radio communication is on open frequencies. You know when your favorite team (or your most hated team) is going to pit, you know how many tires they say they're going to take, you know when problems are developing in the car, you know when they're changing strategy. It's all out there and open to hear — whether you're a spectator, broadcaster or competitor. You actually *feel* like you're a part of the competition.

There's also an experiential part of NASCAR that I haven't felt in other sports. When I stand in the pits inside the first turn and all forty three of the cars race by, there are sounds, feelings and smells that punctuate the experience. The unmuffled roar of the engines lends a living, percussive feel to the rail on which I'm leaning. The bottle of Gatorade I'm holding transmits vibrations through my hand and up my arm. I see the little bits of rubber tire wear, affectionately referred to as *marbles*, bounce around the edges of the track, creating a danger zone as they can cause the car's tires to lose the grip of the track as they roll over them. I smell the unique exhaust that comes from the 98 octane fuel the cars are burning. Unlike the fumes that emit from a diesel engine, these fumes have strangely sweet hints, almost like citrus. I know it's probably not great to inhale the fumes, but to me it *smells* like the track. Combined, it's all somewhat intoxicating. An evocation of power, wrapped in sights, sounds, smells and experience like nothing else.

I wander down pit row during the race and perch in a chair behind the pit box of the #9 Dodge Dealers/UAW Dodge of Kasey Kahne, one of the Evernham Motorsports' entries that Valvoline sponsors. When Ray Evernham retired as Jeff

Gordon's championship crew chief to start his own team, Valvoline signed on as one of Ray's very first sponsors. As an engineer, Ray understood the fluid technology Valvoline scientists could create for him. As Ray says, "it's about how they can get more horsepower out of each *can*." I have always loved that quote. Valvoline hasn't been sold in cans in decades. Unless, of course, he's talking about 55 gallon drums. Now *that's* a can.

The pitcrew members eye me warily, wondering who I am. Am I a competitor snooping on them, watching what they're doing to steal information or technique, to gain some advantage? Though they don't know me personally, they see the "V" on my shirt and take some marginal comfort. The car chief on the pitbox taps Ray on the shoulder and slightly leans his head toward me. Ray looks down and nods reassuringly to the team, signaling I'm OK. He gives me a smile, mouths me a silent "welcome" and gets back to work.

Kasey had qualified on the pole that night and had been solidly leading for much of the race. I switched my scanner to monitor the communication amongst the #9 team members. The race was going well. Kasey was quite comfortable in the car and crew chief Kenny Francis had kept up with the requisite adjustments as the track cooled when the sun went down mid-race. All accomplished under Ray's watchful eye atop the pit box. Kenny was learning from the Master Crew Chief.

Under a caution flag caused by another car that blew a tire and hit the wall, Kenny calls for a two tire pit stop for #9 Dodge. The accelerated wear on the right side tires requires a change of tires every chance you get given the heavy brake use and centrifugal forces exerted in banked short track racing. The left side tires wear less and haven't been changed in nearly 50 laps; yet they're still OK since all the pressure of left turns wears the right tires disproportionately. Maintaining track position at this point is more important than having fresh left-sides. And changing two tires takes four to six seconds less than changing four tires. Four to six *precious* seconds. Seconds that can keep Kasey in the lead.

Given Kasey's pole qualification, Kenny got his choice of pit stalls and picked the very last one before the pit out line. Pit selection is a considered strategic choice and varies by track. Most pit rows are lined up straight, with parking spaces or pit stalls lined along the left side like you'd see on Main Street in any town.

However, race drivers don't parallel park the car. They try to avoid *reverse*. They have to drive in fast and drive out screeching in a mini-race down pit row that is speed controlled to the *pit out line*. Often called the "race off pit row", NASCAR restarts the race after the caution flag is lifted in the order in which the cars exit the pits, or more specifically, cross the pit out line. Some crew chiefs select pit stalls that have empty spaces behind them to make it easier for the driver to pull *into* the pit stall. At Richmond, Kenny Francis likes pit stalls that are easier to pull out of, as he knows track position will be based on crossing that pit out line. The faster you get out of the stall, the faster you get to the pit out line. And maintaining track position is particularly key on a short track like Richmond. So when Kenny got the first choice based on Kasey's leading qualifying run, he picked the very last stall before the pit out line. Kasey can be literally at the pit out line as he exits the stall.

It's just one of a thousand choices a crew chief makes in a given race that can possibly determine the outcome of the race.

I watch as the pit crew readies for the pit stop. Only seven men are allowed to cross over the concrete barrier wall into the pit stall to conduct a pit stop. These seven men, in carefully choreographed steps, endeavor to change four tires, empty two cans of gas into the tank, remove a plastic windshield tear-off, clean the grill to aid air flow to the engine and make track bar adjustments as needed – and do it all in an average 14 seconds or less.

I gaze in amazement as these athletes line up, balanced on the pit wall in their firesuits, helmets and other safety gear, waiting for Kasey to pull the car into the stall. I say *athletes*, because they are. A favored technique for recruiting NASCAR pit crew members is after the NFL Combine, where football players will find out who will and who won't get drafted into the NFL. If you've played football all your life, but somehow fall short of getting drafted, you are a great candidate for a pit crew. You are already in great physical shape, you have lived your entire life executing specific plays with precision, and you understand innately what it takes to perform as part of a high functioning team. You may initially get a job in a less competitive division than cup racing and you work your way up, competing just like anyone else.

As Kasey pulls into the pit stall, the jackman and front and rear tire changers leap out ahead of the car to get to its right side the very moment Kasey skids to a halt. This is the most exposed and dangerous moment for a pit crew member. You're effectively running out into the street while race cars are whizzing by. To say the least, you're vulnerable.

The jackman tucks the seventeen pound jack under his left arm to avoid accidentally damaging the car as he runs around its front end. He smoothly slides the jack under the carriage, precisely under the dayglow arrow painted on the side skirt. He leaps in the air such that his full weight will drive the lever of the jack downward, lifting the car up high enough to remove the tires, all in a single, forceful motion.

The front and rear tire changers armed with air guns slide on their kneepads to a stop in front of the right side tires, using a motion that keeps the air hose from going under the car and possibly getting stuck. Even though it's concrete, they slide across the pit surface like it's ice. With eyes peering intensely at the wheel, in less than 1.2 seconds, each removes all five lug nuts, scattering them across the pit, drops the air gun and pulls the tire away, careful to set it down without it rolling out of the pit stall, lest they face a penalty for equipment leaving the pit.

As the tire changers remove the old tire, in interlocking coordination derived only from endless practice, the front and rear tire carriers carefully place the new fifty-eight pound tire on the lugs with barely enough time for the axle to exhale, and hold it steady while the tire changer fires the air gun to lock the nuts securely in place. Before the pit stop, the tire carrier has carefully glued lug nuts in place on the new wheel, so they won't fall off when carried, but with not so strong a bond that couldn't be broken easily with the force of the air gun. He's also applied a thin layer of oil on the threads for lubricity. To provide the tire changer extra visibility, the tire carrier has taken a bright yellow or pink sharpie pen and colored the front face of the lug nuts when he glued them down. There is no detail too small to over-look, no time saving idea too small to ignore, when your performance is judged in fractions of seconds.

While this has been happening, the gas man has been emptying the first eleven gallon can of gas into the tank, using the gravity feed locking device that limits gas spills. It seems effortless until you consider that he's carrying eighty-five pounds of weight, most of which is lifted above his shoulders. He must complete this in 5 seconds or less.

The jackman is spinning the quick release mechanism which drops the lever and lowers the car's right side, as he slides the jack out and quickly finds his way around the front of the car to perform the same process on the left side. He has to carefully step around the tire carriers as they roll the used tires to a waiting team member leaning over the wall and grab the waiting new left side tires. Meanwhile, the tire changers have already moved to the left side and started to remove lug nuts. The whole process is repeated while the gas man drains another can of gas. And while this is going on, someone has found time to remove a windshield tear off, cleaned off the grill, and inserted a wrench into the rear window well for a couple of turns to adjust the trackbar, hopefully giving the driver more ability to turn the car at 120 miles per hour on this short track.

As the jackman twists his hand to drop the right side, Kasey's new tires are already spinning such that he takes off with a screech as the tires hit the concrete, edging him over the pit out line a half car ahead of Ryan Newman to maintain the lead in the race.

I watched this whole performance with amazement as one of the pit crew sweeps up the spent lug nuts, and while the rest of the crew jump to my side of the barrier wall, with high fives all around, cheering their ability to keep their driver in the lead.

I am reminded of my favorite author, Pat Conroy, who wrote timeless novels like *The Great Santini, The Prince of Tides, Beach Music* and *The Lords of Discipline*. However, it is not those books that I recall when watching the pit stop. It is a lesser known book he wrote called *My Losing Season*, in which he recounted his senior year as a point guard on the basketball team while attending The Citadel military college in the early 1970's. In the book, Pat recalls the way his team performed at its height – the way the players knew each other's moves so well, each other's unique quirks and style so intimately, that they just *performed*. In words only Pat could conjure, he called the way players performed together "wordless alchemy", "resolute beauty...and trust", and "achieving congruence". I am left to only marvel at an author's words and an athlete's accomplishment. "The wondrous night that rises like a starship of hallelujahs and white light." I am in awe.

As I snap back from the netherworld, the pit crew gathers on my side of the pit box and begins watching the replay of the pit stop they just finished, filmed from the pit box's overhead camera. They replay the pit stop over and over, critiquing each subtle move, pointing out steps of slight miscoordination, looking for some way, *any* way, to turn that 13.2 second pit stop into a 12.5 second pit stop. That extra seven tenths of a second could be the difference between Kasey restarting the race first.... or tenth.

"Achieving congruence."

As THE RACE wore on, Kasey was no worse for the wear. In fact, Kasey and his car seemed to get stronger. Kenny kept making the right adjustments to the car, keeping Kasey ahead of the changing track – and competitors. As we neared the final laps of the race, Cup Champion Tony Stewart was getting stronger and stronger also, challenging young Kasey for the lead. Tony is known for stalking competition in the final laps of the race, willing his race car to go faster, finding time no one could have found in each corner, pushing the limits of physics, and eventually reeling his prey in for the kill – like a lion chasing an impala. Tony was heard on his radio once actually saying "here kitty, kitty, kitty", as if coaxing his prey while stalking it, letting the competitor know he was doomed to be Tony's dinner.

And that was Tony's plan for young Kasey tonight. Kasey was only in his second year of cup racing, and only 25 years old; Tony had already won a cup championship and was about to prove the benefits of experience.

The last two laps of the race were excruciating. Tony tried everything he could to pass Kasey. He tried getting a run on the high side coming out of Turn 2 into the back staightaway. He tried diving under Kasey in the Turn 3 corner. He put his right front tire on Kasey's left rear fender to try to shake him loose, make him hesitate, get even the smallest jiggle, just enough to secure the pass.

But Kasey would have none of it. He was not intimidated by the Champ – or if he was, he refused to show it. Tonight would be Kasey's night, not the Champ's. Kasey dove deep into Turn 4 on the last lap, barely in control but keeping all four tires firmly melted to the track, and powered down the front stretch to take the checkered flag, merely a fraction of a second ahead of Tony. The fraction of a second needed to seal Kasey's first Cup victory!

Tony would have to settle for second place tonight with Ryan Newman behind him in third.

Of course, since Kasey's pit stall was all the way at the end of pit road near the entrance to Turn 1 and we couldn't actually see the start/finish line, the pit crew and I were watching Kasey's win on the TV monitor embedded in the pit box, just like anyone at home. When Kasey took the checkered flag, the team erupted in cheers and high fives, screaming with joy as Kasey roared past the pit in exhilarating momentum. Kasey's first career Cup win!! A night he would never forget.

Ray Evernham and Kenny Francis climbed down off the pitbox, hugged the pit crew and high fived anyone willing to high five back. Exultation abounded! The media, lurking outside the pit, anticipating Kasey's win, but also poised to run to Tony Stewart's box in a moment's notice, was all over Kenny for an immediate comment for the adoring TV and radio crowds.

I hung back, since actually, it wasn't *my* win. These guys worked really hard — they were the team, they earned the victory. Honestly, I was just a sponsor tagging along for the ride. So I stepped back from the pit area, preparing to head back to meet Duke, just happy to have personally witnessed the joy of those who had worked so hard in conquest.

As I turned to leave, I saw Ray enveloped in the cameras and microphone. I caught his eye and mouthed "congrats," giving him a thumbs up as I started to walk away. He pulled away from the media for a moment and yelled "hey, Michael, where are you going?" Not even waiting for an answer he grabbed me by the shirt sleeve and said "c'mon, we're headed to Victory Lane!"

With that, I had surrendered myself to whatever came next. We bounced out to the track and saw Kasey doing his first ever Cup Victory burnout. As his tires spun and the tail end of his car wheeled around kicking up tons of white smoke for the cheering crowd, Ray broke into a trot, and then a full sprint of his own exultation down the front stretch. I joined in. What the heck? Why walk to Victory Lane when you can run? Besides, I'd never been there before and needed someone to show me the way.

So we sprinted side by side, two forty-somethings who were fortunately in reasonable physical shape, running down the track, laughing, cheering and exulting the whole way. You would have thought we were a bunch of seven year olds getting out of school for the summer. I looked into the stands and watched some of the crowd actually cheering us on!

We slowed to a jog as we neared Victory Lane where Kasey was pulling the car in and the shower of champagne began. Streamers and confetti shot out as Kasey emerged from the car to celebrate his first cup victory. Hugs all around. TV cameras, strobe flashes, sheer joy. This was Kasey's first win and he'd go on to win six more races in the next season alone, en route to one of the more promising NASCAR careers.

As I stepped out of my body and watched what was going on in Victory Lane, trying to capture the visual and imprint it in my mind forever, I was struck by one overwhelming notion. I looked at Ray and said to myself, "this guys knows what it takes to be a champion."

—⁂—

ON THE FLIGHT home, it was just Duke and me in the jet. Duke was uncharacteristically quiet; happy for Ray, but clearly disappointed in the #10 team's continued lackluster performance. He shared his concerns with me. The same concerns the President of Valvoline and I had been discussing just days before. The President and I had some ideas of what needed to be done. The question we had was how to get Duke engaged in thinking about a serious change for the Valvoline team.

I took a risk, because I thought Duke had opened the door.

"You recognize the problem with the team's performance," I said to him, looking him straight in the eye. "And you also know the solution." I let the comment lay heavily like a fog rolling through the aircraft cabin.

"What, change the driver? Change the crew chief?" Duke looked back at me. The standard answers. Teams changed drivers and crew chiefs so often in response to poor performance, the fall of the NASCAR season was commonly referred to as *Silly Season*. Duke knew that wasn't really the answer. He was toying with me, buying a little space between himself and reality.

"Nope. I mean, I'm far from any NASCAR expert, but it doesn't feel to me like a driver or crew chief change is the answer."

"What then?"

"You know." The air still lay thick, with the obvious, the unspoken.

"Yeah," Duke lamented, as if he was still that ten year boy sitting in that Pittsburgh church confessional. "If we want to get Valvoline back to being a championship team, we've got to partner with a team that knows what it's like to be a champion," he said dreading the reality, forcing himself to acknowledge that change was necessary. He knew, as well as I, that we would never get back to the winning ways the Valvoline brand deserved until we got a new organization and ownership structure that had not the *hope* of winning, but the *history* of winning.

"So what do you think we should do?" I asked, hopeful we were walking the same path.

"Our ownership agreement comes up for renewal at the end of this year. Now is probably the time to make our move." Duke responded.

"Yeah, you're probably right," I replied, feeling the movement.

"I know Ray Evernham wants to expand his operation next season to add a third team," Duke began as the idea formed in his head. "He told me this past week. He's already got the room in his shop. He's got the organizational talent to handle a third team. What he lacks is the sponsorship, the financial support, to make it happen. And he's too dependent on Dodge as both his automotive sponsor, and primary sponsor on both his cars. Too many eggs in one basket with both his sponsorship and manufacturer support coming from the same company. He needs us; we need him. We need to build our new partnership with Ray."

Duke was getting energized, the idea forming simultaneously with the utterance of his words. He put it all on the table. "Ray's won three championships. He and Kasey beat Tony Stewart at his best tonight. Winning is in Ray's bloodlines."

"THAT sounds like a plan to me," I smiled. "But can you make it happen?"

I tossed the gauntlet.

"Does the Pope shit in the woods?" Duke bellowed, with that certain glimmer in his blue eyes, and that certain smile on his face. Classic Duke-ism. I didn't really know the answer to the question of the Pope's bowel habits, but was pretty sure I didn't need to.

After his requisite show of bravado, Duke calmed and gradually turned quietly inward for the rest of the flight. I watched Duke as he stared out of the airplane window into the darkness of the night. The wheels in his mind were turning as to how this could all come together. I allowed him to mull as we silently winged our way back to Lexington.

"Wordless alchemy." "We achieved congruence."

FOUR MONTHS LATER, Valvoline announced its exit from MBV Motorsports and the simultaneous formation of Valvoline Evernham Racing as a 50/50 partnership. Ray Evernham would be the CEO of VER. Its four person board consisted of Ray Evernham, Rick Russell (Evernham Motor Sports' CFO), Duke Dominic and some guy who knew nothing about racing, Michael Elliott. The #10 Valvoline Chevrolet became the #10 Valvoline Dodge.

Game on.

27

There's Nothing Like Daytona

You'd think Captain Rodrigo Ramirez of the Volusia County Sheriff's Department would simply *hate* the Daytona 500. Captain Ramirez's responsibilities include, among others, supervision of the Department's Motorcycle Unit. As you might imagine, in Florida's temperate climate those 18 Harley Davidson motorcycles stay busy all year around. Everything from traffic control to funeral escorts - which are more common than average in Florida. It stands to reason; the more seniors, the more funerals.

For all of Volusia County's law enforcement officials — whether ensconced in 2-wheel or 4-wheel vehicles — major race weekends are a nightmare. Rowdy vacationers, in large quantities, often having perhaps imbibed a little more than advisable, deluge what is normally a quiet beach town. And not just large quantities of tourists, we're talking LARGE quantities. Daytona Beach's population is normally 60,000. During the two weeks in February leading up to the Daytona 500, the city's population swells at least five-fold. The track holds 250,000 people alone; not to mention all the support staff at the track, hotels, restaurants, airports, rental car counters, you name it. Just the traffic alone is hard to manage and that's when people are behaving normally.

When is it that people on vacation behave normally?

If you're a law enforcement official this is not your favorite time of the year.

Unless you're Captain Rodrigo Ramirez of the Volusia County Sheriff's Department. Because if you're Rodrigo you get a special assignment during the Daytona 500: *Duke Dominic*. Let the Daytona Beach Police Department and the Florida State Highway Patrol worry about traffic flow. Let them worry about drunken tourists. Rodrigo and his motorcycle team are on Duke's hip for the week; and if you're on Duke's hip, you're gonna have fun.

IF RACING IS your religion, then Daytona is your Jerusalem. And the Daytona 500 is your Church of the Holy Sepulcher, your Dome of the Rock, and your Western Wall all rolled into one. Racing was Valvoline's religion and therefore Valvoline planned a whole series of events around the annual running of the Daytona 500. With enough events to justify an entire week in the Holy Land.

"There's nothing like Daytona in February," Duke was telling me one chilly January day as we were sitting in his office only a few months after I had joined Valvoline. He sat back, reflecting in his chair like Robert Duvall playing Lt. Colonel Bill Kilgore in the film *Apocalypse Now*, exulting "I love the smell of napalm in the morning."

Only for Duke, it was "I love the smell of 98 octane exhaust fumes in the spring."

And he did. Enough so, that he convinced the entire Valvoline Management Team to spend the week before the Daytona 500 in Daytona. It didn't take too much arm twisting.

The Ashland corporate jet ferried the Valvoline management team toward the Sheltair FBO adjoining Daytona International Speedway shortly after lunch on the Monday prior to the Sunday running of the Daytona 500. Unlike Bristol's compact coliseum-like half-mile track, Daytona International Speedway's 2.5 mile oval super-speedway stretched out so far that they actually had a lake in the middle of the track, large enough for water skiers. It was incredible to see the sheer expanse of the track as the corporate jet glided slowly to a landing on the adjacent runway.

We stepped off the plane into the February Florida sunshine, a welcomed warmth on our faces after a few months of Kentucky cold. As the roar lessened from the jet engines shutting down, our ears were reintroduced to a different roar – that of cars screaming around the speedway at over 200 miles per hour in practice. With qualifying conducted the day before, chiefs and crews had been carefully converting their cars from qualifying trim to race trim overnight and beginning to get the cars adjusted for racing. Even with the engine restrictor plates NASCAR mandated for racing on superspeedways – a speed governor that kept the cars from going so fast they could go airborne if bumped -- the cars still approached 200 miles per hour and their unmuffled exhausts roared with delight.

We were loaded into awaiting vans, adorned with Valvoline stickers, and whisked to the Ocean Walk Resort on the front beach adjacent to Daytona Beach's pier. The Ocean Walk's lobby had already been decked out in a grand red, white and blue Valvoline welcome – banners, life size cardboard cut outs of various Valvoline drivers, balloons, streamers – all in anticipation of the Valvoline guests who were to arrive later in the week.

We were greeted by a combination of Valvoline employee volunteers and Ocean Walk staff and escorted to the two bedroom oceanfront condo selected for each Executive Team member. As I entered my condo and deposited my luggage in the hallway, I was immediately drawn to the 18th story terrace and gazed upon the vast Atlantic Ocean, welcoming the warm sun on my face once again.

Yet, as much as it seemed so, it was not to be a vacation. Despite having lived a mere sixty miles away in Orlando for two years, this was my first trip to Daytona Beach and it was to begin with four days of annual management meetings – *indoors* at the Ocean Walk. As much fun as racing was, we had oil changes to sell and these were the days spent getting aligned as a management team on our primary strategies and plans. Each of our respective business units had been doing serious preparation work for the meeting and our job as the senior management team was to make clear choices about what we would do, and equally importantly *not do*, in running the Valvoline business the next year.

We worked tirelessly until Thursday afternoon when we took our first break to attend the Twin 150 Races, the qualifying races for the Daytona 500. Unlike all other NASCAR races during a given season, the Daytona 500 has a unique qualifying format. In most races the starting order is determined by the fastest qualifying time as each driver takes two individual laps around the track. The Daytona 500 has two-stage qualifying. The first stage uses the standard qualifying format (qualifying time) and it occurs on the Sunday prior to the 500. However, the first stage only determines two things: 1) the *front row* – the pole position and the number two position; and 2) which 43 cars of the 55 or more who attempt to qualify will actually get to participate in the 500.

Both stages are important. First, who wouldn't want to be on the pole of the 500? Winning the pole for the Daytona 500 is feather in any racer's cap. And second, even though the winner of the 500 takes home more than $1.5 million, the car that finishes dead last in 43rd position still takes home $250,000. All race teams, especially the smaller ones, need that kind of coin and desperately want to qualify for richest purse of the year!

Once the 43 car field is set on Sunday, the second stage of qualifying is then scheduled for Thursday afternoon. The field is split into half for two 150 mile qualifying races. The finishing order of the two races sets the starting order for the Daytona 500 field.

Are you confused yet? Just hang in there. There's plenty more to learn.

As we gathered outside the Ocean Walk for transportation to the track, I noticed six police motorcycles lined up adjacent to our vans. I glanced at Duke, who was gathering the crowd, and asked, "Hey, what's up with the Police? Has there been a problem of some sort here?"

"Not at all. Come with me. You need to meet someone," Duke responded with his patented wry smile. That meant he was up to something.

We walked back into the hotel's restaurant where the management team gathered for their meals. There were six uniformed officers of the law currently having lunch.

"Captain Rodrigo Ramirez, I'd like you to meet Valvoline's Senior Vice President, Michael Elliott," and we shook hands. Rodrigo had a gracious smile.

"We sure appreciate all Valvoline does to assist the Volusia County Sheriff's Department in our work," Rodrigo said, still smiling. His smile seemed permanently formed which I thought was a great gift from God.

"And we're happy to support all the great work you do," I responded, having no idea what I was talking about. "Please, finish your lunch. Don't let me interrupt."

And Rodrigo did just that.

As Duke and I headed back outside, I asked, "So you want to give me a clue what all the 'great work' is that we do for the Volusia County Sheriff's Department?" Duke had all kinds of things buried deep in my Marketing Budget and part of my first year's hazing was to unearth what was hidden there. An endeavor that would take years. I nearly considered hiring an archeologist rather than an accountant.

"We sponsor their programs in a variety of ways. You can't pay a police department for their services, but you can *sponsor* activities. So we donate Valvoline hats and apparel for them to use as prizes when they conduct Drug Education programs in schools. We donated the previous van we used to transport the Valvoline Show Car around the country to retail stores, which they now use to transport their motorcycles to Police Motorcycle Skills Competitions. And we donate all the fluids they need for their motorcycles. In fact, I had the guys in the Valvoline R&D labs blend up some very special racing oils just for their bikes – their *secret sauce* -- which helped them take the #1 spot in those skills competitions. Another reason they love us - in addition to how we feed them and take care of them during speed weeks."

"OK, pretty neat public relations. So forgive me for asking this question, but...." I began.

"I know. You're wondering what business benefit we get out of this?" Duke finished my question.

"Yes, you know I'd ask."

"Ha! Just watch over the weekend. You'll see," Duke bellowed.

As the Management Team loaded in the van, with Duke riding shotgun, the six police officers came out of the hotel, put on their helmets, fired up their Harleys with a collective explosion of sweet sound and flipped on their blue lights. Rodrigo looked back at Duke who spun his index finger in a circle signaling "Let's roll!"

Rodrigo lined up his bike in front of the lead van; his first officer behind the second. Two officers stopped traffic in front of the Ocean Walk while two others sped up ahead to halt traffic at the first traffic light.

Rodrigo and his team completed a ballet of traffic stops at every crossing in the 6.3 mile stretch between the Ocean Walk and Daytona Motor Speedway. A pair of cycles would speed up and stop traffic at a crossing ahead of us, while the pair from the previous crossing sped to catch up with us, pass us and do the same at the next crossing. Blue lights flashing, sirens wailing. You would have thought someone important was in tow.

There was: Duke Dominic.

"Are you kidding me?" I asked Duke, leaning forward to tap him on the shoulder in the front seat. "All this just so we don't have to stop at traffic lights on the way to the track?"

"This is just a warm up for the escort they'll be giving our guests all weekend to and from the track," Duke replied.

"You mean that's how our guests will get through the traffic this weekend? By police escort?" I was amazed.

"Yup. Nothin' too good for our customers," Duke crowed. Duke Dominic knew what he was doing.

THE VAN NAVIGATED its way through the front gate of Daytona International Speedway, enveloped in police escort, and pulled to a stop in front of the Sprint Tower. We exited the van as I watched Duke fist bump Rodrigo and mouth to him "see you upstairs."

We piled into the waiting elevators and proceeded to the suite level high above the track. Valvoline's track sponsorship package included not only conspicuous Valvoline signage all over the track, but also access to the double suite situated in the tower directly above the start/finish line. As we entered the air conditioned suite, you could see an incredible panoramic view of the track through the expansive wall of windows. There were two bars set up with awaiting attendants and plentiful snacks, even though we'd just had lunch. Attendants handed us headphones and scanners as we headed through the doors to the private outdoor viewing box. Rodrigo and his team joined us shortly before the Twin 150 races began. I sensed they enjoyed watching the race from that perch. I know we did.

After the races, Duke hosted a cookout at one of Daytona Beach's outdoor restaurants on the water and we were joined by the Valvoline-owned race team and all the race teams to which we provide sponsorship or resources. It was a raucous beer bash and a good release for the six drivers, crew chiefs, crews and support personnel. Rodrigo and his men enjoyed hobnobbing with all the drivers and getting autographs for their kids, while of course, abstaining from the beer. They provided escorts home for the teams.

As always, Duke was the gracious host. Duke reigned supreme.

FRIDAY MORNING WE got to sleep in, which we needed after a very fun Thursday night cookout. As we proceeded through the day we greeted throngs of guests. Late in the morning the Valvoline management team's spouses arrived via Ashland's jets. While this was a nice weekend for them, spouses played a key role in hosting our most important retail customers and Valvoline Instant Oil Change Franchisees, who were also arriving throughout the day with their spouses to the Valvoline decked-out Ocean Walk Resort.

As you might imagine, such a premiere entertainment package for the Daytona 500 allowed us to get the busiest of our customer CEO's to take time from their schedules and join us for the weekend. It gave us hard-to-come-by access to them and allowed us to engage in client entertainment on a level I had never seen before.

The bar in the atrium became the *Valvoline VIP Hangout* and it was always five o'clock at the atrium bar. As dinner time approached, Valvoline guests loaded onto waiting buses and headed to the track where Valvoline had leased the Daytona 500 Experience Attraction for its guests' *exclusive use.*

The Daytona 500 Experience does everything possible to give its guests the feeling of actually racing in the Daytona 500. Guests can operate racing simulators where they get to sit in what feels like the cockpit of the Valvoline Dodge. After racing a Daytona 500, guests can participate in the pit crew challenge where they put on a firesuit, grab an air gun and change tires in a simulated pit stop. For guests less inclined to be so athletic, they have access to Daytona's Imax theater and the Daytona 500 heritage museum where they can experience both the sights and sounds of Daytona's history.

If that wasn't enough, guests got to meet all of Valvoline's sponsored drivers, crew chiefs and team owners along with various NASCAR dignitaries. All while having dinner and drinks. Of course, guests were escorted to and from the track by Rodrigo and his team.

And that was just Friday night.

On Saturday guests were provided a range of options including spa treatments, shopping and golf, not to mention a view of the Nationwide Race (the AAA Baseball of auto racing) from Valvoline's double suite at the track for those who wanted to maximize their racing experience.

When everyone returned to the Ocean Walk Hotel Saturday night, Valvoline hosted a seated dinner and a post-dinner gathering in the lobby bar that rocked late into the evening. It was a great opportunity to thank our customers for their business and to continue the relationships that had been built over many years.

If you couldn't find a way to have fun at this event, you couldn't find a way to have fun anywhere.

IT WAS TWO hours before the dropping of the green flag for my first Daytona 500 and I had to admit that I was really excited. Rodrigo and Team had thrilled the guests with another police escorted thrill ride to the track. I'm not sure who enjoyed it more - now that I watched it for the third time – our guests or Rodrigo and his Team. Regardless, the guests and Rodrigo's Team were all gathered in the double suite on the Start/Finish line at the track, socializing, eating and enjoying the excitement that always precedes NASCAR's Superbowl.

And it felt like the Superbowl. Rock bands performed on a stage where the drivers would be introduced to thunderous cheers. Various Hollywood stars and professional athletes frequented the Valvoline suite to greet guests, take pictures and sign autographs. Everyone was partying and everyone was having fun.

While Duke had been somewhat conspicuous in his absence in the hours prior to the race start, I knew he was busy playing his Designated Team Owner role. He changed fluidly from his host role to ensuring the team was as ready as it could be for competition. The #10 Valvoline Dodge was going through its first pre-race inspection by NASCAR officials and had emerged unscathed. We were either completely clean or had successfully fooled the NASCAR inspectors where we may have had *chalk on the toes*. Every self-respecting crew chief got chalk on the toes. But I didn't want to ask how. That was a crew chief's carefully guarded secret and I provided it the distance and respected it deserved.

Duke was clearly a bit relieved when he walked in the suite, returning to his host duties. He approached Toni and me as we chatted with Valvoline's President and his wife. Duke leaned in and said discretely in hushed tones, "You four need to come with me for a little while."

We weren't quite sure what that meant but it was said in a way that we understood that we clearly did not have an option – nor did we likely *want* an option. Duke had a plan and that was likely to mean good things for us.

As we exited the elevator from the Sprint Tower, a six passenger cart awaited us with Valvoline's Motorsports Manager, Mitchell Hardy, at the wheel. I leaned in close to his ear and said in an undertone, "what's up?"

Mitchell just smiled and said, "you'll see."

Mitchell drove us through the crowd, through the tunnel under the track and into the most deeply roped off areas. The guards at the various gates recognized Duke and waved us through promptly. We passed rock stars, country music stars, and various celebrities of all sorts gathered for the Great American Race. Vanessa Williams, who would be singing the national anthem, Kelly Clarkson fresh from her American Idol run, and even Ashton Kutcher and Demi Moore were spotted from a distance. But it wasn't until Duke pointed out Brad Pitt and his brother getting out of a limo that Toni yelled "Whoa! Turn this cart around!" We all got a good chuckle out of that.

Of course, she was serious.

Mitchell got the cart as close as we could get to the next security barrier and then we moved on foot toward the elaborate stage. We passed through metal detectors and quick pat downs, which I had not seen before at any of the tracks. After all, this was the Daytona 500. Duke positioned us near the main stage, right between it and the pace car. Suddenly, everything in the vicinity of the stage seemed to go into lock-down mode, as security seem to heighten.

At that moment, the track announcer pointed the crowd's attention to a large Boeing 747 approaching from the west. Excitedly, he announced the arrival of Air Force One, carrying President George W. Bush to an unannounced visit to the Daytona 500. Air Force One flew over, dipped its wing in a graceful gesture to the crowd, headed out to sea, and swooped around, landing gracefully at the airport adjacent to the track.

The crowd cheered loudly as the Presidential Limo made its way from the airport to the track - all televised on the big video boards. I wondered just how many secret service agents and law enforcement officials it took to secure a venue as large as Daytona International Speedway with 250,000 in attendance. I later found out that it was in excess of six hundred. Expensive day for the taxpayer. But a joyous day for the NASCAR fan!

The Presidential motorcade made its way down pit row and stopped in front of the stage. The President stood proudly and waved to the crowd as it drew to attention while Vanessa Williams proudly sang the national anthem. As the crowd anticipation grew, the President pronounced *the charge*, the most famous words in motorsports, "Drivers, Start Your Engines!" The 43 engines roared, the crowd cheered madly for the moment it had been waiting, and the President's handlers exited him quietly from the stage.

Duke looked at me and said, "You're up next."

"For what?" I was dumbfounded. He motioned to an open door on the pace car.

"Your seat for the next 10 minutes. Get in now. The pace car is ready to lead the drivers onto the track."

It did not take much prodding to get me to leap in the back seat of the Daytona 500 Pace Car. The honorary Grand Marshall for the race was baseball player Johnny Damon, a native of nearby Windermere, Florida, who was already loaded in the front seat.

The pace car moved into gear and we glided onto the track. The crowd was on its feet and cheering the drivers to the starting line. We picked up the speed necessary to stay on the track's 31 degree banking and headed into the first turn at over 100 mph, followed by 43 anxious drivers. I held on for dear life in the turns as the centrifugal force of the high banking kept pushing me down to the left side of the car. I looked in the front seat and Johnny Damon was holding on for dear life while waving wildly to the cheering crowd. As the car leveled out on the backstretch, Johnny turned around and looked at me and screamed, "Can you believe we get paid to do this for a living?"

I don't think I could have articulated it any better.

———

WE WATCHED THE first 50 miles of the race from the pit of the #10 Valvoline Dodge, which had qualified in the 12th position. Duke had perched atop the pit box and evolved into race intensity. He maintained focus on the race, on the choices the team was making at each stage of the race to achieve victory. After the first pit stop, Mitchell escorted us back to the suite where we rejoined our guests for the balance of the race.

If you ask a NASCAR driver or crew chief what the secret is to winning the Daytona 500, the answer you'll most likely get is to "survive the Big One so you can be around for the scramble at the end". The *Big One* is the inevitable 200 mile per hour wreck that will likely collect you and your car, possibly a dozen or more at a time, and end your race. With the speed of the cars governed by the restrictor plates NASCAR places in the carburetors to restrict air flow, the aerodynamics enables the cars to drive faster in pairs or tightly packed lines - called *drafting*. So racing at Daytona is often conducted in packs…one driving mistake in the pack, one blown tire, one excessively hard bumping in the draft — and the Big One occurs. And, as a driver, your day is over and your car becomes scrap metal. Often, there are multiple Big Ones, collecting as much as half the field. So driving in the Daytona 500 is a perilous existence.

Given that drafting occurs all over the track, there's no way to predict exactly where or when the Big One will happen. If you can effectively manage the draft and be part of a speed train, you can often move from the 30th position to the Top 5 in short periods of time. As a result, a variety of strategies emerge to avoid the Big One, ranging from trying to spend as much time near the front (which is why you want to qualify well) to laying back deep in the pack, but staying on the lead lap, so you can set up the right train and emerge later in the race. Rarely is anyone's strategy to stay mid-pack; yet that can easily happen to you when there are 43 crew chiefs making constant choices on car adjustments in real time.

The #10 Valvoline Dodge, driven by Scott Riggs, managed to avoid wrecks all day despite being solidly mid-pack for most of the race. With about 50 laps left in the race, Duke abandoned the pit box and came to the suite to bid farewell to our guests. The President of Valvoline and I had already done so, excusing ourselves early because the Ashland Board of Directors is meeting the next day, we had a key presentation to finalize and we had to get back to Lexington that night. Had the #10 Valvoline Dodge been leading, I assure you that there's no army in the world that could have pulled Duke out of there.

The six of us headed down the elevators, lead by Rodrigo and his team, to the van awaiting us at the bottom of the elevators. As we got in the van, the driver had the race playing on the radio. We were only driving a short distance since the FBO is adjacent to the track and the Ashland jet awaited us there.

As we exited the track, Scott Riggs adroitly joined a fast moving train and moved into the Top 10 with less than 5 laps left in the race. Things can change fast in this race. And they had. Then, the unexpected – the Big One happens! We listened intently to the radio as we pulled into the FBO only to find out as we exited the van that the caution flag was out, freezing the field. Fortunately, the #10 Valvoline Dodge had escaped the Big One unscathed. We breathed a sigh of relief and all fell out of the van and ran into the FBO to watch the balance of the race on the big screen TV.

"Rodrigo's going to stay with us, just in case we need an escort back to Victory Lane," exclaimed Duke, ever the optimist. Rodrigo and his men joined us as we gathered behind two couples in the FBO, already sitting on couches watching the final laps of the race. I knelt behind the woman sitting on the couch with my eyes glued to the screen, breathing heavily with excitement. I caught myself and stepped back for a moment so I wasn't literally breathing down her neck.

The TV announcer indicated that NASCAR called a "green white checkers" finish to the race. That meant that when the race restarted there would be a two lap scamper to the finish line. Scott Riggs restarted in the Top 10 and made the right choice of which train to join as various ones emerged throughout the first lap. As the white flag dropped signaling the final lap, Scott positioned himself well and moved into the Top 5 along with Jeff Gordon, Jimmy Johnson, Dale Earnhardt, Jr., and Kurt Busch. Three cup champions, the most popular driver in the sport driving at the track where his famous father was killed….and, yes, the young driver of the #10 Valvoline Dodge. We were whooping, we were screaming, we were loudly cheering Scott on…dreaming of the possibilities we had only once imagined for our new team.

As the drivers moved into turn three, the Top 5 separated themselves from rest of the field, divided into two trains – one with two cars and one with three. Scott was in the middle of the train of three, hugging the outside of the track, where he hoped to find a way to slingshot to the finish line coming out of turn four. The cars were all bobbing and weaving, jostling for position, trying to gain a head of steam coming out of the final turn. The front two cars endeavored to get ahead of each other while simultaneously blocking the cars behind them. A tough challenge. The back cars were trying to find a way to pass the leaders, faking a move to the right and then perhaps darting to the left. There just isn't that much width to the track and no one could tell what the other drivers would do. The tension was excruciating!

Scott tried to move to the outside of Kurt Busch but Kurt threw the block. Dale Earnhardt, Jr. tried an inside move on Jeff Gordon who successfully blocked him, too. Meanwhile Jimmy Johnson was out of luck with nowhere to go. The track was too narrow. The blocks end up paying off that day and Jeff Gordon slid past the start finish line with Dale Earnhardt hard on his bumper, merely a fraction of a second ahead of Kurt Busch who was being pushed by Scott.

A fourth place finish for Scott and the #10 Valvoline Dodge in the Daytona 500! Not as a win but a helluva good finish! We cheered, we smiled, we were thrilled!

But not enough to head back to the track. We had a plane to catch. Air Ashland.

We bid Rodrigo thanks and farewell as our pilots lead us out to the awaiting Citation jet. Even with our well-planned departure, we still had a forty-five minute traffic jam on the ramp as the raft of private aircraft departed.

As we taxied, all facing each other inside the aircraft, I exclaimed "what an awesome finish! What a great race! I've never felt anything like that before!"

Toni responded, "Me, either. That was incredible!" And then as she calmed, Toni added, "The race finish was pretty cool. And I have to say that Demi Moore looked much better than I expected and a heck of a lot better than Ashton Kutcher. He looked pretty scruffy. Like he needed a bath." She scrunched her nose as she always does with anything that doesn't appear clean to her. I knew that expression well.

"What are you talking about?" I asked, incredulous that she wasn't as focused on the race as I was. But then again, it wasn't her *business*. So I softened, "When we saw Demi and Ashton earlier today, they were pretty far away. How could you see them that well?"

"Earlier today?" she responded. "No, I'm talking about in the FBO."

"In the FBO?" I asked. I had no clue what she was talking about.

"Yes, you remember those two couples sitting on the couches when we rushed in to watch the end of the race? One couple was Demi Moore and Ashton Kutcher waiting to leave."

"What? You're joking me! No way!"

"Yes. In fact, you were crouched right behind Demi, nearly touching her."

"Get outta here. You're pulling my leg."

"She's not joking," said Duke and laughed, "you weren't 'nearly touching her.' You were breathing right down her neck! You really didn't notice her?"

"Seriously, I only saw two things in that room: the TV on the wall and the box of Krispy Kreme doughnuts under it on the table! I hadn't eaten in hours and I was starved!"

Everyone broke out laughing and Duke bellowed to Toni, "I think you can feel pretty good about your marriage when your husband likes doughnuts more than he likes beautiful movie stars."

———

As we winged our way back to Lexington, we all began to settle into the flight after the exciting finish to the race. As things got quiet, I looked at Duke who was still smiling.

He glanced over at me and asked, "Was it a good day?"

"I'd call a fourth place finish at the Daytona 500 a very good day for our race team."

"Yes, it was. I'm glad to see the team get off to a good start. We needed that. But I wanted to know if *you* had a good day?"

"The best, Duke. The best. Thank you very much."

Duke sat back with a satisfied smile. The Duke reigned supreme.

Epilogue

Bristol Revisited

THE ONLY THING Michael heard was the voice of Bristol Motor Speedway's President Jeff Byrd, echoing through the stadium, "...and I'm proud to introduce the Senior Vice President of Bristol Motor Speedway's newest sponsor, Michael Elliot of The Legendary... Valvoline... Company!"

Michael had not prepared himself to address the crowd. He thought it was pre-arranged with the track that he would simply smile and wave once introduced. It would be easy enough. Smile and wave. Like a cheerleader in the Rose Bowl Parade. The only choice he'd have to make was which wave he'd use: the *hinged hand* wave or the *screwing in the light bulb* wave. It was all in the wrist motion. That was the choice he was prepared to make.

The choice he was not prepared to make was what to say to the crowd - as he had no prepared remarks. But that was not the way Jeff Byrd wanted it. Jeff insisted that Michael address the Bristol crowd and promptly introduced him to do so. Whether Michael liked the idea or not; whether Michael was prepared or not.

Michael had no choice but to walk calmly up the stairs to the stage, doing every-thing possible to collect himself, while trying not to notice his all-too-rigidly smiling face projected on the four-sided Sony JumboTron screen towering above him. He focused only on the polite applause of the crowd and the beaming smile and out-stretched handshake of Jeff Byrd.

What would you do in this situation? How would you react when faced with the prospect of having to address 165,000 people with no prepared remarks? What would you say? What could you say? Anything? Would you feign laryngitis? Or would you simply collapse in a heap right there on the stage?

Strangely, a deep calm came over Michael as he approached the microphone. Time seemed to stand still as the world decelerated into incredibly slow motion. Instead of intense panic, Michael experienced a contemplative calm. It felt like he called *time-out* on life and began to reflect upon how he ended up in this very spot on this very day.

He marveled at the bizarre set of circumstances that produced the evolution of his life, that led to this particular moment. How in the world did he traverse the expanse of time that began with that young kid and The Plan to today where he was facing 165,000 dedicated race fans? What was the string of decisions, circumstances and twists of fate that led him from the pleasant streets of Charleston through the gardens of *Mr. Jefferson's Academical Village* through the decayed sidewalks of Cincinnati's Over The Rhine to the ovals of NASCAR?

He considered the myriad interdependent steps along the meandering path of his life that brought him to this very moment. Would he be standing here if he hadn't gotten the mistaken job offer from P&G? Would Michael have ever met Charlie if P&G hadn't moved him from Paper Products to Beauty Care on that very first day of work? Would Charlie have ever become an executive recruiter to obtain the Valvoline search assignment in which to place Michael if Charlie hadn't left On Target on that fateful day? Would Charlie have ever considered Michael for the Valvoline job if they hadn't figured a way to rekindle their friendship? Would Michael have ever considered a job outside of P&G if he had taken the *golden handcuffs* promotion? Would Valvoline have even been interested in Michael if he hadn't obtained the work and life experiences outside of P&G at On Target, ProtoCall, Main Street Ventures, ConnectMail and Stablehand Advisors? What if Michael had never met Matthew and taken those opportunities to expand his business experience?

Could any of this have been possible without the disjointed array of complex and seemingly random connections, happening in the order they did? What an intricate tapestry of events his life had become. What an unpredictable and unforeseeable collection of circumstances, people and timing it had taken to bring him to this very moment on the journey of his career - facing a huge crowd with nothing to say.

It seemed that in life, things rarely work out according to plan. Perhaps it's the alternatives to the plan that hold the possibilities.

And that's the exact moment in which Michael experienced a sensation that might only be described as a *revelation*. He flashed on a quote from a 1970's era poster he had once seen and dismissed as the pop-philosophy of the time. Yet the quote may have been the simplest, most accurate piece of philosophy he had ever rejected. For it never made more sense to him than at this very moment.

The poster simply said "Life Is a Journey, Not a Destination." The meaning of this moment was less THAT he was here, but more about HOW he got here - and where he might still go.

HOW he derived so much meaning from his various work experiences - his cubicle tales - and by extension his life, less from where he was at a given point along the path and more by the journey itself.

HOW by letting go of The Plan, he had garnered more friendships, life experiences, and fun than he might ever have thought possible under the controlled and limited elements of The Plan.

HOW the path was one he never could have designed, not even dreamed could bring him to this moment. That the fabric of his journey was simply undesignable, *unplannable*.

HOW his own story — his career and life path - wasn't remotely about the title he achieved or the resume he had compiled or the companies he had helped to build. It wasn't about failures or successes. It wasn't about the way it came about nor the way it turned out.

It was simply and remarkably about the journey. About the joy of the journey. It was really all about.... *enjoying the ride*.

How trite. But how true. After all, if you didn't enjoy the ride, why would the destination be worth attaining?

Michael began walking effortlessly toward the microphone as if he were carried along on a cloud. He released a deep sigh, less to compose himself than to express the sense of cathartic contentment he was experiencing at that very moment. The satisfaction of this simple moment in life brought about in the most bizarre of circumstances. The satisfaction that brought him a strange and unwarranted comfort as he stood on this lonely stage. It was only then that he gathered his energy and the words began to flow exuberantly from his mouth as he embraced the awaiting crowd.

"It's Saturday Night, Bristol!" he roared into the microphone with a fierceness even he did not recognize, engendering a thunderous response from the ready-to-party crowd.

"And at local tracks all around America, Saturday Night means one thing: short... track... racing!!" More applause from the crowd. They were instantly *with him*. A love of short track racing is why they were here.

"Valvoline has been proud to sponsor short track racing at local tracks for more than 100 years. So it only seems fittin' that Valvoline should sponsor the greatest short track of them all...Bristol....Motor...Speedway!"

"That is Valvoline's way of thanking YOU...for supporting US...for over a century. So enjoy the race tonight Bristol Fans, and most of all, from all of us at Valvoline, enjoy the ride."

"Yep," he smiled as he stepped back from the microphone and surveyed the cheering crowd. "P*lease* enjoy the ride."

AUTHOR'S NOTES

I CAN'T HELP but step back and marvel at some of the ridiculous things that have happened to me, thanking God that I've endured life with my body, mind and sense of humor largely intact. The stories contained in this book are wrapped loosely around the concept of work. But, honestly, work as a concept is really just a vehicle to accomplish my primary goal: to tell some stories. Which, not coincidentally, is what I've tried to do at many cocktail and dinner parties over the years. Much to my wife's chagrin. Storytelling is a wonderful art, of which I am only a novice, still learning. Who doesn't love a great storyteller? I hope to be one someday.

The stories contained herein are real. They all really happened — or are at least *99 44/100 % Pure* (that's an Ivory Soap reference for readers who are not P&G aficionados). The tiny *56/100* of a percentage point that is fictional would generally fall within the following three categories:

Names – The names have been changed to protect the innocent -- and even the guilty. Yes, even Chip Sharp and Denise Sobel deserve some level of anonymity. That said, I suspect people who know me will probably be able to figure out not only who Chip and Denise are but perhaps also some of the other colorful characters. I hope inclusion in this book doesn't offend anyone. I tried to tell stories that would be mostly positive or at least neutral, and hopefully not negative. As to the stories of Chip and Denise, which are unapologetically negative, I'm sorry if their cover is blown. My only defense is to offer the following:

1. As Walt Disney has proven, every great story needs a villain;

2. I didn't write anything that didn't *actually* happen; therefore, if any of the stories I told reveal publicly some behavior that embarrasses them, then

3. Please remember what the great philosophers say: karma's a bitch.

Beyond the anonymous, I made liberal use of characters whose names are in the public domain, because, quite honestly, it made it more *fun* to tell the story. Does anyone want to read a story about a pouty and spoiled fashion model no one's ever heard of? Really? I wouldn't find that interesting or fun. Just sad.

Time Shifting — There are times when I told a story that didn't happen quite at the specific time in which it occurs chronologically in this book. To be clear, the story *did* happen; and it *did* happen to me or people I know. It just didn't happen at the point in time where it occurs in this book. Sometimes I did it so the book flowed better. Sometimes I did it because this book is intended to entertain, not to provide a *tell all* and potentially embarrass anyone unintentionally. So, on occasion, I *rearranged* some history to avoid that. Hey, it worked for Fred Flintstone; why not for Michael Elliot?

Story Shifting — I'm not even sure if *story shifting* is a real term; perhaps I just made it up because it seems to logically parallel the concept of *time shifting*, at least for me. What I mean by "story shifting" is that I took a story that happened to one person and attributed it to another person. For example, the James Brown story did actually happen; it just happened to my cousin Terry Richardson not the character in this book. I couldn't resist a story so rich and funny! As such, the story begged to be told, it just *needed* to be told. So I was compelled to find a device with which to tell it. Monday morning stories worked for me as such a device. Hopefully, for you too.

Otherwise, I believe everything else contained in this book really happened as described. I know it's hard to believe. But, at times, as I note in the book, real life is truly more interesting than fiction. At least, that's the way I've found my life to be. You simply couldn't make this stuff up.

Debts of Gratitude

I owe huge debts of gratitude to a number of people who made this collection of stories possible. First, I owe thanks to the handful of people who actually took time to read the early drafts of this book and either share their reactions with me or simply offer encouragement: Rita Solomon, Terri Solomon, Gary Solomon, Maury Levine, Gail Richardson, Marc Fisher and our children, Jake & Mimi Solomon, Josh Solomon, and Mikey Solomon. Thanks also to George Molinsky and Margaret Lawson of the law firm of Taft, Stettinius & Hollister in Cincinnati who have not only given me good advice and friendship over the years, but will also hopefully keep me out of trouble on this project. And thanks to Lynn Purdom who helped me to craft many of the unique phrasings of the character Duke Dominic.

I owe a special debt of gratitude to two people in particular: Barbie Stern and Andy Solomon. Barbie and Andy invested months to provide me with meticulous comments and edits, page by page, that made the book markedly more readable. For that, I'm sure we are *all* grateful. Only true friends would invest that much time and energy. Thank you very much.

I also owe thanks to a few people from whom I borrowed true stories for this book. As noted before, my cousin Terry Richardson shared with me the priceless James Brown story. My good friend Eli Hyman, proprietor of the famed Hyman's Seafood in Charleston, shared with me the story of hiring a driver for his aging father Meyer (who now rests in peace). Buddies Jerry Felix and Ron Binkouskas always howl at dinner when telling the $99 suit story. It never seems to get old. When I initially heard these three stories, I laughed until I cried. So I couldn't imagine creating a collection of entertaining stories without including them. Thanks, guys.

I also need to thank my good buddy Larry Kuhlman who not only provided me the quote "Life is better with a soundtrack," but also with great assistance in getting cover art created and the manuscript drafts digitally assembled and printed. It truly takes a village and in this case, The Graphic Village in Cincinnati, Ohio.

My inspiration to even contemplate writing a book came, in part, from some of the great contemporary authors whose works I have had the pleasure of reading, and in some cases, whose styles I have borrowed at times. These masters include: Pat Conroy, David Baldacci, Lawrence Sanders, James Patterson, Dorothea Benton Frank, Ken Burger, Steve Martini, Stuart Woods, Jack Higgins, Daniel Silva and John Grisham. You all have provided me with endless amounts of both entertainment and inspiration. The world owes you much, as do I.

The last group of people I want to thank are all those who serve as characters in this book, many of whom have been dear friends over the years. So many of you are the colorful characters of my life and that color is the gift you offer the world. I consider it an honor to have captured a snippet of it. I'm fortunate to have crossed paths with you and I'm proud to have the honor of sharing your color with the world too (at least in black and white print).

Finally, I owe the greatest debts of gratitude to my parents, Rita and Melvin "Bones" Solomon, for the life they have created for me; and to my wife, Terri, who not only put up with this passion project for the four years of our life I have invested in it, but also for putting up with me for three decades – and all the craziness my meandering career has inflicted on our marital journey. I am indeed a very fortunate man. To borrow a phrase from the book, I am *way over-chicked* and proud to wear the label.

Thanks to any and all readers who have gotten this far. You honor me by allowing me to share my stories. And please remember to enjoy the ride.

About the Author

Walter H. Solomon has more than three decades of business experience and has served as a C-Suite officer in both global *Fortune 500* companies and hypergrowth *Inc. 500* start-ups. He is also active in the not-for-profit world, having served on ten boards of directors and as an officer for more than half of them. He brings these experiences to his humorous collection of true workplace stories in *Cubicle Tales*.

Solomon has lived along the salt marshes of Charleston, South Carolina, in the elevations of the Blue Ridge Mountains of Charlottesville, Virginia, among the seven hills of Cincinnati, Ohio, and amidst the bluegrass horse country of Lexington, Kentucky. He and his wife Terri have three grown sons, a delightful daughter-in-law, and a border collie grand-dog.

Made in the USA
Lexington, KY
17 March 2014